City of Sediments

City of Sediments

A History of Seoul in the Age of Colonialism

Se-Mi Oh

STANFORD UNIVERSITY PRESS

Stanford, California

Stanford University Press
Stanford, California

This work was supported by the Strategic Research Institute Program for Korean Studies of the Ministry of Education of the Republic of Korea and the Korean Studies Promotion Service at the Academy of Korean Studies (AKS-2021-SRI-2200001).

Printed in the United States of America on acid-free, archival-quality paper
Library of Congress Cataloging-in-Publication Data
Names: Oh, Se-Mi, 1975- author.
Title: City of sediments : a history of Seoul in the age of colonialism / Se-Mi Oh.
Description: Stanford, California : Stanford University Press, [2023] | Includes bibliographical references and index.
Identifiers: LCCN 2022030213 (print) | LCCN 2022030214 (ebook) | ISBN 9781503634800 (cloth) | ISBN 9781503635524 (paperback) | ISBN 9781503635531 (ebook)
Subjects: LCSH: Colonial cities—Korea—History—20th century. | City and town life—Korea—History—20th century. | Seoul (Korea)—History—20th century. | Korea—History—Japanese occupation, 1910-1945.
Classification: LCC DS925.S457 O43 2023 (print) | LCC DS925.S457 (ebook) | DDC 951.95—dc23/eng/20220629
LC record available at https://lccn.loc.gov/2022030213
LC ebook record available at https://lccn.loc.gov/2022030214

Cover design: Michele Wetherbee
Cover image: Kelvin Kyung Kun Park, *Space Time Machine*, 2015. Courtesy of the artist.
Typeset by Elliott Beard in Latino URW 9.75/14

For my son Ben Dojin
In memory of my father

CONTENTS

NOTES ON ROMANIZATION

This book employs the modified McCune-Reischauer system for romanizing Korean. Exceptions are made for well-established romanization of names for Korean authors who published using a different romanization. Following the standard practice for Korean and Japanese names, the surname is placed before the given name, and a comma is not used to separate the two. The romanization of Korean place-names also follows this modified McCune-Reischauer system unless the English name of the place is well established, as in the case of Seoul. Exceptions prioritize the context in which the name is found. For instance, if a Korean name is part of an official name of an organization or title, it follows the romanization of its official name. Place-names during the colonial period were subject to different readings, but this book generally reads them in Korean when there is no textual context to guide the reading. Japanese readings and romanized Korean are also indicated when relevant.

ILLUSTRATIONS

ACKNOWLEDGMENTS

Creating this book has been a long journey. Looking back, I might have felt a little too comfortable being in a perpetual state of rehearsal. I did not always know what I was looking for, but I searched hard. This book made me grow. Along the way, I met people who encouraged me and lent me a hand. This book would not have been possible without their immeasurable generosity.

I have benefited enormously from being part of the community in the Department of Asian Languages and Cultures at the University of Michigan. Youngju Ryu invested in this project from the beginning and worked tirelessly to help me see it through. She also helped my prose to be readable. I am proud to call her my mentor, colleague, and friend. My mentor Donald S. Lopez Jr. provided his expert advice as author and editor and answered every question that I brought to his attention with care and kindness. Susan Juster reminded me to prioritize my sources above all and provided support at every step of the way. I am truly touched by her thoughtfulness. Nancy Florida taught me how to think hard in her own graceful way, and Christi Merrill's encouragement came at a crucial time and helped me out of stasis. The beautiful translation of Japanese poems in this book is by Erin Brightwell, whose sense of humor was just the medicine for routine departmental life. I would also like to thank Christopher Hill for stimulating conversations inside and outside of the classroom and for his faith in my sedimentary model of history. I share the importance of aesthetics with Abé Markus Nornes, who helped me with big and small things related to publication. Deirdre de la Cruz is my friendly next-door neighbor who was kind enough to share her copyeditors with me. I will never forget when David Rolston generously brought books on *ŭigwe* to my department colloquium talk. Nachiket Chanchani and Jahnabi Barroah Chanchani provided much-needed afternoon walks in the woods and relaxing coffee breaks. Emily Wilcox shared invaluable insights from her own experience. Xiaobing Tang spend much time going over big ideas with me and served as a departmental reader for my manuscript workshop. I appreciate his feedback and helping me edit down my thoughts. I would also like to thank everyone who offered feedback at the manuscript workshop, including Ben Brose, Sonia Özbey, and Erick White.

I am most indebted to people who read my manuscript at various stages and provided important feedback. I would like to express my very special gratitude to the two anonymous readers of the manuscript. Not only did their insightful comments help me take my manuscript to the finish line, but they also instilled a sense of direction in me for the path ahead. I am humbled by their generosity. My sincerest gratitude goes to Takashi Fujitani and Suk-Young Kim, who graciously read my manuscript at an early stage and provided meticulous and thorough feedback during my manuscript workshop. Thanks to their help, the revision process was enjoyable, as I learned a great deal from seeing things from different angles. I am very grateful to Albert L. Park for his help on many aspects of writing and publishing. He was generous with his time and offered helpful feedback, always bundled in positive energy. If I can choose anyone with whom to spend Christmas Eve, that would be Kyeong-Hee Choi, as she combed through my manuscript. Her laser eye for the smallest details and the big picture helped me restructure my manuscript. Jisoo Kim kindly went over all things related to Chosŏn for chapter 2 and was never too far away when I needed someone to talk to. Good food and good company can always enliven intellectual exchange. I especially appreciated conversations with Kim Baek Young whose seminal work on Seoul became a launching pad for my own research. We put our heads together about what to make of the insignias; I am happy to say that I think I figured it out. Seo Youngchae always had exquisite taste for conversation and cuisine. Of the many brilliant ideas he brought to the table, his advice to think complex and write simple stayed with me.

My education at Columbia University played a critical role in making me the scholar that I am today. I would like to thank Laurel Kendall, Charles Armstrong, Eugenia Lean, Carol Gluck, Madeleine Zelin, and Nicholas Dirks, who shared their wisdom with me. I am particularly indebted to Theodore Q. Hughes, who never spared his encouragement when I needed it the most. His comments about my dissertation really being about visual culture set me on an intellectual quest that proved so fruitful. It turned out that I also went back to my roots when I read Paul Ricoeur with my late advisor JaHyun Kim Haboush. Her instruction to me during one of our last conversations was that I write a book that I wanted to set a high bar for me. I strove to emulate her examples in scholarship. I have also come to rely on the counsel of Andre Schmid, Henry Em, Chris Hanscom, Janet Poole, Jin-kyung Lee, Atsuko Ueda, and Hiromi Mizuno. I am grateful for their guidance over the years, some even going back to my undergraduate years. I would also like to thank Sun Joo Kim, Carter Eckert, David McCann, Shigehisa Kuriyama, Andrew Gordon, and Ian Miller, for enriching my yearlong stay as postdoctoral fellow at Harvard University. There are too many names to mention from that vibrant community of postdoctoral fellows and graduate students, but I would like to give a shout-out to my Seoul comrades, Jun Uchida and Todd Henry. My time at New York University and the University of Wisconsin, Madison, was a crucial phase as I explored new approaches in visual studies. Through seminars and conversations, I have benefited from the input and support of Xudong Zhang, Rebecca Karl, Yukiko Hanawa, Tom Looser, and Moss Roberts; and Steven Ridgley, Nicole Huang, Louise Young, Viren Murthy, Yuhang Li, Rania Huntington, Charo D'etcheverry, and Adam Kern.

I have been fortunate to have many opportunities to share my project through invited talks, conferences, and workshops, all of which constituted the most productive phase of my research and writing. For the chapter on Kojong's funeral, I am grateful to Yi Song-mi for sharing her unmatched knowledge about *ŭigwe* and to Park Jeong Hye and Burglind Jungmann for the helpful exchange at the Hahn Moo-Sook Colloquium at George Washington University. I would also like to thank Hŏ Ŭn for organizing a conference that explored the role of visual mediums as historical sources at Korea University, and Chelsea Foxwell for inviting me to her photography seminar at the University of Chicago and treating me to the most stimulating discussions. I would also like to thank Jini Watson Kim, Ellie Choi, the late Hyung Il Pai, and Hyung-Gu Lynn, with whom I shared panels at the Graduate School of Design and Visualizing Cultures conferences at Harvard University. At the workshop that Steven Chung organized at Princeton University, I tested out my ideas about commercial signage. I would like to thank Cha Seung-gi, who kindly affirmed my semiotic approach, and Nayoung Aimee Kwon, who rightly pointed out how our writing should reflect the sources that we use. Michael Kim and Chung Kŭnsik brought together scholars working on the Japanese empire for a conference at Yonsei University where I felt right at home and became energized. Over summer breaks spent in Seoul and during my stay at the Kyujanggak Institute for Korean Studies at Seoul National University, I learned a great deal from Park Tae-gyun, Baek Moon Im, Kim Ye-Rim, Kim Hyun-joo, Shin Hyun-joon, Lim Jie-hyun, and Yi Sang-u, and became replenished in the company of Ju Hui Judy Han, Kelly Jeong, Jina Kim, Kyung Hyun Kim, Serk-bae Suh, Sunyoung Park, Christine Kim, James Kyung-Jin Lee, Jonathan Zwicker, and Daniel O'Neil.

One thing that I can boast about my life in Ann Arbor is the close-knit community at the Nam Center for Korean Studies. The Nam family and the former director Nojin Kwak, as well as the current director Youngju Ryu and all the core faculty, including Y. David Chung, Dae Hee Kwak, Jaeeun Kim, Ungsan Kim, and Soyeon Kim, ensure that this is a nurturing community inclusive of all family members. Kelsey Langton, Evan Vowell, Kate Klemm, and DoHee Morsman are the pillars of the center and provide a truly welcoming place for colleagues, friends, kids, and babies. Yunah Sung and the library staff at the University of Michigan library provided every resource that I needed in the most expedient way. Katherine Faydash and Danielle LaVaque-Manty copyedited the manuscript; Katherine read multiple versions of the manuscript and offered insightful editing comments at every stage. Juhn Ahn worked through my impossible romanization and citations, and Erin Brightwell also proofread my romanization and translation of Japanese. Kaeun Park did a Herculean task with all the images that appeared in this book. I could not have done it without her help. Thanks to Joo Young Lee's careful notetaking, I could revisit all the helpful comments from the manuscript workshop. I would also like to thank Kenneth Ross Yelsey, Dafna

Zur, Eugene Park, and Jun Yoo for providing help as the manuscript was ready to be sent out.

I would like to thank the wonderful team at Stanford University Press, Tiffany Mok, Kapani Celeste Krikland, and Sunna Juhn. I owe much to my editor Dylan Kyung-lim White. He had a magical way of making the publication process smooth and efficient, and so enjoyable. I am grateful for his faith in my project and sharing a vision. I want to extend my very special thanks to Kelvin Kyung Kun Park for creating the artwork for the cover and interpreting the ideas of the book so beautifully and compellingly: this book would not have been complete without it.

The research and writing of this book were supported by a Fulbright-Hays dissertation research fellowship, a Korea Foundation postdoctoral fellowship at the Korea Institute of Harvard University, a Kyujanggak fellowship from the International Center for Korean Studies at Seoul National University, the junior faculty nurturance fund from the Nam Center for Korean Studies at the University of Michigan, and the Strategic Research Institute Program for Korean Studies of the Ministry of Education of the Republic of Korea and the Korean Studies Promotion Service at the Academy of Korean Studies. A previous version of chapter 2 appeared in Korean as "Ŭirye, yŏksa, sagŏn: Kojong changnye wa yŏksa ssŭgi" in *Yŏngsang maech'e ro saeroun yŏksa ssŭgi*, edited by Hŏ Ŭn (Sŏn'in, 2015).

I would be remiss if I did not mention my immediate and extended family whose lively online chats made their presence feel near despite the physical distance that separates us. My mom Sarah Oh and elder Eric Yu spent hours on end on FaceTime to keep their grandchild entertained, and my grandmother Hye Sik Choi was the source of steadfast support. I would like to extend my thanks to the Steiner parents who provided a safe community especially during the pandemic. Francisco Sanin's wisdom and support also uplifted me. For Elise Prébin, Jimin Kim, Lucy Lee, Connie Kim, Elizabeth Yoon, Lee Eunjoo, Lee Sona, and Kim Najeong, friendship knows no distance or passing of time. I want to thank Juhn Ahn for his effort with childcare during the last stretch and his parents, Ahn Eui-chan and No Young-han, for their encouragement. Two very special people anchored me throughout the process: my son Ben Dojin Ahn and my late father Rev. Mongŭn Jinhwan Oh. Ben's unbounded curiosity opened new worlds for me, and his strength during difficult times inspired me. The memory of my dad, how he lived his life with dedication and left this world with utmost dignity, kept me focused on what is truly important in life. I missed him at every step of this journey, and I felt a great sense of loss when I could not be there for my son during the busiest times. I dedicate this book to these two beautiful souls whose love I would like to reciprocate. And last but not least, to my fur babies, Bernie (we miss you so much) and Volcano, thank you for warm hugs and bright smiles.

City of Sediments

Introduction

Can the city write history? Can it become readable as text, a discourse on time? Can the city have an epistemology of its own? Premised on the idea that historical writing is always organized as narrative and time is always produced through the mediation of space, this book offers a history of Seoul under Japanese colonial rule (1910–1945) that lays bare its own textual formation in and through space. This is not a history that traces changes in space over time but a history that reveals complexities and contradictions of its own construction. The city of Seoul, in this history, emerges not just as a product of the historical forces that shaped it but as an interlocutor that articulates the contested field of power and its epistemological operation. The exploration of the city as method starts with the 1926 competition for a new insignia. With that, this book extends the investigation of Seoul beyond the material into the discursive.

In 1926, a contest was held for a new design of Seoul's insignia. The winning design, selected by a panel of twenty-eight judges from over nine hundred entries submitted by almost five hundred individuals in Korea, Japan, and Manchuria, featured a simple, geometric redesign of the earlier insignia, which had been in place since 1918 (figure I.1).[1] This earlier design had featured the Sino-Korean graph *kyŏng* (*kei* in Japanese) from Seoul's official name under the Japanese rule, Kyŏngsŏng or Keijō, inside a circle with eight small rectangles jutting out from the circle's edges.[2] The resulting cogwheel stylized the city walls with four major gates and four minor gates. In the new insignia, the Sino-Korean graph was replaced by a hollow circle in the middle, and the cogwheel around the graph *kyŏng* supplanted by two arcs at the top and bottom, each with three equidistant squares jutting outward. These two arcs, which thus rendered graphically the Chinese character for mountain (*san*), were purportedly meant to visualize two mountains to the north and south—Pukhansan and Namsan. But the overall effect created by replacing the cogwheel with these arcs was to give the impression of opening up the city walls. This was certainly the view expressed in an article in the newspaper *Tonga ilbo*, which stated that the old design was inadequate for representing the city's rapid development because it depicted Seoul as a city enclosed by walls. In contrast, the openness of the new design would be the key to articulating Seoul's future. The new insignia pointed to the possibility of outward, radial expansion, to be touted as "an ideal structure suitable for a modern city."[3]

These two insignias represented Seoul in different ways, in terms of topology (space) and history (time). Two main features of the 1918 insignia were the cogwheel and the graph from Seoul's name, together representing Seoul as a walled city and the capital city—an identity rooted in place. The 1926 insignia, on the other hand, was one rooted in history, giving a sense of how Seoul had changed and would change over time. Moving away from the iconic representation of 1918 (i.e., the stylized

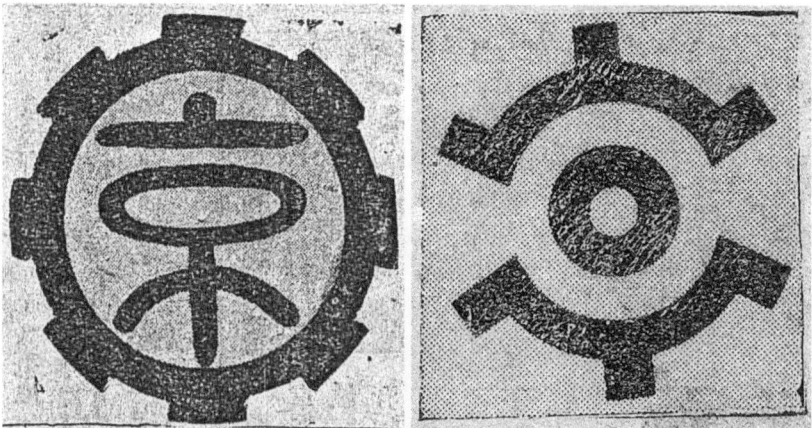

FIGURE I.1. Insignias for Seoul, from *Maeil sinbo*, June 18, 1918, National Library of Korea (left) and *Tonga ilbo*, September 26, 1926. Reprinted with permission (right).

city walls) and toward a more symbolic design, the insignia were to work also as an index sign for the city's future via the radial lines indicating an outward expansion.[4] This was a vision of the city articulated from an urban planning perspective, in which urbanization was synonymous with modernization. And yet the future of Seoul was articulated in the image of the past, or to be more precise, in terms of its contrast to the past. While other top entries (figure I.2) retained little resemblance from the older insignia and instead explicitly visualized outward growth with direction pointers and even a spiral, the winning design was a revision of the older design, which served as a reminder of what came before and how it had changed. The new design was an evolution of the previous one, not something radically new; Seoul was not to be reinvented as a modern city but would develop from its current form by disavowing its identity as a walled city. The 1926 insignia was not about representing Seoul's identity through emblems unmarked by time; it was about narrating a change. At the core, the new insignia was itself a piece of history writing, concerned above all with a seamless transition from old to

FIGURE I.2. Announcing the awardees for Kyŏngsŏng insignia design, from *Maeil sinbo*, September 26, 1926, National Library of Korea, Seoul.

new, from walled city to modern city, and with articulating Seoul's past
through a lens of particularity and its future in the image of universalism. It first created an image of the city in the bygone era and, through
a remaking of that image, put the present in motion toward the future.

This history writing was not based on intimate knowledge of the city
itself. Rather, the story of Seoul as told through these insignias presented
a past that never was, a myth that fabricated the conditions under which
the new insignia narrated the development of Seoul. Consider Seoul's
city walls, for which construction began in 1395, when Seoul became
the capital of the Chosŏn dynasty (1392–1897). For five centuries, the
city walls allowed Chosŏn monarchs to secure their power practically
and symbolically by providing a fortress and regulating the movement
of people and goods. When attempts at modernization began at the end
of the nineteenth century, however, the city walls became one of the
earliest targets. Under the advisement of Collbran and Bostwick Co.,
the Hansŏng Electricity Company was established in 1898, and shortly
afterward, a streetcar route opened between the West Gate and Ch'ŏngnyangni, and then between the South Gate and Yongsan. With the introduction of streetcars, the city's eight gates that had opened and closed
at regular intervals were left open at all times to accommodate increased
foot and vehicular traffic. In 1907, citing the impediment that the walls
posed to traffic flow, King Kojong issued a permit to demolish the walls
on one side of the South Gate, and by 1909 the walls on both sides had
been completely removed. The East Gate met the same fate in 1908.
Seoul's walls had been taken down and two of the city's most important
gates disconnected from the walls even before Japan annexed Korea in
1910. The reality of Seoul, therefore, was that it had long stopped being a
walled city by the time the cogwheel insignia became its official symbol
in 1918.

Nor is the image of Seoul as a city confined within walls unproblem-
atic. To be sure, during the Chosŏn dynasty, the capital city was called
Hanyang tosŏng or "the Walled City of Hanyang," but this included areas
within the walls and outside them (figure I.3). The area outside the walls,
Sŏngjŏsimni, became officially part of Seoul in 1461 and constituted a
vital part of Seoul's administration, economy, and culture thereafter.
In fact, it was only in 1910, with Japan's annexation of Korea, that the
city became limited within the area that had been circumscribed by the
walls.[5] The 1918 insignia omitted this history of how Sŏngjŏsimni was

expelled from the city proper. The 1926 insignia then built its expansionist model upon this historical inaccuracy, hiding the violence that had radically altered the shape and function of Seoul, and further erasing Sŏngjŏsimni from memory. The walled city of Seoul, so central to the vision of change put forward by the 1926 insignias, was merely a ghost. The evocation of a feudal, premodern image of Seoul served to lay down the foundation for narrating the inexorability and inevitability of historical progress. So, while the 1926 insignia depicted the city as opened up and expanding as a result of modernization, it hid the colonial violence of undoing the old capital's spatial logic and silenced the histories of different locales to naturalize the epochal change from premodern to modern.

Yet another fiction is the character *kyŏng/kei,* physically present in the 1918 insignia and alluded to in the 1926 one. Kyŏngsŏng/Keijō was the official name chosen for Seoul, then called Hansŏng, when Korea was annexed by Japan. The names Kyŏngsŏng/Keijō and Hansŏng came

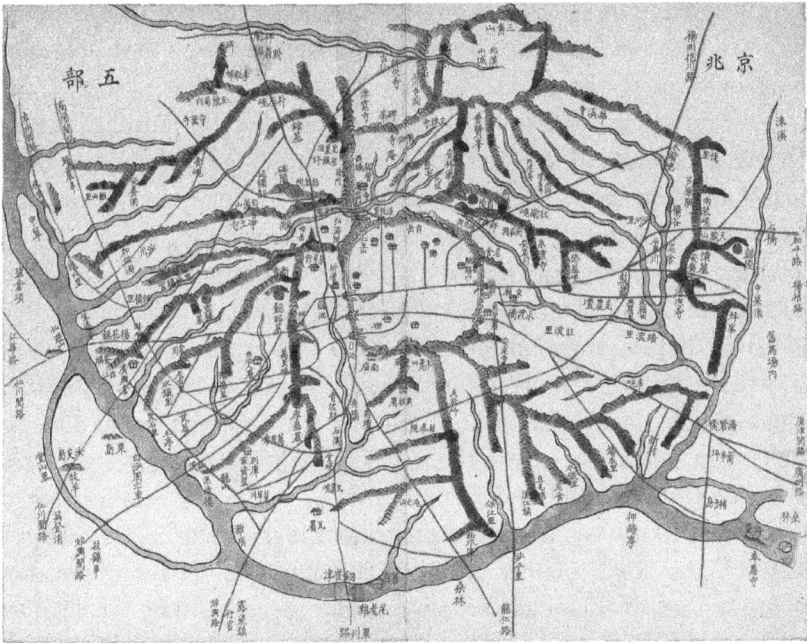

FIGURE I.3. Kim Chŏng-ho, *The Map of Five Districts of the Capital* (Kyŏngjo obudo), from *Taedongyŏjido,* 1861, woodblock print, 400 x 671 cm, Seoul History Museum.

to point to different political powers that rationalized the space into an urban form at different times in history, and the change from Hansŏng to Kyŏngsŏng/Keijō came to signal the end of one era and the beginning of another. However, since the Chosŏn dynasty, Kyŏngsŏng had been one of several official and vernacular names used for Seoul, including Hanyang, Kyŏngjo, Kyŏngdo, Susŏn, Changan, Chungang, Chaegyŏng, and Sudo, as well as Sŏul (Seoul). None of these names disappeared, and they all continued to be used during the colonial period, including Hansŏng.[6] Moreover, whereas Kyŏngsŏng/Keijō functioned as a proper noun in the insignias—a name—the word *kyŏngsŏng* as a general noun simply meant "capital," so it had been used to refer to any capital throughout history. Only during the Taehan Empire was *kyŏngsŏng* used as a proper noun that referred to Seoul as the capital of Korea while *sudo* was used to refer to capital cities of other countries. The singular nomination of Seoul through Kyŏngsŏng/Keijō in the insignias is thus a result of privileging that name over the others in use and the history of the name Kyŏngsŏng itself—that is, a result of colonial erasure. In becoming Kyŏngsŏng/Keijō, Seoul forcibly disavowed those other names and subsumed the multiple histories and practices on the ground to validate the idea that its name was new when in fact it had become intimately attached to the place of Seoul over a long history.

How do we write, then, a history of a city that has morphed across time with this web of names, shapes, and forms? Describing Seoul's historical development from a premodern capital to a modern colonial city would simplify all these complexities and replicate the very process of colonization that the city endured. Instead, any attempt to understand the multiplicity of Seoul, temporal or spatial, must be a deconstructive endeavor that estranges any appearance of a transition from premodern to modern as stable. It should also question how such history writing became instrumental in naturalizing colonial intervention and masking its violence. If we look to the traces of the material past—sediments of earlier times, buried under and lost to the sprawling urban space of Kyŏngsŏng/Keijō—we can find clues about the many forces that shaped the city. The "real" history of Seoul, therefore, has to excavate those layers and unearth residues whose recalcitrance disturbed the signs of modernity and colonial domination. For this reason, to build the history of Seoul, one must unbuild it first.

In both insignias, the violence committed to the city was discursive, driven by a modernity that deceptively pronounced its force to be inescapable while it took history to be the main agent of its mythical narrative: colonial power was all but invisible in these insignias, and changes were rationalized as modernization. This reveals an important facet of Japanese colonialism, one that operated through discourse about urban space, modernity, and history. Political oppression, economic exploitation, and a culture of violence were the inevitable results of reshaping, redistricting, and renaming Seoul. However, we can locate the workings of colonialism not just in the physical changes to the city but also in the discursive practices that produced a narrative about Seoul's past, present, and future and normalized the developmental narrative of modernity. Because Japanese colonial power was exercised in and through this writing of history, with the city as its text, this book takes a spatial approach in writing a history of Seoul. History writing and spatial practices are not always comparable, but any abrasion that can be caused by their suturing can prove to be rewarding, if it leads to a recognition that any discourse that claims an identity of the two different forces is, like the insignias, a product of power and its mythical property. To cause discomfort is to defamiliarize our habits of historical (or historicist) thinking.

To this end, I use the name Seoul as the most inclusive nomination that allows inquiry into the many forms and aforementioned complexities of the city. To see the city both as a space and a text within which history can be unpacked is not to endorse an ahistorical approach but to freeze the forward trajectory of time, the kind of temporality that history is culpable of creating, and thereby recuperate the time-knot that has been assimilated into a historicist narrative. Therefore, in lieu of a history of Seoul that details the processes of historical change over time, this book takes Seoul as a method through which history writing can be brought to the surface. The city, in other words, becomes the site for the practice of turning the material traces of history into text—language, image, and narrative. It views historical time as a function of space and approaches the spatial practices and discursive space of Seoul as history writing. Its goal is to map the processes of textual formation through which the telos of history was inscribed in space and to reveal the disjunctures and multiplicities that were concealed by the colonial intervention. This will lead to a history that treats the city as a set of categories for analyzing the questions pertinent to epistemology that frame much of our historical discussion today. Rather than take history as a methodology for investigating urban space, in other words, the book takes urban space as a methodology for studying history.

The City That Escapes Naming: Modernity and Its Visual Properties

The big question that confronts anyone seeking to write about Seoul under Japanese rule is how to define coloniality and how to speak of modernity in that context. What the insight gained from the insignias tells us is that modernity and colonialism always went hand in hand in Seoul. This entanglement can also be noted with respect to the name Kyŏngsŏng/Keijō. Kyŏngsŏng had been in use long before the Japanese anointed it the official name of Seoul, but the difference in the colonial context was that it could now also be read in Japanese as Keijō. In practice, both versions were used, not just in translation but as proper nouns in their own right. In Korean-language publications, for example, the name Keijō often appeared in the Korean vernacular script, *han'gŭl*, as *keijo* (게이조). Kyŏngsŏng and Keijō were used interchangeably, but at times they did not always mean the same thing, as can be seen in a 1927 article published in *Tonga ilbo*. "Is it Kyŏngsŏng or Keijō?," the fifth installment in a series reviewing the economic condition of Korea, offered a rather grave assessment. Seoul could no longer be considered the center of the country due to the expansion of the Japanese settlement from South Village (Namch'on) out into North Village (Pukch'on), where the royal palaces and the elite *yangban* establishment were located: "Kyŏngsŏng is no longer the center of Chosŏn nor the center for the people of Chosŏn. Rather, it is the center for Chōsen. It does not belong to the people of Chosŏn, but to Japan. If the economic situation looks thus, the other aspects of the city will surely be the same. The city must now be called Keijō, not Kyŏngsŏng."[7] The alarm expressed about the trend of Japanese expansion had much to do with the fact that Seoul had been the capital city of the Chosŏn dynasty before colonization, unlike many other colonial cities in the world that became urbanized for the first time under colonial rule. However, rather than scrutinizing continuity (Kyŏngsŏng was a name already in use), this article located a historical rupture (Kyŏngsŏng became Keijō). The two readings of Seoul's name thus gained two different identities in this article: Kyŏngsŏng referred to Seoul before colonialization and Keijō to Seoul under Japanese colonial rule. In so doing, the article repeated the same kind of historical process analyzed in reference to the insignias, but from a different perspective that saw the change as neither inevitable nor a sign of progress, but of loss. The article inadvertently ended up identifying the trajectory of the city through the same future image as the colonial discourse.

Beyond the denoted meaning of the words in print, the text's composition reveals an even more complex picture. Kyŏngsŏng/Keijō is a name that derived from the same Chinese characters, which can be read either in Korean or Japanese. The title of the article thus rendered the names in han'gŭl and katakana, Japanese syllabaries primarily used for words of foreign origin, respectively: "Is it Kyŏngsŏng (경성) or Keijō (ケイジヤ ウ)?" But in the body of the article, which was written in the Korean mixed script (kukhanmun), a script that combines Chinese characters with Korean inflections, the name appeared in Chinese characters (京城). The result was that the Chinese characters were not open to multiple readings but had to be read as Kyŏngsŏng in the context of the Korean mixed script. In doing so, the article privileged the Korean reading of the characters and claimed in effect that its name written in Chinese characters, the name that had been in use throughout history, was the sole property of Korea and its history of diglossia. In contrast, the word Keijō, always written in katakana and thus divorced from the Chinese "original" by the virtue of the latter's exclusive connection to the Korean reading of Kyŏngsŏng, was marked with visual and aural distinction. The alien appearance of katakana in the body of the Korean mixed-script text underscored the estranged identity that Seoul gained as the only word in "foreign" script. This "foreignness" is what undercuts Seoul from becoming a bona fide "Japanese" city under colonial rule, but points to something else whose origin cannot be traced within the shared linguistic or cultural sphere by Japan and Korea—modernity.

The fact is that Seoul became a city befitting the title "colonial metropole"[8] not as a "Japanese" city per se, but as a modern city. A 1936 article in Taehan maeil sinbo reinforced this view, touting Seoul, with its more than two hundred thousand residents, as a city on par with other global cities (kukche tosi).[9] Indeed, familiar expressions of modernity across the globe were abundant in Seoul. But a characterization of Seoul as a city of "cosmopolitan" appearance involves high-stakes debates about how to speak of modernity in a non-Western and colonial context. Several of these issues can be glimpsed in a short essay, "Impressions of Keijō," written by a Japanese traveler in Seoul about his encounter, in the colony, with familiar objects and sites of the metropole. The traveler marveled at all the amenities and conveniences, such as streetcars, streetlights, and telephones, and at the hustle and bustle of modern girls and modern boys strolling under neon lights. The splendor of modernity was on full display in Seoul, particularly in the Japanese commercial district of Honmachi, so much so that the writer compared it to the Ginza district of Tokyo. The familiarity of Seoul, however, caused the traveler to feel a sense of discomfort, leading him to lament that modernity in Seoul was mere imitation and a reflection of a culture with no foundation.[10] The source of his unease was the temptation to view modernity in Seoul as a radical alterity to the metropolitan modernity, be it in Japan or in the West. The resemblance between metropolitan and colonial modernity made it difficult to do so, leading the writer to condemn Seoul's modernity as a copy instead—a disingenuous and incomplete version of modernity (figure I.4).

Was Seoul's modernity a mere copy, with no structures to support its superficial manifestations in the plethora of things? And if it was, does that make Seoul's modernity incomplete, a product of undisciplined imitation and unsophisticated understanding of culture? On one level, the question is about the mimetic. Seoul, an impression, or a copy of the metropolitan modernity, is seen as a product of borrowing of a culture that predates colonization. On another level, modernity existing on the surface level of "thingness" can be disregarded as nothing but a superficial imitation of the metropolitan modernity without a material (read actual) foundation in the colony, political economy or otherwise. These are the questions that also entered into the debates of "colonial modernity" in the past decades, which explored the overlapping and simultaneous instances of colonial and modern projects.[11] The foremost goal was to "make visible how globalizing colonial or imperial capital inhabited and reconfigured space, all space; not just some space."[12] Colonialism was not a dark side of modernity, but an integral part of capitalist expansion. And yet the emphasis on the global capital, as well as the characterization of "colonial," produced many works whose sole goal was either proving or disproving the premises of colonial modernity and also in-

FIGURE I.4. Photo featuring an aerial view of Seoul, 1925, 19.4 x 27.2 cm, Seoul History Museum.

vited criticisms about how this concept would apply to different contexts marked by varying degrees of colonial control.

Rather than litigating the question of modernity in the colonial context of Seoul in material (evidential) terms or demonstrating the coeval temporality of the metropolitan and colonial worlds, this book turns its attention to the question of epistemology. Once we foreground the inquiry in how our discourses have also been framed by modernity and its epistemological operation, the more important question, for us, is: Where does the traveler's desire to locate an alterity in the similitude of forms he found in Seoul come from in the first place? Put differently, where does the impulse to distinguish modernity in the colony from modernity in the metropole come from, and how does that distinction come to be articulated? To think intentionally about epistemology is helpful because it not only adds a dimension to the production of conditions that we historians study, political or otherwise, but also challenges the way we frame our discourses: how *we* talk about modernity in the colonial context. This eventually brings attention to how any attempt to talk about the non-West has already been subsumed by the self-articulation of the West within its field of knowledge production, the West's "refusal of its self-delimitation."[13] For this reason, Achille Mbembe warned about how Africa had always been discussed through a "negative interpretation" in the metatext about bestiality wherein the problem lies in how the West has developed its own self-image.[14] Similarly, colonial and postcolonial cities came to be characterized in terms of lack, which Sarah Nuttall and Achille Mbembe elaborated through the example of Johannesburg: the metanarratives of urbanization and modernization situate African cities in the context of global modernity without agency to contribute to that modernity. So, a meaningful investigation of African cities, or any other colonial cities, would have to entail "a profound reinterrogation of Africa in general as a sign in modern formation of knowledge."[15]

The West's knowledge production of modernity—its own fantasy about its existence—forecloses the non-West altogether, and this is the main process through which colonization occurs. The operation entails what Peter Osborne has called "historical totalization," a term introduced in his elaboration of Reinhart Koselleck's conceptualization of *neuzeit*.[16] *Neuzeit,* as a historical period, breaks from the previous epochs and defines the quality of historical time by distinguishing the period's own time from the one that preceded it. This is a striking difference from ideas based on the specificities of an epoch. *Neuzeit* defines itself as a philosophy of movement and as qualitatively better than what came before (progress) and allows for qualifications such as "earlier than" and "later than" rather than simply "before" and "after."[17] By "ascribing to temporal sequence a function creative of knowledge," therefore, "historical truths, by virtue of their temporalization, became superior truths."[18] More important, modernity as totalizing category was made possible through rationally (temporally) ordering its (spatial) other in its discourse, which Dipesh Chakrabarty observed in terms of how history and historical development (historicism) became a stagist theory of development that privileged Europe in what he called a "first in Europe, then elsewhere" temporal frame.[19]

The spatial unfolding of this temporal logic of universal history is modernizing and colonizing at the same time. In that sense, the process through which Kyŏngsŏng became Keijō was not simply a change in land ownership or government, but a change in epistemology. The process underscores how Seoul became foreclosed in modern knowledge production, how the city came to be situated in the metropole's self-imagination and in the subsequent figuration of metropole and colony. If we recognize how modernity orders noncontemporaneous times in a linear progression of time, we can better understand the double-edged sword of universalism that excludes as it includes: colonialism is an inherent impetus of modernity and integral to the totalizing and foreclosing force of modernity. In this regard, we can talk about the cosmopolitan expressions of Seoul noted in the traveler's essay as a product of Japanese colonialism operating through the discourse of modernity. Modernity itself was the mode of power for Japanese colonialism; the universal discourse of modernity and history was a strategy of colonization. In that light, modernity is not a condition brought about by urbanization but the totality of the processes through which colonial power discursively formulated itself in the urban space.

From this perspective, our subject of inquiry should not be whether Seoul was modern, or whether Seoul's modernity was genuine or a copy, but rather how modernity came to articulate itself as universal. For this reason, the book locates modernity's discursive practice and self-articulation in the urban space and asks how knowledge about modernity was produced through the urban form. For this, I draw from Timothy Mitchell's proposal for rethinking modernity as *staging*, not as a stage. Mitchell argued that the most salient characteristic of modernity is that the modern is staged as representations—image-making practices and social practices such as architecture, urban planning, literature, tourism, entertainment, and disciplinary mechanisms, which led him to formulate modernity as "world-as-picture," a mere copy that defines itself by what it lacks, by the gap in time and space that separates it from its model, but at the same time claims that the world it replicates is complete in itself.[20] Modernity in Seoul, like elsewhere, was manifested visually—a staging. To locate the energy behind staging, this book starts its inquiry in architecture, which sported "cosmopolitan" styles, useful for unpacking the question of copying. More important, architecture lends itself as a text wherein its visual forms were instrumental in producing a discourse, a concept and an idea which we often call the zeitgeist.[21] I explicate this further through the concept of monumentality.

In Seoul, the most important aspect of monumentality was the spatial reordering of the city through erasure. Key monumental structures of Japanese colonialism were strategically placed and built directly on the grounds or in close proximity to monuments to the Chosŏn dynasty's monarchs. Such an effort to undo the symbolic importance of the Chosŏn monuments was most notable in the construction of the new Government-General Building on the grounds of Kyŏngbok Palace. The building's construction began in 1916, shortly after the 1915 Industrial Exhibition, when a large portion of the palace was gutted. When it was completed in 1926, it dwarfed the remainder of the palace, which by then existed only in sections. Japan's construction of new architecture on palace grounds was a powerful way of visualizing colonial violence and dominance over space. However, the old palace was not completely removed, and surviving in a state of ruin, it presented a base for the purposeful superimposition of the new monumental architecture for Japanese colonialism. Rather than expunging the "old" other, the process of erasure pressed it into a relation with the "new" so that two different temporalities could be configured in one space—one pointing to the future promised by the universal time of modernity and the other to the Korean past of a particular time. When the two temporalities were incorporated into a historical narrative, Japan and Korea occupied different places in the linear progression of time, one advanced and the other lagging behind. This was a historical narrative that was also a colonial discourse. Modernity was part and parcel of Japanese colonialism, and it even appears that outside of modernity, colonial power and colonial difference could not have been articulated. Colonial discourse that is enveloped in the logic of modernity does not necessarily do away with the hierarchy of colonizer and colonized in the shared pursuit of universality. Instead, it resignifies colonial difference in temporal terms so that one is "modern" and the other is "not yet modern." The not yet modern is to be distinguished from the not modern by its participation in modernity's temporality, but its possibility of becoming modern is foreclosed from the start by modernity's very logic, which blurs the boundary between the colonial subject's desire for modernity and that of the colonizer: the colony will catch up, in time.[22] *Desire* is the key word here because this "indoctrination" was not didactic. Rather, modernity in Seoul, as elsewhere, was spectacular. The semblance of order would be achieved by associating architecture with certain events, times, and people through its visual properties. The superfluous figuration of modernity was essentially phantasmagoric because the identification and distinction between the metropole and the colony were based on the same desire, which was a key tenet of coloniality.[23] In all this, the city was the stage for such fictionalizing about modernity and its progress, the making and masking of reality.

In this way, Japanese colonial discourse rejected a localized concept of culture and prepared the conditions for Korea's participation and subjugation in the universalized realm of modernity. Consider again the traveler who lamented Seoul's modernity as a copy. It was his familiarity with modernity that made it difficult for him to separate Honmachi of Seoul from Ginza of Tokyo. Seoul under Japanese colonial rule became not a Korean city, a Japanese city, or an Asian city—it was a modern city that exhibited familiar forms and expressions of universal modernity where the question of origin mattered little. So, what the Japanese traveler saw as the lack of cultural particularity in Seoul was not a product of undisciplined imitation or unsophisticated understanding of culture but an outcome of Japanese colonialism that was operating within and through the totalizing discourse of modernity. The various signs of modernity in Seoul substituted for the "real" without specific reference to an origin in place or time and created a world in which images were the main producer of concepts. These images conjured up a Korea where the universal condition of progress would come in time, allowing the colony to belatedly catch up with the metropole. In this way, the boundary between coloniality and modernity became indistinct: the colonial subject's desire for the universal was precisely what alienated that subject from the promise of the universal.

Toward a Sedimentary History: Methodology and Sources

The practical question that confronts us is how we pursue a mode of inquiry that recuperates historical possibilities from the methodological and categorical limits that have shaped the study of Seoul. What would a history written from the position of the marginalized, excluded, and subsumed look like? It would certainly have to be critical of any impulse to see Seoul as the alterity of the universal or to locate it within its scheme of becoming. This book finds a potential for critical inquiry in the city itself and explores the very energy that escapes naming to unleash the multiplicities of the name, whether Kyŏngsŏng or Keijō, or something else. Any use of name, therefore, would have "to unfix rather than to fix the meaning."[24] That is, this history would resist the unchangeable

finality of utopian politics of modernity and move toward an urban poetics.[25] To present the entangled (not linear) processes of Seoul's construction, demolition, reconstruction, remembrance, and metamorphosis,
this book adopts space as an ordering principle and organizes itself in
the model of sediment, to uncover what lies beneath the manifold representations of the city's overlapping, conflicting, and layered slices of
life. The goal of this model is to present coeval processes that complicate
the usual scheme of cause and effect. Here, the common usage of the
term *sediment*, which refers to layers accumulated over time as matters
deposited earlier settle to the bottom, seems to be at odds with the temporal remaking of this model. The physical sediment does exist in Seoul:
the urban space of Seoul today is built upon layers of its many pasts,
some of which occasionally attain visibility and are kept visible behind
glass windows on the streets.[26] But because a purely physical notion of
sediment that spatializes a linear temporality in successive layers is not
adequate for capturing the multiplicity of time, this book uses sediment
as a speculative model to deploy against the linear temporal trajectory
of modernity.[27] This is in part to respond to the way the architectural
practices of Japanese colonialism operated through erasure and layered
its monuments over the five-hundred-year-old capital, all to narrate the
arrival of the "new." By sedimentary history, therefore, I propose a model
of inquiry that challenges the kind of temporalization of space by the
architectural practices of Japanese colonialism that turned the city into
a historical narrative. If we think of colonial power as operating on the
premise of the "textualization" of space—that is, the flattening of multiple
temporalities into a linear teleology—then we can turn this very mode of
power on its head by overlaying different layers atop one another.

    The sedimentary model of history takes inspiration from an illustra-
tion that appeared on the cover of the magazine *Pyŏlgŏn'gon* in July 1933
(figure I.5). With the title, "Modern Picture of the Twelve Thousand Peaks
of Kŭmgang Mountain" (*Modŏn kŭmgang manich'ŏnbong*), the cover illustration styles itself as an imitation of a traditional genre of painting
and presents a kaleidoscopic montage of a modern cityscape replete with
restaurants, cafés, movie theaters, and so on, all adorned with signage in
different scripts. This eclectic assortment highlights Seoul's modernity
through linguistic diversity and presents a view of cosmopolitanism that
does not privilege the West. Playing on the title, the illustration arranges
these establishments in the form of a mountain with multiple peaks. Two

smaller peaks (one of which is in silhouette) show a grimmer view with signposts that read "a duel arena" and "a suicide spot" and convey a sense of despair, juxtaposed against the abundance of hedonistic pleasure in this imaginary map. A chapel stands on the highest peak with a banner hung from its bell tower that reads: "Heaven is near." From the chapel, we can conjecture a satire of the message of salvation: promise and despair are two inseparable effects of modernity.

That chapel is significant for another reason; it reminds me of Paul Virilio's description of history as a landscape, which draws on Ecclesiastes: "For God, history is a landscape of events. For Him, nothing really follows sequentially since everything is co-present. From the smallest fact to the greatest historical event, there is nothing wonderful before him."[28] Viewed from the chapel, the imaginary position of the divine, the city lies before us neither as a chain of events nor even multiple strata that lead to the summit in successive moves, but as a panoply of many different events that coexist with no particular relation to one another. The same imagery of a nonlinear history appears even more powerfully

FIGURE I.5. Cover of *Pyŏlgŏn'gon*, July 1933, Yonsei University Library, Seoul.

in Walter Benjamin's well-known discussion of Paul Klee's painting *An-gelus Novus,* in which the angel sees history as "rubble on top of rubble" piled before his feet rather than as a chain of events.[29] Unable to keep his outstretched wings from closing as a storm rages at him, the angel is transfixed by the horror of history, which Benjamin identifies as prog-ress. The goal of sedimentary history is to heed these critiques of history and to visualize heterogeneous moments as traces of copresent time. In place of teleological narrative, which would inevitably privilege the question of origin, causality, and progress, a sedimentary history deploys an *architecturalization of history* through which time and space can be reconfigured, arranging events on top of one another by overlaying their surfaces rather than enumerating them one after another.

What these layers of the sedimentary history consist of are not simply events that usually make up a history: they are conceptualized as surfaces. This is to acknowledge that Seoul under Japanese rule was spectacular and phantasmagoric, so this book brings due attention to the *visual* dimension of the city and begins with architecture. On one level, the function of the architectonic allows an examination of space and surface in relation to each other. On another level, such a methodology works to replicate the experience of modernity from the marginalized position because while modernity was exhibited on the exterior of ar-chitecture, access to the interior of the monumental buildings was often denied to colonial subjects. Accessibility connotes privilege. When access is denied to a certain group of people, so is their potential to functionally transform the architecture. Here, Giuliana Bruno's conceptualization of the surface is helpful. She sees the surface as a mediator between the interior and the exterior because it is something that is configured as architecture and functions as a form of habitation.[30] So, I define surface as a space that the subject inhabits through sensory experience in visual, oral, auditory, and haptic registers, that are both material and imaginary. All of these surfaces also make up the visual dimension of the city, and I use the term *visual* to include, by relying on W.J.T. Mitchell, the interplay between visual and verbal signs, the sensory and the semiotic, the visi-ble and the invisible, and the synesthesia of auditory, tactile, and haptic, as well as everyday practices of seeing and showing, all of which amount to "the dangerous supplements" to hegemonic discourses.[31] Accordingly, the surfaces of sedimentary history consist of not only material objects detectable through sight but also extend to the mediascape as well as the soundscape of chatter, rumor, and noise. These surfaces are in turn overlaid atop one another and made visible on each level: the "cosmopolitan" ornaments dressed up Japanese monumental architecture, whose monumentality lay as much in manifestation as in erasure; commercial signage made up another visual and oral layer through its prominent "Asian" scripts and varied reading practices; the cacophony of language play, as well as rumor and gossip, haunted the senses and made up the underlayers of the city.

Then, what sources would help to enliven the experience of the city, uncover its visual, auditory, and imaginary surfaces, and capture the fragmentary, aleatory, and multiperspectival views of the urban life? If we understand the archive as a function of fields and institutions that endow it with truth claims, we will have to look beyond the usual sources available to us via colonial archiving. The sedimentary history instead gathers moments, pieces, and slices of urban life and deploys them to "carry over the principle of montage into history."[32] They are from texts and objects in mass circulation, which lend themselves for a study of words, word-images, images, and objects: postcards and maps (chapter 1), a commemorative photo album and journalistic photography (chapter 2), commercial signage and advertisement (chapter 3), gramophone recordings (chapter 4), and reportage in magazines (chapters 5 and 6).

These sources cannot easily be classified but prove to be effective mediums of capturing the speed, motion, and mood of urban modernity. They did so, not simply through the content that they described, but through the form they took. For this, I call them *metropolitan miniature*, drawing on Andreas Huyssen. Metropolitan miniature, referring to a body of short texts published in the feuilletons, is a product of the advent of the new media—photography and film in particular—that centrally focused on the question of perception and how the verbal and visual interacted. For Huyssen, these *modernist* texts regarded urban space as underpinning modern life and highlighted the sensory experience, as well as the dream images, so the visible world was always shadowed by what was invisible, the urban unconscious.[33] These texts were called "unstorylike stories" and many other things. Underscoring the difficulty in defining these texts with a single name, Ernst Bloch once lamented in a letter to Siegfried Kracauer, "If only we had a name for the new form which no longer is a form."[34] For this reason, Huyssen claimed that metropolitan miniature was essentially an anti-form, which was begotten from experimenting with the visual.[35]

There is no specific genre term that applies to such a diverse body of texts circulating in the everyday on which this book relies, but more often than not they were known simply as *iyagi* or "stories." Though they seldom showed any adherence to genre conventions or formal considerations having to do with writing, iyagi showed keen awareness of the new mode of seeing produced by new mediums such as film and photography. They also adapted to sound technologies such as gramophone, as well as new forms of sociability in print such as review roundtable (chapter 3) and interviews (chapter 6).[36] The interaction between the verbal and the visual was what distinguished iyagi from other casual stories about the urban life on the one hand and from literature on the other; they owed their existence to the speedily changing modern city with rapid circulation of words and images through the print and sound media. And much to the chagrin of the day's language reformers and intellectuals, they contained a strong trace of colloquial, spoken language—the language of the marketplace and the everyday. In this regard, iyagi in their multiple reiterations posited themselves as "anti-form" against literature as well as social science. This is why I call them metropolitan miniatures. What connects the different authors and historical contexts between Huyssen's feuilletons and this book's iyagi is how they engaged with the modern city, grappled with the new visual experience, and most importantly, experimented with the form of writing. The anti-form of the metropolitan miniature offers a critique of established narratology, epistemology, and even ontology, and certainly history writing. Therefore, I attempt to find the meaning of being modern not in a formulable articulation about modernity but in the raw experience presented in anti-form.

Being modern is not simply being in the modern world; rather, it is about critical engagement with the very logic of modernity and the experience that it shapes. The forgotten surfaces of the city, which may be inconsequential and insignificant to a teleological history, are what the book brings to the fore by stacking surfaces on top of one another in a sedimentary history composed of montage of urban life. It traverses many boundaries of material and immaterial, visual and verbal, visible and invisible, monumental and mundane, and image and sound to explore how the city was represented in image and text, reverberated in

the soundscape, and was experienced in lived time. In presenting a mul-
timodal overlap and layering of life through different sensory registers,
the book also writes its history in a way that creates a bricolage of these
unremarkable anti-forms instead of relying on data-driven sources to re-
construct city life in Seoul—all in the hope of shifting the urban terrain
by layering figural over discursive, *syuzhet* over *fabula*, *parole* over *logo*,
moment over monument, chance over design, fragment over totality, de-
viance over defiance, and play over discipline.

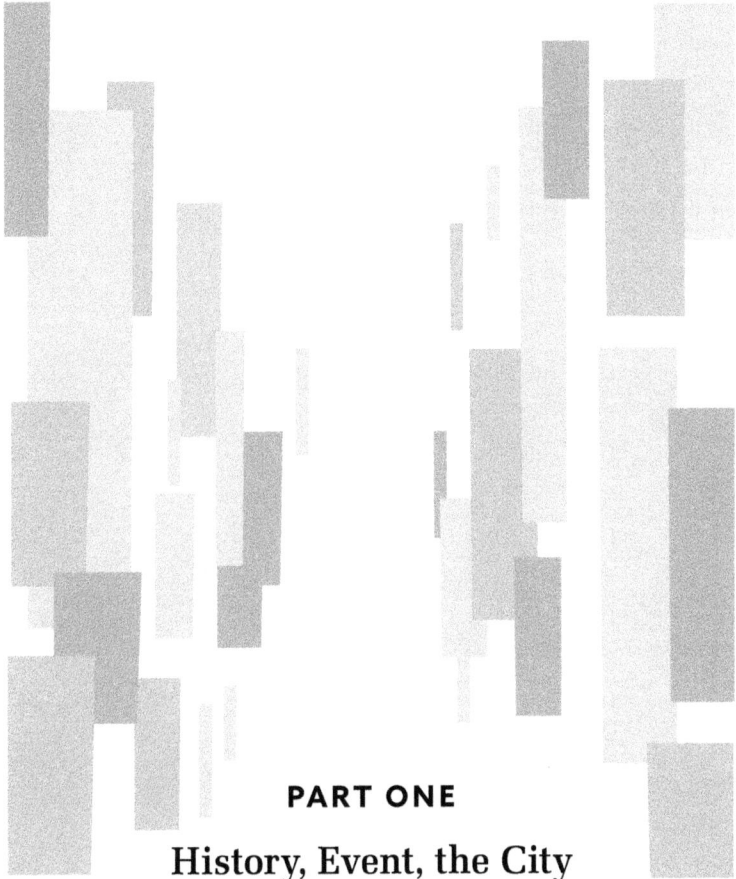

PART ONE

History, Event, the City

1

Figuring History through Architecture

AN URBAN SYNESTHESIA

On October 9, 1925, *Tonga ilbo* announced its plan to run a photography series called "The Photograph That I Want to See" in which readers would recommend photographs of any type for the newspaper to print.[1] Over a little less than two months, the series ran fifteen photographs, several of which were related to the past monarchy. The second installment, published on October 29, also featured a monarchical palace in an article entitled "Kwanghwa Gate of Kyŏngbok Palace" (figure 1.1). It appeared in a collage of two photographs placed on an offset diagonal. The photograph at the top showed a view of the new Government-General Building, still under construction. At bottom right the photograph showed Kwanghwa Gate in front of the Government-General Building. Because of the way the two images were overlaid, Kwanghwa Gate partially blocked not one but two views of the Government-General Building. This presentation is a curious choice because it was Kwanghwa Gate that was to be removed and relocated to the eastern part of the palace, where it would not obstruct the view of the new structure when it was completed. The accompanying text did not explicitly state a reason for relocation other than dozens of readers wanted to see Kwanghwa Gate once more before it was moved. But by juxtaposing the two buildings, the paper not so im-

意注題課眞寫

FIGURE 1.1. Views of Kwanghwa Gate, from *Tonga ilbo*, October 20, 1925. Reprinted with permission.

plicitly signaled the culprit of this tragedy and conveyed a sense of loss, reluctance, and even resistance on the part of Korean onlookers.

Kyŏngbok Palace suffered incremental destruction throughout the colonial period. Even before annexation, some parts of the palace came to be used as gardens by the Japanese, and four thousand rooms had been auctioned off to Korean and Japanese buyers.[2] In 1912, according to the Urban Improvement Ordinance, the hilly road called Hwangt'o maru between the crossroads in front of Kyŏngbok Palace and Tŏksu Palace was flattened to build a plaza, and the palace opened to the public in the following year. In 1915, a major catalyst for the palace's demolition was the Industrial Exhibition, which destroyed much of the palace to accommodate new exhibition structures.[3] In particular, the area in front of Kŭnjŏngjŏn was cleared to build Exhibition Hall No. 1, a massive structure tall enough and wide enough to enshroud Kŭnjŏngjŏn. In 1916, shortly after the closing of the exhibition, the construction of the new Government-General Building began in the largely emptied out palace. Intentionally located on the site of Exhibition Hall No. 1, this new building also blocked the view of Kŭnjŏngjŏn, one of a handful of buildings that survived colonial dismantling along with Kyŏnghoeru and Kwanghwa Gate.

That Kwanghwa Gate prevented an unobstructed view of the new monument to Japanese colonialism was a thorny issue. The Government-General initially planned to destroy the gate, but when it announced its plan in 1923, it met with strong resistance from Koreans as well as from Japanese ethnologists like Yanagi Muneyoshi.[4] Despite huge projected costs, relocation of the gate began in September 1926 and was completed fourteen months later. The outcry over the gate's relocation was undeniable. An article in *Tonga ilbo* in 1926 bemoaned the fate of Kwanghwa Gate, saying it had been a prize of Eastern architecture and a gateway to the palace central to the Chosŏn dynasty in modern times.[5] Another editorial in 1927 also lamented the destruction: "Disturbing a single stone (of Kwanghwamun) is like skewering the deep depths of our hearts. . . . We can only watch as our precious traditions are uprooted."[6] It defended Kwanghwa Gate as the last structure built by the hands of Korean people—an outcome of their sweat and labor—and compared its relocation to physical harm done to the bodies of Korean people. The editorial thus likened Kwanghwa Gate to a pair of glasses through which one can see the past and future, as well as "a world of ten thousand flowers visible only to Koreans."[7]

The scale of colonial violence against Kyŏngbok Palace and Kwanghwa Gate is often described in terms of the scale of the Government-General Building itself. The mammoth structure was a towering presence; it was the only five-story building in Seoul at the time, occupying 6,922 square meters, with another 31,749 square meters of open space, lawns, and gardens.[8] An illustration published in an article reviewing the Cultural Rule (1920–1937) in *Kaebyŏk* in 1925 emphasized its domineering presence by juxtaposing it uneasily with Kwanghwa Gate and straw-roofed houses (figure 1.2). The illustration clearly contrasts the Government-General Building and Kwanghwa Gate in terms of style and scale in a way that symbolizes dominance and violence, also obvious in the common Korean dwellings that are dwarfed by it. The handwritten text in the illustration reads: "If you compare the new building for the Government-General and Korean houses, we can easily understand the state of the governance."[9] The Cultural Rule was little different from the previous Military Rule (1910–1919) and was as oppressive as its new architecture.

After the liberation, the Government-General Building was repurposed as the Central Office by the Republic of Korea and later as the

FIGURE 1.2. Illustration of the Government-General Building, from *Kaebyŏk*, March 1925, National Library of Korea, Seoul.

Museum of Korean Art. Kwanghwa Gate was destroyed during the Korean War; it was not until December 1968 that Park Chung Hee oversaw its reconstruction. The new Kwanghwa Gate was awkward. Whereas the original structure was largely wood, the new one was made of concrete, steel, and stone. It featured signage in vernacular Korean, presumably Park's own calligraphic work, and was intentionally positioned in alignment with the former Government-General Building, slightly off its original axis. Undoubtedly, the restoration of Kwanghwa Gate was meant to support Park's authoritarian regime by sanctioning him as the bearer of Korean history; and that history also had to affirm the trajectory of developmentalism set by Park's regime. Many critics detested the concrete structure but justified it as a representation of Korea's modernization, in contrast to the wooden structure that did not outlast the harmful effects of history. Michael Kim thus argued that the new Kwanghwa Gate ultimately signaled Korea's indigenous modernity, not the restoration of its past.[10] It was nationalism, not traditionalism, then, that guided the reconstruction of Kwanghwa Gate.

Traditionalism received attention during the 1990s, when the Government-General Building was completely removed. Kim Young Sam's election pledge to remove the building was carried out in 1995 on the anniversary of liberation with fanfare and fireworks. It was not without controversy, and at the crux, the debate revolved around whether the physical removal of architecture can rewrite or even rectify history. Some even questioned which history was being erased, since the building had long served as the Central Office for the South Korean state. The rationale behind the building's removal, though, really reflected an even more fundamental issue. According to Jong-Heon Jin, the destruction of the Government-General Building was intended to restore the "national spirit." This was based on the argument that the colonial state's demolition of Kyŏngbok Palace was intended to eliminate the symbolic space of the Chosŏn dynasty, itself guided by principles of geomancy (*p'ungsu*).[11] This understanding of the spatial geography of the Chosŏn dynasty, according to Jin, called for a return to the traditional, not just a correction of the past, as a major component of the history writing that would unify competing nationalisms.

Arguably, the Government-General Building has been the single most contentious site of history in modern and contemporary Korea. It served as a symbol of colonial dominance during and after the colonial period, and the subsequent efforts to restore Kwanghwa Gate and Kyŏngbok Palace were intended to articulate Korea's own developmentalism as well as to revive tradition as a motor of Korea's nationalism. Most stunningly, the rewriting of history all took place in the urban space, not history books. How, then, should we conceptualize the relationships between the urban space and history, and between architecture and urban space? Jong-Heon Jin rightly described the urban landscape as text and imagery—he called it the "urban symbolic landscape."[12] In this conceptualization, however, one object stands for the entirety of historical narratives of colonialism and the colonial discourse of power. This kind of reading makes architecture vulnerable to the politically charged rhetoric that guided the demolition and reconstruction of the palace. Instead of identifying the function of architecture as symbolic, therefore, this chapter emphasizes its relationship to the surrounding environment. In this approach, domination is not noted simply in what the building symbolized but in how it created a stark contrast to the remaining palace structures. It also pays attention to how urbanization linked the building to its surroundings and examines a structure not in isolation but *in connection with* its environment. In other words, situated architecture in the flow of connection and disconnection opens up the possibility of exploring the discursive functions of architecture and urban space with a specific focus on conduits of movement. Therefore, in moving away from symbolic readings of architecture that reinforce the rhetoric of colonial domination, this chapter complicates the history of colonial rule by presenting the city's evolution as a narrative space via urban restructuring and architecture, as well as through visual representations of travel such as maps and postcards.

Rewriting Space: Temporality of Erasure

Kyŏngbok Palace was not the only palace that suffered an unfortunate fate. As early as 1908, a zoo and a botanical garden were built on the grounds of Ch'anggyŏng Palace, destroying many original structures. In 1911, a museum was added to the site, and the palace opened to the public as Ch'anggyŏng Garden (*wŏn*). In 1922, cherry trees were planted, and in 1924 the garden opened for nighttime cherry blossom viewing. Hwan'gudan, the altar that served as the main stage for the founding of the Taehan Empire, was demolished to construct Chosŏn Hotel in 1914. The hotel's lobby was built atop the altar, so only the three-story pavilion Hwanggungu survived, relegated to the garden. Tŏksu and Ch'angdŏk, two palaces that served as residences for Kojong and Sunjong, remained largely intact until their deaths. After Kojong died in 1919, most functions of Tŏksu Palace became ineffective, and the building of a new city hall across from the palace was proposed in 1920.[13] As for Ch'angdŏk Palace, renovation projects were discussed after Sunjong's death in 1926, and in 1927 a road was constructed that pierced the border between Ch'angdŏk Palace and Chongmyo—direct violence against the sacred ancestral shrine and the monarchy.[14]

Considering that many colonial cities around the world were urbanized by their colonizers, the question arises as to why Japan would choose an active, already-urbanized capital city for its colonial center. The measures required to deconstruct the monarchical palaces were costly. Moreover, full-fledged urban planning proved difficult when contending with the complex forces that shaped the city's landscape, including the five-hundred-year history of the Chosŏn dynasty, the Taehan

Empire's incipient modernization efforts, and the remnants of the settlement of Western imperialists and other foreigners. Kim Paeg-yŏng noted that Japan's selection of Seoul as the capital was neither an automatic nor a natural process. Seoul was not a port city, so its inland location did not lend itself to easy access from the metropole. Moreover, the concentration of resistance forces there made it costly both politically and socially to develop, administer, and manage the city.[15] But Seoul had to be the colonial capital because of the power that it exerted as a traditional city as well as the persistent resistance of the Taehan Empire and the monarchy. Therefore, Japanese colonial rule altered the fundamental structure of Seoul's urbanity but without stripping its status as capital. In short, the Japanese colonial government worked to change Seoul's identity and function, not its status.[16] Evidence of this is found in the shrinking of the boundaries of Seoul to within the city walls to the exclusion of Sŏngjŏsimni, and in the development of a gourd-shaped city, including a Japanese military base in Yongsan. The new boundaries accommodated the economic center in South Village and the military center in Yongsan while creating a political center in North Village, thus breaking Seoul into a duality, suffocating the traditional center in the north by violently restructuring the city from the south. Kim called this process "violent assimilation."[17]

South Village had grown at the periphery, at the foot of Nam Mountain, which was called Chin'gogae or "muddy hills," because of frequent flooding. Whereas North Village had been home to the power holders of the Chosŏn dynasty, South Village had been occupied by poor *yangban* and scholars, and later by Chinese migrants and merchants. As Japanese migration to Korea steadily increased during the 1880s, around 1885 Japanese migrants began to form a settlement in the area. They established the Consulate, the Office of the Settlers, and the Office of Commerce in 1887 to protect their economic rights and shift commercial power away from the Chinese. They attempted to expand their settlement to Chongno but met with resistance from Korean and Chinese merchants.[18] Thus, rather than leave Chin'gogae, an unsuitable muddy hill in the eyes of any urban developer, they decided to transform it into Ponjŏng/Honmachi, a new center worthy to bear the name of the Japanese settler community. The Urban Improvement Ordinance of 1912 was introduced to tackle the road construction that would modernize the area and take advantage of its proximity to the South Gate. It proposed the renovation and construction of twenty-nine roads, most of which were located around the Japanese settlement.[19] The reform paved and straightened the narrow zigzag pathways that first separated pedestrian walkways from the road, including the road connecting the South Gate, South Gate Railway Station, and Hwanggŭmjŏng Street (today's Ŭlchiro).[20] While access to the south aided the economic and commercial activities of South Village, another newly extended road, T'aep'yŏng Avenue, played an important role in connecting South Village to North Village. The road's construction began in 1912 and was completed in 1914 through several projects that expanded the avenue from Kwanghwa Gate into a sixty-meter-wide thoroughfare that reached the South Gate and eventually Kyŏngsŏng Station. Along the way, it intersected with all major streets, including Chongno and the newly widened Hwanggŭmjŏng Street. The Road Planning by Urban Reform in 1919 extended the artery southward to the Japanese military base in Yongsan, eventually connecting all military, commercial, and political centers in one stroke. This north-south thoroughfare was an important enabler of the colonial government's penetration of the heart of the city and the development of the city into the gourd shape mentioned earlier. Equally important was that as the main artery linking the two zones of the city, it rendered ineffective the traditional east-west urban axis through Chongno. Following the example of T'aep'yŏng Avenue, other vertical conduits from Chongno were created, which included Tonhwamun Avenue, to connect the Tonhwa Gate of Ch'angdŏk Palace to P'il-dong, and Ŭiwŏn Avenue, to connect Ch'anggyŏng Palace to Taehwa. These newly constructed roads formed a grid, connecting South Village to North Village and "opening up" the city.[21] By 1929 and 1930, the road grid was completed; it changed little with the 1934 urban planning project, which focused mainly on extending the city's outer limits and rezoning neighborhoods and new industrial zones.[22]

In South Village, the center of the Japanese settler community was located at the intersection of Namdaemun Avenue and Ponjŏng Avenue, where the Japanese consulate and Offices of Japanese Settlers and Commerce were built in 1897. With the construction of Kyŏngsŏng Post Office and the Bank of Chosŏn in 1912, which gave the area its name— Sŏnŭnjŏn or Senginmae, literally meaning "the square in front of the Bank of Chosŏn"—it also became the financial and economic center for South Village, whose importance was elevated in the 1930s with construction of the Mitsukoshi Department Store. Except for the Shinto

Shrine built in Nam Mountain near the settlement in 1925, the trend that followed the development of South Village's commercial, financial, and economic apparatus in the 1920s was the moving out of public and administrative buildings, and in this, the year 1926 was pivotal. In 1926 the new Government-General Building was completed on the grounds of Kyŏngbok Palace. The same year saw the completion of City Hall, which had been relocated from Sŏnŭnjŏn to a site previously occupied by the Keijō Newspaper building across from Tŏksu Palace. Other key leisure and educational facilities, such as Kyŏngsŏng Stadium and Kyŏngsŏng Imperial University, were also completed. And of course, the city's new insignia was announced in 1926.

The relocation of key political installations in North Village functionally separated it from South Village, cementing the identity of South Village as an economic center and North Village as a symbol of political domination. All of the major development that occurred around 1926 signaled the dominance of the main north-south axis and the beginning of the northward expansion of Japanese settlers.[23] In this light, the relationship between North Village and South Village has come to be viewed differently by some: Chŏn U-yong, for instance, explained it as a strategy not of invading space in North Village but of alienating.[24] Todd Henry characterized it as assimilation, which also revealed the multifaceted workings of colonial governmentality, particularly in public spaces.[25] Kim Paeg-yŏng insisted that Japan did not treat North Village as an object of hostility and obliteration but as "remnants" and "ruins" to be assimilated and accommodated.[26] Inevitably, there exist tensions between domination and assimilation, assimilation and alienation, and alienation and accommodation, but if we add another component—time—we can see these seemingly contradictory forces in a new light. The fact is that this spatial duality was marked with a distinctive temporal characteristic that privileged South Village. That is, the urban space of Seoul by the mid- to late 1920s produced a discourse about time that resulted in a gaze split between modernity and tradition. In that bifurcation, North Village was forced to cast itself as "traditional," "old," and "not yet modern"—all this a result of colonial domination, but more of forcing the colonized into a relation with the colonizer as evidence of assimilation. Yet the outcome of assimilation was alienation, both from what the colonial subjects desired (universal modernity) and from what they desired to leave behind (particularity).

This was most pertinently seen in architecture, as evident in the contentious debate surrounding the Government-General Building. And yet the building was not merely a symbol of domination; it also created that new temporality that is modernity through its strategic location vis-à-vis Kyŏngbok Palace. This was a temporalizing process that was achieved through the *sous rature* ("under erasure," or striking out as in text that is x'ed out but still visible) of monarchical architecture.[27] Despite demolition, key buildings from the palaces survived and came to persist *sous rature*, crossed out but visible, by new colonial monuments: the zoo, garden, and museum at Ch'anggyŏng Palace stood alongside what remained of the palace and the adjunct Ch'angdŏk Palace; Hwanggungu became accessory to a hotel; and Kwanghwa Gate, Kŭnjŏngjŏn, and Kyŏnghoeru stood overwhelmed by the imposing Government-General Building. As they existed in fragments, severed from wholeness and denied the possibility of regaining wholeness, their legibility was a reminder of absence. As remnants, they were constant reminders of what had disappeared and the power that caused its disappearance.[28] They were indeed ruins. They did not simply represent a dynasty in shambles but allowed it to undergo resignification as the end of an era, a past interrupted by the advent of the modern. In other words, the palaces symbolizing monarchical power were inadequate in the "modern" Korea that was led by Japan; nevertheless, they were necessary to announce colonial power and, more importantly, the arrival of the "new" era.

A further extrapolation of the concept of ruin is helpful to better understand the temporalizing process of erasure. A postcard from a collection called *The Hundred Views of Keijō* (Keijō hyakkei), discussed in detail later, illustrates this. It featured Chosŏn Hotel, which was shown in two contrasting images: the baroque-style structure of the hotel on the left and Hwanggungu, the only building preserved when the site's altar was destroyed, on the right (figure 1.3). The side-by-side images could have invoked the violence of colonization. However, Hwanggungu appeared lit by electric lights along with the illuminated fountain as if consecrated by modernity. The modern technology tempered the effect of violence and created an evocative scene in which the present and past coexisted harmoniously. Three poems that appeared along with these images illustrate this by evoking a pleasant, romantic, wistful ambience in the clear water, the cool shade, summer twilight, the sound of cicadas, and falling leaves:

How pure the water!
How fine the shade the trees cast!
For so long as they,
At least, are with us . . .

Unbearably sad
Summer twilight falls
On the ruins of the old fortress
As cicadas cry
And withered leaves drop.

Splendid
Though I know naught of
Their past—
The stone steps
And lovely maiden's tears.[29]

Along with the picturesque image of nature, another type of architectural ruin is presented: the old fortress (city walls) and the stone steps.
These are what one would typically count as ruins, remnants of architec-

FIGURE 1.3. Postcard of Chōsen Hotel, from *The Hundred Views of Keijō* (*Keijō hyak-kei*), c. 1925–35, 9 x 14.2 cm. Source: Busan Museum.

ture surviving in decay, unlike Hwanggungu, which was presented in its pristine form, beautifully illuminated.[30] The stone walls and steps were a reminder of the "brute, downward-dragging, corroding, crumbling power" of nature that would eventually win over the human's artifice, and thus is a reminder of the passage of time.[31] In contrast, the exquisite presentation of Hwanggungu was the extolling of the power that could resist the passage of time. Hwanggungu with no signs of decay then invites the question of how we can even consider it a ruin. The answer can be found in how Hwanggungu came to signify more than time past. What it signified is a past frozen in time—a primordial past.

The Korean architecture *sous rature* was presented as the artistic achievement of Korea, and Japan was the custodian of Korea's tradition. This past was a pan-Asian dream in which the past was tamed and exoticized for imperial self-articulation and consumption. The mood of reflection in solitude and silence in the poems underscores this point. The poems were essentially written in a voice of an imperial subject of melancholy and narcissistic mourning. Taylor Atkins called it an "epistemology of loss," in which "the times of loss and nostalgic longing for a purer cultural self are central to Japanese experiences of modernity."[32] Through an epistemology of loss, colonial access to Korea gave Japan an opportunity to mediate its own historical and modern identity. The ruin, in other words, was "a sign of survival" but "not its own survival, but the survival of the possessor," for which Susan Stewart pointedly argued that "it is the possessor, not the souvenir, which is ultimately the curiosity."[33]

Although such a view of history through a nostalgic lens might appear to undercut the writing of history that progresses through the teleological trajectory of time, Janet Poole reminded us that nostalgia, essentially rooted in a desire to return to what is now lost, is an attempt to conceive of a future.[34] Svetlana Boym similarly spoke of the temporality of nostalgia as a "future-past" that is not always retrospective but prospective.[35] For this reason, nostalgia is not antimodern but an integral part of modernity. Moreover, nostalgia is not merely a symptom of individual emotion or an expression of local longing "but the result of a new understanding of time and space that made the division into 'local' and 'universal' possible."[36] In short, nostalgia is a "historical emotion" and a "side effect of teleology."[37]

Undoubtably, the transformation of Seoul into a colonial city is a testament to the colonial power that violently rewrote the spatial practices of the previous dynasty. The result, was, however, much more complex than domination, assimilation, or alienation. What this example of entangled relationship of modernity, history, and nostalgia shows is that modernity, its temporal and spatial logic, was at the heart of the colonizing process. When modernity is allowed to become a critical component in understanding Japanese colonialism, Korea's place vis-à-vis Japan is articulated in temporal terms, not as a past no longer relevant in the present but a past useful for the articulation of future. Then, *sous rature* was a process that prepared Korea's incorporation into the colonial discourse of power, first by signaling the colonial undoing of space and then by being integrated into an emotive narrative that constructed modern subjectivity. The next sections thus turn their attention to the surface matters of architecture for a closer look at this different (discursive) mode of operation for colonial power—how the textual reading of architecture entailed the production of an emotive landscape.

Ornamentality: A Journey into Interiority

A key component of discursive production through architecture was the contrast achieved by colonial monumental architecture to the Korean architecture under erasure. Colonial architecture in Seoul was grandiose in scale and elaborate in presentation, subjecting Chosŏn monuments under erasure to a sharp contrast of scale and stylistic difference. Most Japanese colonial architecture in Seoul followed the Beaux-Arts style, drawing on the nineteenth-century building styles of Europe. The key feature of this style was a reference to the past through the "eclectic ornamentation used to camouflage new materials."[38] Japanese colonial architecture thus incorporated the latest techniques to modernize construction but still plastered the façade with decoration to dress up the modern in the glory of the past. Early examples of this are found in the Bank of Chosŏn and Kyŏngsŏng Post Office, which faced each other on Hwanggŭmjŏng Street. Built between 1907 and 1912, the Bank of Chosŏn was a white granite building in the Neo-Renaissance style, designed by the architect Tatsuno Kingo. Kyŏngsŏng Post Office, built between 1913 and 1915, was designed by Ichiro Nomura, featuring a signature baroque-style dome and the arched entablatures of red and white bricks.[39] During the 1920s, new materials such as steel-reinforced concrete were introduced, making it possible for monumental architecture to achieve a truly monumental scale.[40] Key buildings from this decade—Kyŏngsŏng Station, City Hall, and the Government-General Building—were larger and taller than previous buildings. For instance, Kyŏngsŏng Station, on which construction began in 1922 to replace the modest two-story wooden structure of Namdaemun Station, and was completed in 1925, was an impressive three-story structure occupying 5,222 p'yŏng.[41] It used masonry for exterior walls, reinforced concrete for the slab, concourse, columns, and basement, and a steel truss for the roof. It was adorned with Palladian-style exterior with an ornate Byzantine dome, Diocletian windows, and a rusticated façade. Symmetry, reinforced by the centrally located entrance, was an important concept that represented authority based on rationality and power. City Hall, built from 1925 to 1926, was a four-story building occupying 2,502 p'yŏng. Following the neoclassical style, the front of the building was symmetrical, with a central tower and a dome. Its decoration was much simpler, and it had a streamlined geometric composition, drawing its monumentality more from the construction of a single large open space. And yet it also featured a veneer of added Lysine coating on the brick walls that gave the appearance of artificial stone.[42]

The Government-General Building, built between 1916 and 1926 and designed by George de Lalande, a German architect who completed the basic design between 1912 and 1914, and Iwai Chōsaburō and Sasa Keiichi, who took over after de Lalande's sudden death in 1914, is a significant building architecturally as much as politically (figure 1.4). It was the first to incorporate reinforced concrete for the entire structure, which upon its completion propelled a stylistic shift from neoclassical to international around 1926.[43] This five-story structure revealed major characteristics of Neo-Renaissance style, especially emphasizing symmetry and geometrical proportion. It achieved monumentality by aligning its central axis with the street, creating harmony with urban planning.[44] Symmetry was repeated throughout the building: a copper-plated dome was placed atop the center and turrets on each end; the front entrance was central and counterbalanced by two auxiliary entrances facing each other; the front was divided into four sections punctuated by horizontal strapworks; and the courtyards were laid out facing each other, and another courtyard was prepared in the back of the building to create the same scale of void space as the loggia in the front. As for the finishes, the walls between the columns were filled with masonry, and the exterior

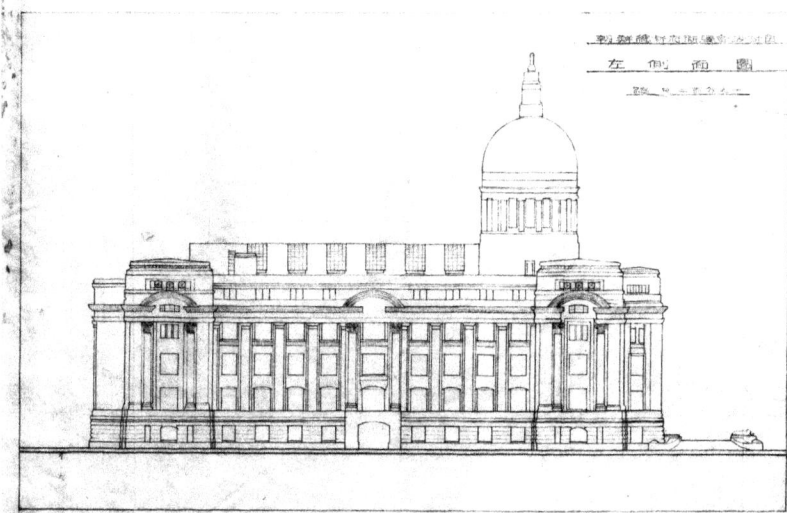

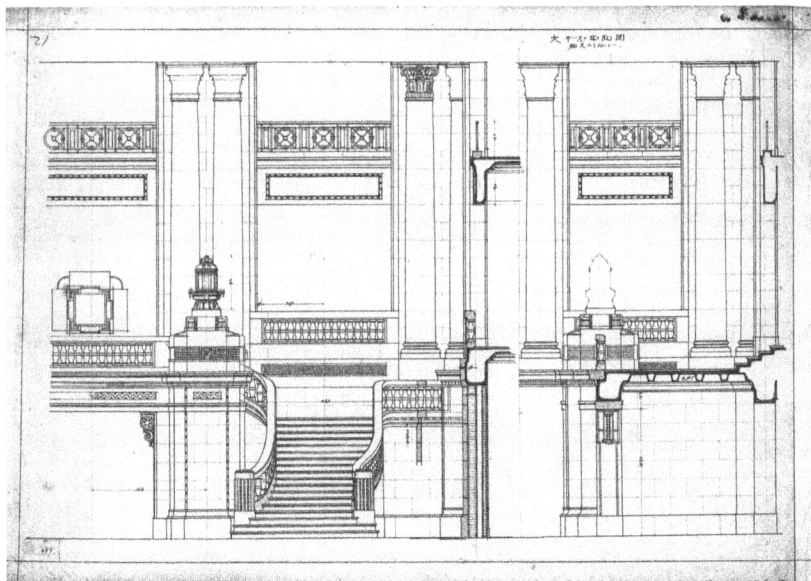

FIGURE 1.4. Surveyed maps of the Government-General Building, c. 1915–1925, National Archive of Korea.

walls were plastered with granite. The foundations of the walls in the courtyard were covered with granite, and other walls had an artificial stone façade. Granite finished the surfaces inside as well, while orders, shafts, and railing decorations used marble plaster. Decorations were elaborate on the exterior and interior of the building. The porch was offset to the front and supported by orders and shafts, as was the dome. Dentils decorated the top of the building on all sides. Loggias on three sides of the building featured iron railings with ornate decorations. The loggia openings, framed by segmented arches, had different designs on each floor above the second one. Inside, a pedestal on the second floor featured eighteen pairs of Corinthian columns decorated with entablature, cornice, frieze, and architrave, and the barrel vault on the third floor was done in the style of the Pantheon.[45]

From the splendor noted in the guiding principles of symmetry, balance, and proportion, as well as ornamentation more elaborate than that of the Bank of Chosŏn or Chosŏn Hotel, the Government-General Building was built to impress. Technologically advanced and aesthetic, it was touted as the representative achievement of modern architecture by Japan: "The new building is a blend of modern science and art and reveals the highest level that such a union can attain. This building is Japan's and Asia's pride and it is also the symbol of a Korea entering the dawn of a new age."[46] Nishizawa Yasuhiko, who did not fail to mention that no traditional Japanese architectural style appeared on the façade, offered a similar assessment of the building: the construction seen in the Kahn Bar and concrete and steel frame represented strength; the hallway in the middle created by the shape of the Chinese character *il/ ni* for Japan showed a utilitarian side; and the influence of neo-baroque style seen in the symmetry, dome, and projected entrance, as well as the detailed attention given to the loggia and columns, were all attributes of its aesthetic quality.[47]

A Korean architect, Pak Kil-yong, who designed Hwasin Department Store and the main hall of Kyŏngsŏng Imperial University, would have taken issue with this analysis. Critical of the implementation of eclectic European styles that emphasized the façade, Pak argued that architectural beauty could not be judged by outer appearance alone. Rather, the goal of architecture was to address the spiritual needs by attending to practicality and functionality, not to style. Efficiency was the highest value in modern architecture, and the resources spent to beautify the

exterior were considered unnecessary or superfluous: "As society progresses, the inner structure of architecture becomes focused on practicality and rationality. Ostentatious display (hŏsik) on the exterior will
not have any impact on the people. The most modern architecture will
no longer be restricted by so-called styles determined by the façade (oe-
buyangsik). Individual function and efficacy of the building will be the
only goal of the most progressive architecture."[48] For Pak, architecture
in Seoul sported romantic and irrational styles of the previous era, emphasizing surface matters (oegwanjuŭi hyŏngsik) even as it purported to
respect science and rational thinking. This impeded the development
of Korean architecture.[49] So, he offered a blistering comment about the
Government-General Building, pointing out a contradiction between its
form and style: "Despite the fact that this is a reinforced-concrete structure, it is a kind of Renaissance style building. The lobby located in the
center protrudes to the front and has multiple stone columns that were
very costly to build. These are needless decorations that have no architectural function. It must have originated from the fact that this building
was built to impress and overpower."[50] Pak asserted that the building's
decorative style was a perfunctory decision to imitate a style from a
prefeudal past that had no meaningful existence in a modern society:
"Civilized beings of modern times do not need architectural styles of the
past."[51]

Kim Paeg-yŏng argued that Japanese colonial architecture's incorporation of Western styles epitomized how Japan adopted the technology,
system, and modes of Western imperial powers in its urban planning.
For Kim, although the forms showed similitude to the Western world,
internally they demonstrated the cultural inferiority of a non-Western
imperial power that had internalized the superiority of Western culture.
In short, this was an indication of an imperial power that had also experienced cultural colonization.[52] Likewise, Kim Chin-song explained
what appeared to be the indiscriminate adaptation of culture as "distinction through imitation," in which the anxiety of being left behind reflected the anxiety of being alienated from civilization.[53] These critiques
are valid, but the use of classical styles without a site-specific referent
in modern architecture is not unique to Japanese architecture, as Japan
was a non-Western culture imitating Western cultures. Emphasis on the
facade was a feature common across the nineteenth century and, according to Janet Ward, also a characteristic of Weimar architecture of the

1920s, which inspired a functionalist critique and a movement of façade renewal to advocate streamlining and unembellished surfaces.[54] What these critiques grappled with, in Korea or Germany, was what the surface created—a tale of modernity that was all about enchantment, seduction, and fetishism. Seoul's modernity, as elsewhere, existed on the surface levels of materiality, which Lewis Mumford poignantly described as a "corrupt veneer, a false 'municipal cosmetic' whose 'monumental façade' concealed rather than revealed."[55]

To better understand how architectural ornamentation produced this kind of fictive history writing, we can turn to examples from the postcard collection *The Hundred Views of Keijō*. Published by Taishō Photo Studio, the collection was composed of thirty-two postcards that included one hundred views of Seoul: a panoramic view of the city, historical sites such as palaces, people, and customs of Seoul, and the modern infrastructure of Japanese colonialism. The collection differed from other postcards or travel literature focused on Korean ethnography that were more consumption- and leisure-oriented.[56] In these, the usual itinerary centered on the so-called eight most famous sites of Seoul: Kyŏngsŏng Station, Yongsan Station, the South Gate, the Government-General Building, City Hall, the Shinto Shrine, the Nam Mountain Park, and the Botanical Garden.[57] The range of sites and topics that *The Hundred Views of Keijō* covered was much broader, crossing different sectors of politics, the economy, the military, education, and culture, and it included many sites not usually part of travel guides. In doing so, it created a disparate space from that of tourism, in tandem and in tension with it, and functioned almost like a comprehensive visual geography of Seoul.[58] Moreover, architecture was its central focus, so it gave an exhaustive and detailed photographic presentation of the buildings in Seoul. But because this collection was still intended for mass consumption, the attention to details did not amount to colonial archiving; rather what it produced was a discourse about Seoul.[59]

The collection developed an unlikely formula for such discursive production. This was achieved by inserting poems and songs alongside photographic images, as seen in the earlier postcard featuring Chosŏn Hotel. The texts were Japanese *waka* or Korean folk songs. Together, the textual elements were instrumental in conveying a contemplative tone: some were nostalgic, and some others were melancholic and even nihilistic. For instance, a postcard featuring Kyŏngsŏng Station (figure 1.5) showed photographs of Kyŏngsŏng Station at top, Namdaemun Avenue seen from the station at bottom left, and Yongsan Station at bottom right. The poems and Korean folk song read:

> *The successor to*
> *Kan'yō (Hanyang)'s distant past,*
> *the capital is*
> *flush with eternal splendor . . .*
>
> *With its old hometown*
> *in the distant kingdom of*
> *far Kōrai (Koryŏ)*
> *even summertime is sad*
> *for the poor mountain cuckoo.*
>
> *Now the mountains are ablaze*
> *Where do my travels take me?*
> *Off to Chinju I go*
> *to the waves of the Nan (Nam) River.*[60]

FIGURE 1.5. Postcard of Keijō Station, from *The Hundred Views of Keijō* (Keijō hyakkei), c. 1925–35, 9 x 14.2 cm. Source: Busan Museum.

While the images featured colonial architecture related to the railway, the poems and songs curiously included place-names specific to Korea such as Hanyang, Koryŏ, and Nam River in Chinju. All evoked memories of national resistance: Hanyang was the official name of Seoul for the Chosŏn dynasty; Koryŏ was a dynasty that fought against the Mongol invasion for more than forty years; and Nam River in Chinju was where *kisaeng* Non'gae committed suicide by plunging into the river with her arms wrapped around a Japanese general during the Hideyoshi Invasion. And yet by casting all these places in a reminiscent light, they came to signify a past that was lost and could not be recovered. This is starkly different from numerous other postcards that celebrated the grandeur of colonial architecture in a single glamour shot or contrasted modern buildings and amenities with the premodern and feudal lifestyles of Korea. In these cases, image and text produced a united message in which the imperial subject was either a collector of knowledge or a consumer of exotica. In this collection, there seems to be some dissonance between text and image. The images were about sophisticated modern architecture, and the words were about the past; the images showcased the material condition of Seoul while the words described the inner voice. The text did not provide objective information about the image but was singularly concerned with conveying subjective feelings. Yet there is a discernible empathy and even solidarity between the colonizer and the colonized, and even between the images of modern architecture and the texts describing a longing for forgotten history.

Another postcard featuring the Government-General can further support this point. It arranged four photographs from top to bottom showing Taep'yong Avenue, the dome of the Government-General Building, the Governor-General's residence, and the gate to the residence (figure 1.6). Each image was accompanied by a poem, and a Korean folk song translated into Japanese sat next to the photograph of the Government-General Building's dome (the second poem):[61]

> *With the holiday*
> *there is not a cloud in sight*
> *along the lakeshore.*
> *Clear and white shines the sunlight*
> *sparkling atop the water.*

I plant them in the garden
and how they, the flowers, grow!
Their lush leaves in profusion
reach over the fence.
"Let's look again today," think
those who walk along the road
and smitten with the flowers,
while away the day.

The trees embrace and
hide me, while their leaves' trembling
pacifies and soothes.
How at ease my heart does feel
in "Mien" Garden at dawn.

The crimson column
once again has come to life.
The servants, taking turns,
have set alight the lanterns
and gathered them all here.[62]

The poems and the song created a seamless blend and showed a reciprocity and harmony between actions of the speaker and others: the speaker plants flowers, and strollers are enchanted by them; the gleaming leaves clarify the mind of the speaker, and the servants light the lanterns. Such consonance is notable in bridging many distinctions between emotion and action, nature and city, self and other, and the colonizer and the colonized. It was meant not to equalize the power dynamics between the colonizer and the colonized, but rather to incorporate colonial subjects into that in-sync subjective process of introspection and action of the imperial subject: even the servants light the lanterns.

Here, the emotive landscape was a reflection of a different presentation of architecture; that is, how architectural surface creates a subjective reflection. In that regard, the way the images show the architecture of the most powerful political body in colonial Korea is noteworthy. Unlike the usual full view of the Government-General Building, to exude a commanding aura, it appears distant and indistinct over the horizon in the first photograph; the building that was shown in full frontal views

FIGURE 1.6. Postcard of the Government-General Building, from *Hundred Views of Keijō* (Keijō hyakkei), c. 1925–35, 14.2 x 9 cm. Source: Busan Museum.

was the Governor-General's residence instead. Specifically, the second photograph, in lieu of a commanding view of the Government-General Building, shows a close-up view of the ornament on top of its dome. The dome, one part of the building, does not necessarily stand in for the whole building, functioning as an icon. Rather it demonstrates how the ornament produced "the material urban reflection" through which a discursive subjectivity was formed.[63] The onlooker viewed the building in fragments and in turn arranged those fragments into an aggregate view, the architecture, which attests to a narrative construction at the core. Through the subject's engagement with the fragments of images, the material surface of architecture was turned into a reflective space, which was also a textual space activating two different subjectivities of vision and writing.

Proponents of ornament praised it as aesthetic achievement, and critics saw it as unnecessary to the function of the modern architecture. However, ornament becomes more than design or decoration, neither useful nor useless, but a space where vision was turned into cognition and cognition into emotion. Through ornament, in other words, the textual space on which ornament existed was transformed from expressive to experiential process, mobilizing the subject to reflect on reality by means of these abstract forms. In this regard, the coexistence of the cognitive and emotional in these postcards can be explained as a sign of a subject engaging with the two-dimensional surface of architecture. The poems in effect narrated how ornaments became an interface between the observer and the surface and were turned into a contemplative, self-reflective, and emotive space through a simulated sensorium. The beholder teetered between sense and sensation and between thought and emotion, creating what appeared to be a misalignment of vision and experience. However, this subjective position was not a disoriented one; it was endowed with rationality, which enabled the assemblage of fragments of the city into abstracted meaning. Because subjective formation took place on the surface of architecture, the surface becomes an important analytical site. In the synesthesia of this physical, material, and imaginative space, the history of colonizing Seoul folds against itself as the city is violently rewritten through the erasure of architecture and in turn rematerialized in the eyes of the observer. The next section will further explore another aspect of the visual presentation of this postcard collection and discuss how this narrative production relied on a modern subjectivity born out of travel and kinetic vision.

Architecture and Kinesthesis: Panorama and the Cinematic

At the crux of the narrative production of architecture was a new mode of seeing prepared by the modern city, namely the panorama. This section probes the evolution of the panorama in Seoul, specifically through the lens of travel maps and postcards, and explores the role of motion in the production of emotion. Crucial in understanding this new visual experience is the word *kyŏng* ("views"), an important medium of visualizing the colonial power that subsumed Korea, whose roots are also found in modernity. A prevalent image of Seoul that appeared across travel literatures, especially in maps and photographs, is a wide, high-angle view of the city that presented the "whole" view (chŏn'gyŏng) of the city. Many postcards published from 1911 to 1929 presented photographic panoramas that captured the landscape of Seoul. The panorama was usually taken from a position in the mountains and oftentimes required that multiple postcards, which were published as a collection, be lined up horizontally for a broader view of the city. This total and limitless scene was not a natural view, however, but an "expanded" one that demanded recognition of the position of the observer and validated its position as the overseer.[64] According to Theodore Hughes, the panorama was the logic behind the visual regime of Japanese colonialism: "The colonial remaking of the urban space underway in the 1920s and 1930s indeed operated by way of a visual regime tied to the 'panorama of evolution,' the material restructuring of the city itself as a panorama, a kind of permanent colonial exposition."[65] For this reason, the perspective of the panorama changed over time to favor the position of the colonizer.[66] Before 1926, most photographs of the city were taken from Nam Mountain, placing Kyŏngbok Palace and Pugak Mountain in the center with East Gate and West Gate visible at their sides. Postcards published after 1929, however, were taken from An Mountain, overlooking the city center from the west. This did not necessarily privilege the position from the south, where the Japanese settlement was located, but it made visible the new north-south axis from the Government-General Building to City Hall to the Shinto Shrine, as well as the newly refurbished Hwanggŭmjŏng.[67]

This shift of perspective from south to west is also noted in maps. *Tour Guide Map of Keijō* (Keijō yūran annaizu) (figure 1.7), for instance, depicts the natural terrain of Seoul from a perspective similar to the earlier photographic panorama from Nam Mountain. It shows an expansive view of the city from the mountains in the north to the Han River in the south. The viewing point here was from above (pugam), which simulated the photographic panorama and presented a more realistic perspective than the bird's-eye view (chogam) and was still suitable for representing the pleasure of the surveyor overseeing the city in its entirety (as the literal meaning of the word pugam is "to overlook"). It also featured drawings of mountains and rivers, as well as key buildings. The realism was tempered, however, by geometric lines and figures as well

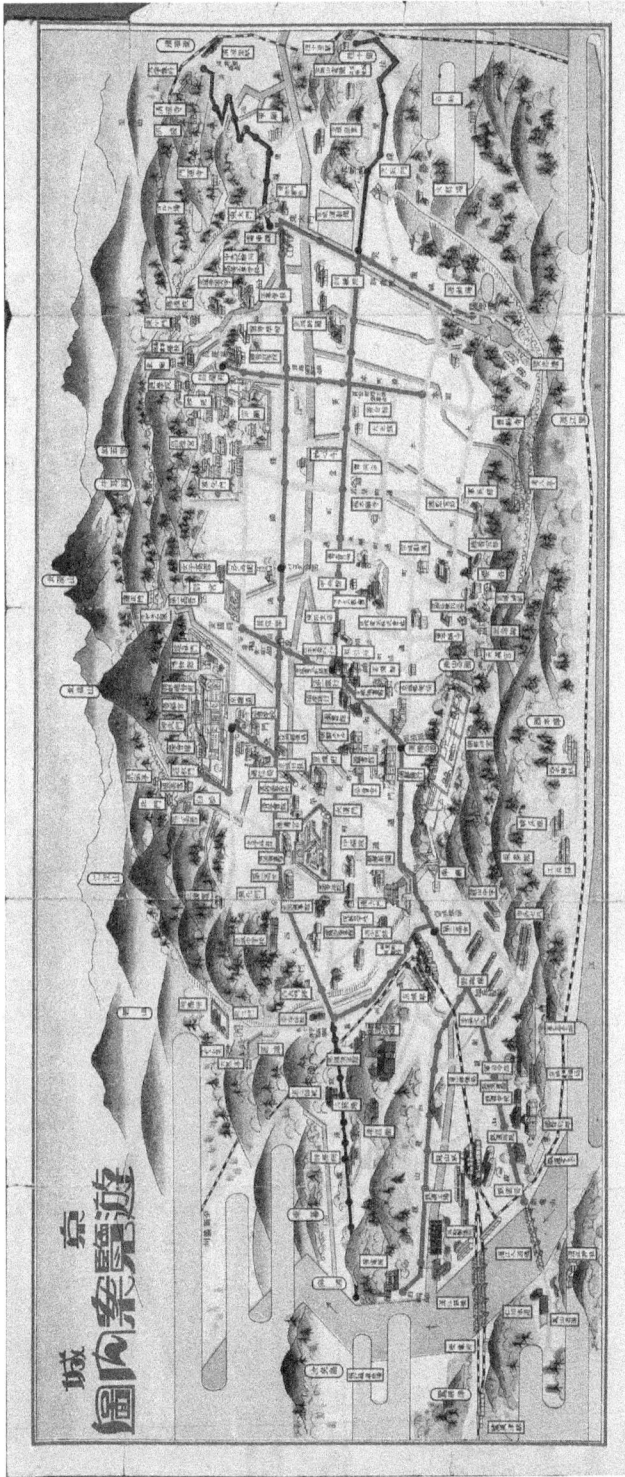

FIGURE 1.7. *Tour Guide Map of Keijō (Keijō yūran annaizu)*, 1920s, 20.3 x 46.3 cm, Seoul History Museum.

as the pictorial and diagrammatic representation of places. Straight red and blue lines indicated streetcar routes for local and long-distance services, respectively; these were marked with place-names shown in boxes contoured by red lines; streetcar station names were written in red ink without the encasing box.[68] Through detailed description of the streetcar routes and stops, it supplied the viewer in a position of power with the means to know the places—their names and locations—and a possibility for intimacy with the place through knowledge. In this way, the map functioned as a reference for facts, supplier of knowledge, and shaper of travelers' experience of the city on the ground; travelers could see their movement being framed as part of a seamless, mechanized movement by streetcar and could experience the imaginary, whole view of the city. It was a visual representation uniquely suited to fulfill the desire for power and familiarity at the same time.

In this context, *The Map of the Chōsen Exhibition* (Chōsen hakurankai zue) of 1929 (figure 1.8) shows a shift in perspective from south to west, also noted in the photographic panorama. It shows a similar composition of realistically depicted natural terrain and buildings as well as a diagrammed view of roads and streetcar routes, but instead of an aerial view of the city from the south, it created the effect of overlooking the city from an imaginary point on a western mountain. The result was, ironically, a more "realistic" view of Seoul that showed a more three-dimensional view of the mountain peaks. The previous view from the south overlaid South Village in front of North Village, resulting in a rather flattened image of the city. The imaginary western perspective also turned the north-south axis of the city around the main horizon of the map and made the difference between North Village and South Village, presented side by side, more pronounced. T'aep'yŏng Avenue, the main artery of Japanese colonialism, as a result, became more noticeable as the horizontal axis of the map. The map showed Kyŏngbok Palace in a disproportionate scale because it was the site of the 1929 exposition, but its prominence was mediated by a symmetry created by South Village, the Shinto Shrine, and Nam Mountain at the other end of the map.[69] And the repositioned mountains opened up the horizon and presented a more unbounded image, limitless and vast—a more potent way to articulate the position of power. The result of this innovation was an articulation of colonial power through the visual rendering of space—a product of the

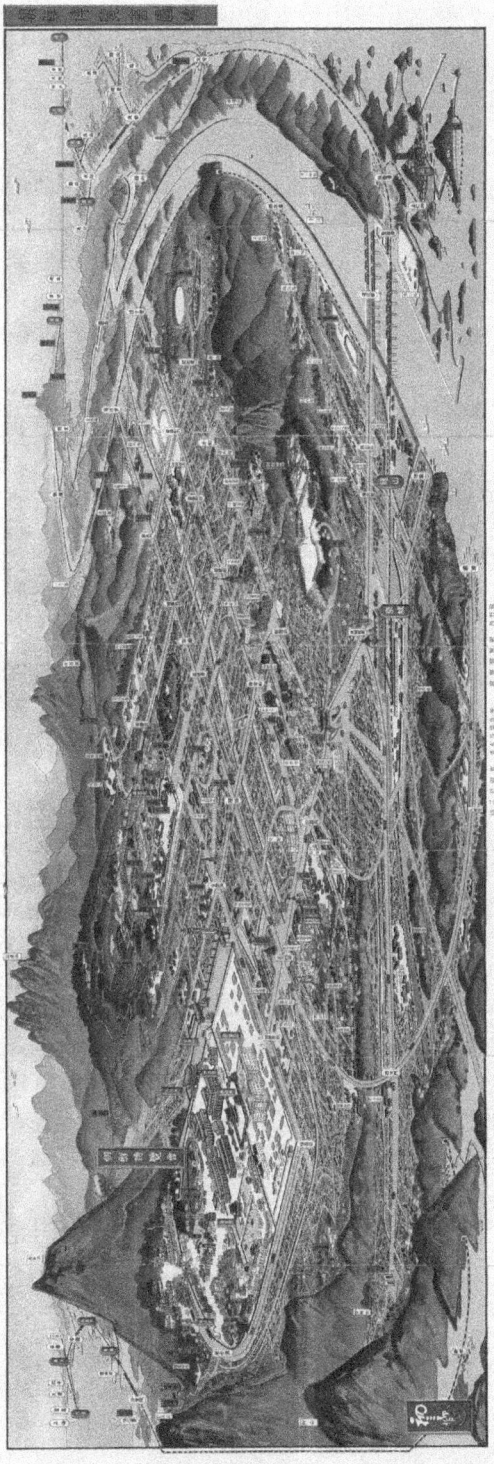

FIGURE 1.8. Yoshida Hatsusaburō, *The Map of the Chōsen Exhibition* (Chōsen hakurankai zue), 1929, 9.2 x 28.2 cm, National Museum of Korean Contemporary History, Seoul.

imperial gaze and its ability to colonize space through inspection and, more importantly, through representation.

The panorama was a product of nineteenth-century curiosity and appetite for the ever-expanding world under imperialism, and it was useful for making visible the newly acquired colonies and imposing the illusion of order for the colonized. It was a de facto utopian view because it presented a limitless world with no obstacles, one made possible only by broadening the vista and applying an omniscient view. Kim Kye-wŏn thus called the panorama "a metaphor of utopia," rather than simply a method of recreating and representing the landscape.[70] The power of the panorama is found, Kim argued, in its ability to universalize the self (the West) while simultaneously displacing the Other (the non-West) to the distance and observing it with a sweep of the eye, which in the end allowed the imperial subject to call itself "modern."[71]

Here, we can seize on the coproduction of spatial distinction and temporal difference between colonizer and colonized, which is a modus operandi of modernity, and translate the spatial metaphor of "the sweep of the eye" in temporal terms—as history arranging events into order. According to Angela Miller, the driving impetus of the panorama was "to give to two-dimensional representation a narrative structure, by means of continuous unfolding of time through space."[72] The image of space in the panorama functions as an image of time by ordering it in a linear narrative of development and historical progress, which is a view of history "as a series of unfolding scenes fluidly connected, giving to audiences the illusion of mastery over random, distant, or otherwise incomprehensible events."[73] This is a powerful iteration of the panorama that "captured not only spatial extension but the passage of time and the grand sweep of history."[74] The possibility of historical contingency was minimized as this new medium rationalized the view through a reality effect, which was in fact "an expedited, edited, and misleadingly simple passage through a simulated reality."[75] The panorama, creating a sense of order by arranging events and creating a reality effect, was historicist at the core. Therefore, Miller compellingly declared that in the panorama, the pedagogical (supplier of knowledge) was turned into the propagandistic (producer of history).[76]

At this point, we can turn our attention to a feature prominent in both the 1928 and 1929 maps: streetcar routes. Through them, we can explore how the limitless view of the panorama was not solely the work

of a surveyor in a stationary position at a mountain top or of an imaginary omniscient gaze—it was deeply rooted in the modern urban space
and the new visual experience that it created. In modern times, urban
space became exceedingly fragmented, so the self-evident wholeness
of the panorama was a result of "an imaginary unity and coherence
to an external world that, in the context of urbanization, was increasingly incoherent."[77] That is, the panorama was essentially a composite
view of fragments arranged into a whole. Narrative was a key agent that
achieved the seamlessness of the panorama, and the panorama was a
product of a fluid movement and kinetic vision. Hence, the roads, streetcar routes, and railway prominently featured in the two maps became instrumental in imagining the course of movement and thereby simulating
the effect of movement. *Guide Map of Keijō* (Keijō annaizu) is another example (figure 1.9). This map featured a more "modernized" depiction of
the city in which information took precedent over a perspectival view of
the landscape. Its perfectly geometrical grid was irrespective of Seoul's
terrain or scale in determining distance and position, and most details
about the places disappeared, setting the streetcar routes against a blank
space. What it entailed was a kind of visual mapping of the city—from
South Mountain to Pugak Mountain, paved city-center roads, streetcar
routes that linked North Village and South Village, the thoroughfares
filled with monumental architecture—as a way of vicariously experiencing the moving panorama along the routes of travel. In this context, the
two photographs of Kyŏnghoeru of Kyŏngbok Palace and the square in
front of Chosŏn Bank offer an important clue about how to read the map.
The two images created a view of the city through a contrast of tradition and modernity, colony and empire, and old and new. The binary
was then used to compose a narrative about the passage of time through
the traveler's movement through space; that is, the seeing subject was
the one who created a continuum of images through motorized travel.
The traveler was the "mobilized subject," as Theodore Hughes put it, who
transformed "fragments into function" in which the montage of images
collected on the ground became a seamless, moving panorama.[78]

These images were cinematic in their proclivity to create out of montage a seamless panorama. Here, Giuliana Bruno helps us understand
the working of "spatial storytelling," in which a new mode of traveling
and viewing architecture reshaped the relationship between space,
movement, and narrative.[79] Cinema had a "kinetic origin" because it

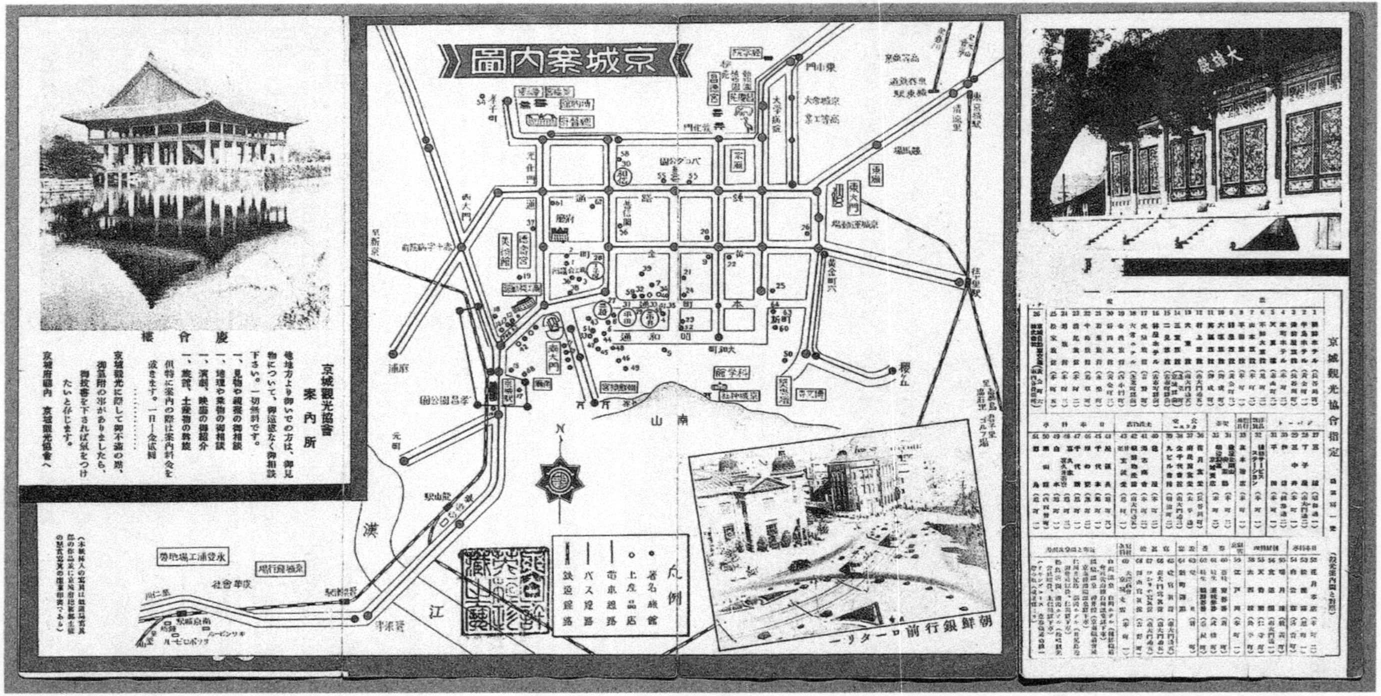

FIGURE 1.9. *Guide Map of Keijō (Keijō annaizu)*, late 1930s, Seoul History Museum.

created a system linking disparate objects by an observer in transit, in search of the picturesque.[80] For this reason, architecture and cinema were intimately tied to each other, and mobility, the essence of these new architectures of modernity, was a form of the cinematic. At this point, we can discuss the mediums of travel map and postcard in relation to each other. The postcards in *The Hundred Views of Keijō* were sold as a collection, and as a collection they offered curated images to tell a story, one related to the next. Many of the postcards, roughly one-third of the collection, were collages of multiple photographs, at times organized by type (e.g., schools) or place (e.g., different views of the Shinto Shrine). Yet more often than not, the relationships among the images had to be imagined by the collector. Assisting the narrative production of the personalized geography was the text—the poems and songs. The image and text forming a narrative in these postcards can thus be considered a function of "paracinema," a technique of assembling images from noncinematic modes such as magazines to imitate cinema's vision in motion.[81] In this, the interplay of different images in the collage, as of image and text, simulated a sense of motion and kinetic vision. In that regard, the cinematic becomes an important lens through which we can understand the aforementioned postcard about the Government-General Building, which arranged the four photographs in a zigzag, conveying a sense of motion (see figure 1.6). The photograph at the top showing T'aep'yŏng Avenue set the stage for the following photographs, as the perspectival view of the winding road presented the thoroughfare not as a spatial component but a conduit of movement that framed the narrative path for the images to follow. With the Government-General Building and its residence located on its north end and south end respectively, the postcard was essentially a narrative of travel along this road, while the camera (the kino-eye) zoomed in and out from the architecture along the way, as seen in the close-up shots of the dome of the Government-General Building and the residence's gate.

Another example is seen in a postcard featuring two views of the square in front of Chosŏn Bank—one from South Gate looking toward Chongno at the top right and the other from City Hall facing Mitsukoshi Department Store at the bottom left (figure 1.10). Together, the photographs demonstrate opposite viewpoints from south and north, but when side by side, the Post Office would connect to complete its view, essentially simulating an effect of a camera panning 360 degrees around the plaza. This postcard, therefore, was a panorama—a collection of fragmented images to be cognitively assembled by the collector. Even more, numerous passersby on foot and wheels, as well as automobiles and a streetcar, created a feeling of bustling movement, essentially turning the square into a boulevard. The vanishing point in the top photograph pointed to the continuous path stretching to North Village, so when the image panned from the top photograph to the photograph in the bottom, it simulated movement out of the north to South Village—that is, out of the past to the future. Each photograph was also accompanied by poems, and the reference to a time past in the first poem supports how the spatial movement created by the cinematic also produced a temporal transition toward modernity:

(left)
Along the roadside
the crickets flock together,
chattering away.
Such longing do I feel for
that which is no longer here!

(right)
I bring the blade of
summer grass up to my mouth,
and in that moment
my heart is overcome by
such hesitation indeed![82]

FIGURE 1.10. Postcard of the square in front of Bank of Chōsen, from *The Hundred Views of Keijō* (Keijō hyakkei), c. 1925–35, 9 x 14.2 cm. Source: Busan Museum.

The emotive tone in these poems can now also be explained as products of a kinetic vision. Here, Bruno's formulation of the relationship between vision and motion into that of vision and emotion is instructive. The picturesque is essentially a cinematic practice "to engage the passenger's imagination and incite her (e)motion."[83] In this, the effect of viewing upon the contact between the observer and architecture is where the sight turns into feelings: "Here, the eye is epidermic, it is a skin; sight becomes a sense of touch."[84] This led Bruno to discuss the experience of the mobile subject as *haptic*. Contact is a function of the skin—a surface—and a sensory interaction of kinesthesis. Bruno thus called this kinetic subject the passenger rather than the passerby, to underscore how the kinetic became kinesthetic, how a sensory voyage became a voyage to the interior.[85] In this regard, the distant view of Namdaemun Avenue framed by the columns of Kyŏngsŏng Station (see figure 1.5) becomes poignant. Although the photograph at first glance might seem misplaced, the subjective view was a reminder of the haptic gaze of a traveler whose voyage to a distant land in the colony was manifested in the sensorial experience expressed in the poems and the discovery of interiority. The passerby-turned-passenger demonstrates how the cinematic was capable of producing self-reflection and turning the passage through urban space into an emotive process. What it entailed was a discursive production not of ideology but of sentimentality and sensibility, in which history and the passage of time were articulated through the spatial practice of "site-seeing."[86] This was a colonizing process because it tamed other impulses of the spatial dimension of architecture, constantly interfering with the linearity of narrative, but as much a product of modernity and urban experience. Thus, the discursive production in the travel maps and postcards attests more than anything to a desire to control the spatial reordering, sequence of movement, and ways of seeing of the imperial subject, while affirming a subjectivity firmly rooted in the modern, urban setting.

* * *

By way of conclusion, I turn to two images that illustrate different positions of colonial subjects in this context. One is from a travel postcard (figure 1.11), which depicts three Korean men looking at Kŭnjŏngjŏn. This audience hall of Kyŏngbok Palace stands severed from the rest of the palace under erasure; and stripped of its function, it is presented as a ruin, impeccably preserved as an artifact of the past. The three men wear traditional garments, in synchrony with the object of their gaze, but they appear eerily distanced from it. This feeling is accentuated by their placement: rather than occupying the same palace ground as the building, the person in the foreground is positioned in the blank space of the postcard, highlighting that distance rather than being relegated to the past along with the monument in ruin. That spatial distance is also a temporal distance that positioned the Korean onlookers in a disparate time, thereby underscoring the sense of alienation from their own history. The object of their gaze belonged to the past; even for Koreans, the

FIGURE 1.11. Postcard of Kŭnjŏngjŏn, 14.2 x 9 cm. Source: Busan Museum.

gaze belonged to the modern. Korean colonial subjects also had nostalgia for their past, albeit from a position of disprivilege.

The other image is a 1927 painting, *Landscape against Mount Pugak* (Pugaksan ŭl paegyŏng ŭro han p'unggyŏng) by Kim Chu-gyŏng, to show how a colonial painter negotiated his position as the mobilized subject (figure 1.12). The painting depicts a winding road through a neighborhood where City Hall, completed the year before, appears behind unassuming buildings. The painting has a perspectival view, with colors and brush techniques characteristic of modern impressionistic paintings. It earned a special prize at the Art Exhibition of 1927 for its skillful rendition of the modern urbanscape. However, some also criticized it for juxtaposing a modern landscape with a bucolic one, creating an awkward assemblage of local and colonial elements.[87] The source of the criticism is where the critical potential of this painting is found. The painting's mishmash of colonial architecture, buildings of untraceable style and unidentifiable names, old walls, and nature does not amalgamate into a system of order marked by distinct spaces or times. City Hall, which

FIGURE 1.12. Kim Chu-gyŏng, *Landscape against Mount Pugak*, 1927, oil on canvas, 97.5 x 130.5 cm, Museum of Modern and Contemporary Art, Seoul.

usually appeared in colonial representations in an unobstructed view from the thoroughfare, laid open at its front, is seen here behind unknown buildings and an old wall along the right side of the street. Bright white, the wall occupies most of the passerby's right side and to its left, a tree hangs over the buildings, narrowly avoiding a blocked view of City Hall. These two elements of nature and local history envelop and frame the view of City Hall, also aided by the mountains in the background. Unlike the Japanese travel literature, the unromantic view of the local could not be incorporated into an articulation of the teleological history of the colony and the empire. The ruin in this painting is no longer an aesthetic concept, but a specter of the past copresent now.

The painting also shows a cityscape from the position of the figure on the road who occupies the center of the foreground. From her standpoint, which also overlaps with viewers' point of view, buildings appear to be overlaid in front of each other, with little space between them. In this form, it is virtually impossible to draw a sequential relationship among the buildings and create a contrast that would entail a temporalized landscape. In this way, the painting visualizes urban development as an overlaying process that entails a jumbled montage of buildings of different styles, materials, and forms. Although the perspectival view of the street indicates movement in one direction, the multilayered composition of the surroundings hampers discursive formation and denies a sequential transition from tradition to modernity and from local to colonial. As such, the painting privileges the view of the beholder rather than that of the urban planner. A modern girl wearing a white dress and holding a red parasol, the colonial-modern subject of this painting asserts her modernity. Yet she does not return the gaze of the viewer and refuses to become an object to be viewed, instead insisting on her ability to see and instructing viewers to see from her point of view of nondiscursivity.

Section 2 and section 3 further explore instances of colonial subject's engagement with the discursive production of colonial power, but first, the next chapter continues to examine the prominent medium noted in this chapter—photography—by taking a close look at King Kojong's funeral and discusses how the ways of seeing a ritual passage through the city was controlled and entailed a history writing.

2

Ritual, History, Memory

PHOTOGRAPHING KOJONG'S FUNERAL OF 1919

One day in late February 1919, Mary Taylor, the wife of United Press International (UPI) reporter Albert Taylor, checked into the Severance Hospital to give birth to their son. Coincidently, this celebratory occasion took place when the crowd who had gathered to mourn the death of King Kojong started a mass protest for Korea's independence, the March First Movement. In her memoir, Taylor recalled witnessing the funeral procession on March 3 from the window of the hospital.[1] A crowd from all over the country had gathered all night long, dressed in white funeral clothing. The path of the procession was lined with wooden torches, "ten feet high and as thick around as a man's body."[2] Japanese soldiers and Koreans with wooden paddles also stood along the path to keep the crowds back. At the head of the funerary procession were bearers who carried on their shoulders empty sedan chairs draped in brocaded silk. Next came the colorful main banner that hung on a crossbar along with lanterns and bells. There were also white paper banners, which Taylor described as obituary addresses on bamboo poles, carried by bearers who wore bright blue muslin and black hats with red horsetails hanging over their brims. They were followed by the royal red umbrella and the empty chair of state, and behind them were masked dancers who chased away evil spirits, the master of ceremonies atop a white horse, and his attendants. Then came two great catafalques supported on huge trestles by at least a hundred bearers dressed in mourning sackcloth. The bearers moved in rhythmic step, singing a slow and measured dirge. It was explained to Taylor that two identical catafalques were prepared to confuse the spirits. Ropes fastened to the biers were pulled back and forth for the same reason. It was at this point in the procession that people let out a wail (*aigo*). The catafalques were followed by paper horses (*chuganma*), fifteen feet tall. At the rear of the procession were mourners in rickshaws and the Japanese police, who followed the procession on horseback. With this vivid account, Mary Taylor wrote a devastating assessment of the funeral: "If the Japanese expected this truly Korean funeral to make the Koreans forget their sufferings, they were gravely mistaken. The silent throngs that watched their last emperor go to his fathers must have been filled with hate and despair because not only had their demonstration failed and thousands lost their lives but now their last emblem of freedom had gone with the passing of their emperor, who was without a successor."[3]

Taylor's account offers a rare insight into the elaborate ritual of the royal funeral, of which her husband, Albert Taylor, also left many photographs. Albert Taylor was also instrumental in spreading the news of the March First Movement overseas and sending a copy of the Declaration of Korean Independence to his bureau when his wife found it in a bundle of papers left by her nurses under the coverlet of her bed.[4] The Taylors' entanglement with the funeral and the March First Movement is truly exceptional because no other records offer such a detailed account of both events. Even more so, it is difficult to find references to Kojong's funeral and the March First Movement together, even though the two events occurred almost concurrently. There are some eyewitness accounts written by foreign missionaries in Korea at the time, but these documents focus exclusively on either the March First Movement or the funeral.[5] There also exist several official records about the funeral, but these records do not mention the March First Movement. In Korean historical scholarship, both in English and Korean, there is a glaring silence when it comes to the funeral of Kojong, with most scholarship giving attention to the March First Movement.[6]

In this light, Mary Taylor's note about the mood of the funeral is noteworthy. She considered the death of Kojong as equally, if not more, devastating to Koreans as the "failure" of the March First Movement and did not hesitate to call Kojong the "last emblem of freedom" for Koreans.[7] It is indisputable that Kojong's death was significant, and yet his legacy was much more complicated. Speaking of his death as a historical rupture—the end of an era—has to consider the five-hundred-year-old dynasty in its full complexity, as well as Korea's own attempt at modern nationhood at the turn of the nineteenth century. Moreover, Kojong had been largely absent in public since his dethronement in 1907, while his son Sunjong took on symbolic official duties. The funeral brought Kojong into the public arena once more. So, the question loomed large as to how Korea should mourn a king in a country now under Japan's annexation. To make matters worse, rumors surrounded the cause of his death; he had fallen ill unexpectedly in late January and died the following day. His sudden death was attributed to a hemorrhage or heart attack, but a rumor of death by poisoning spread quickly and eventually became a catalyst for the March First Movement, which was orchestrated to take place close to the day of Kojong's funeral procession. On March 1, thousands of protesters filled the streets of Seoul and marched through the city shouting, "*Manse!*" and calling for Korea's independence. Although the protest was nonviolent, the Japanese police suppressed the movement with brute military force. Two days later, with chaos and violence still in the air, the funeral procession took place as planned, and tens of thousands of people flocked to pay their respects to the late king.

This was a moment in which the monarch's death was interlaced with the birth of a modern public demanding Korea's sovereignty. Korean nationalism was evoked from the sense of loss, and the memory of the deceased king was being resurrected, if not rewritten. The question becomes why the Government-General decided to go ahead with the funeral only days after the outbreak of the March First Movement. Was it to alleviate the rising tension among the mourners-turned-protesters and to give in to their demands for proper respect for the deceased king? If so, why did Mary Taylor think that the funeral did not offer any consolation to the Koreans? For this, Takashi Fujitani's influential study on the construction of the modern Japanese nation through public imperial pageantry offers an insight. Fujitani showed how imperial rituals and ceremonies in Meiji Japan, including the funeral of the emperor, reinvented the emperor as a visible modern monarch whose domination of the landscape in imperial and military progress produced a sense of a disciplined modern society.[8] These official cultures of rites, symbols, and

customs constituted what Fujitani called the "folklore of the regime"—
mnemonic sites where the materiality of signs was as important as verbal
signs. The role of pageantry in producing a shared sense of national community became more problematic in the colonial context of Korea. In a
study about Sunjong's imperial progress of 1909, Christine Kim showed
how the Resident-General attempted to replicate in Korea the nation-
building strategy of Meiji Japan in the hopes of promoting coprosperity
between Japan and Korea. This event took place under turbulent circumstances resulting from the insurgency of the righteous army (ŭibyŏng),
but rather than successfully steering Korea from militant resistance to
imperial harmony, it only incited and affirmed nationalistic passions in
Koreans.[9] If the lesson learned was that these mnemonic sites uninten-
tionally reinforced the image of the monarch in the national imagination of Korea, what can we say about Kojong's funeral being staged in
such a public way?

The answers to this question lie in the details of how the spatial and
visual politics of the funeral were managed to simultaneously render
Kojong as a figure to be venerated and check his relevance to the Korean
nation. The body of the dead king moving spectacularly through the
city was a carefully orchestrated site of narrative production, and it is
through that narrative that the potential of the royal pageantry was cur-
tailed. In other words, the end of an era had to be articulated through the
visual signs of the funeral. Therefore, this chapter treats the funeral as
a media event and analyzes the funeral and visual records of it. Of particular interest is the role of photography, a new medium through which
the funeral was represented.[10] In the colonial context, photography is
often discussed for its central role in the construction of the archive and
the colonial production of knowledge.[11] Some photographic records of
Kojong's funeral do fall into these categories, but this chapter brings photography into the realm of a mnemonic site, discussing how it produces
a particular spatio-temporality through narrativity. Therefore, instead
of approaching photography in terms of archives, this chapter explores
how photographic images write history. The question, then, is not how
images represent a historical event, but how they produce a historical
event and a notion of history. This is important because photographic
records of the funeral existed parallel to the age-old ritual performance
of the royal funeral, a visual medium in itself, and the genre of recording
for rituals, called ŭigwe (Royal Protocol of the Chosŏn Dynasty).[12] Thus,

this chapter first discusses the details of Kojong's funeral, then examines three different types of visual records of the funeral—*ŭigwe*, photojournalism, and the commemorative photo album—to show how different mediums of visual representation rendered the funeral as ritual, history, and memory.

The Funeral

Rites and rituals were integral to the moral universe of the Chosŏn dynasty, and they occupied an important place as a means of governance equal to the law. Preserving rites and rituals, in short, was crucial to ensuring the continued ideological stability of the dynasty. Early in the dynasty, rules about the rites were established through manuals, the earliest one being *Sejong Sillok Orye* of 1451, which was followed by *Kukcho Oryeŭi* of 1474. All royal and state rites strictly adhered to the rules established in these manuals, which propagated Neo-Confucian values through practice and in doing so made visible the ideal principles of the dynasty through material symbols. JaHyun Kim Haboush described grand state rituals as "cultural performances" in her discussion of the ritual controversy in the seventeenth century.[13] Many debates on rites contributed to the production of specific practices and to a set of symbols, customs, and performances, which culminated in the publication of *Supplementary Treatise on Funerary Rites* (Kukcho Sangnye Pop'yŏn) in 1752 and 1758.

Royal funerals, reserved for the members of the royal family, were possibly the most intricate rites of the Chosŏn dynasty. The first stage immediately following the death of the person lasted until the corpse was prepared and placed in the mortuary hall. During this time, succession matters were handled and the grave site prepared. The second stage involved the departure of the bier from the mortuary hall to the grave site, as well as the burial, and the third stage consisted of a three-year mourning period during which rites were performed at the ancestral shrine. When the king died, a temporary bureau, the *togam*, was established and its officials selected. Under the direction of the prime minister, three branches of the bureau were established: *kukchang togam*, which oversaw the entirety of the funerary rites; *pinjŏn togam*, which managed the mortuary hall, dressing of the corpse, and funerary clothing; and *sallŭng togam*, which was responsible for the burial site. The funeral proceeded

in the following sequence: the establishment of the *togam*, the preparation of the mortuary hall, the donning of the mourning garments for the
chief mourner, the departure of the coffin, the lowering of the coffin, the
return of the mortuary table to the palace, and finally the disbanding of
the *togam*.

Kojong died at the age of sixty-seven on January 21, 1919, in his residence at Tŏksu Palace.[14] Immediately after his death, the three *chugam*
(*ŏjang chugam*, *pinhonjŏn chugam*, and *sallŭng chugam*), replacing the
previous *togam*, began preparing for the funeral following the royal rites
detailed in *Supplementary Treatise on Funerary Rites*.[15] However, on January 27, the Government-General intervened: "The funeral of the Great
King Yi, recipient of the Supreme Order, shall be a state funeral."[16] In
this simple edict, there are many clues about Japan's intentions. Kojong,
for example, was referred to as "the Great King Yi" (Yi T'aehwang), a title
given to him after his dethronement. It was customary for Chosŏn kings
to receive a temple name for their funeral (*myoho*), a title either granted
by the Chinese emperor or dedicated by the king's officials. In Kojong's
case, since he declared himself emperor of the Taehan Empire, all of his
ŭigwe records referred to him as Emperor Kojong (Kojong T'aehwangje),
but the Japanese edict used a title that underscored Kojong's demotion to
nominal king. As King Yi, he is referred to by only his surname, without
any reference to the dynasty or empire over which he reigned. More interesting, he was referred to as a recipient of the Supreme Order (*taehu-
nwi*; J. *taikun-i*), the highest rank in the imperial bureaucracy of Japan.
Similarly, since the founding of the Taehan Empire, the state funeral was
called *ŏjang*, or "funeral of the emperor," rather than *kukchang*, used for
the king or queen, but the edict used a term that reverted this initiative
begun by Kojong himself. These titles and names indicate how precarious Kojong's status was, as it was being affirmed and negated all at the
same time: this was an attempt to recognize the status of a king while
subjugating him to the imperial order of Japan and precluding any possibility of elevating his position to that of the head of a nation.

With Japan's intervention, the funeral was arranged by the Office of
Funerary Rites of the Imperial Household Agency, in accordance with
Japanese imperial rites. The three *chugam* operated under the directives
of the Imperial Household Agency, and all the offices were headed by Japanese officials, except for the vice chief of funerary rites, Cho Tong-yun,
who assisted the chief of funerary rites, Ito Hirokuni. With this change,

the mortuary hall in Hamnyŏngjŏn, where Kojong passed away, was re-decorated in the Japanese style, and a Japanese imperial funerary ritual *hōkokusai* was performed on February 9, 1919, with Japanese dignitaries in attendance. The funerary procession, which was the most spectacular and public part of the funeral, and took place from the Taehan Gate of Tŏksu Palace to the burial site of Kŭmgok Hongnŭng, also saw many changes to tradition. Attendants donned different mourning attire: chief officials were in Japanese-style mourning attire, high officials and attendants in full military uniform or tailcoat adorned with badges and medals, in contrast to Korean officials and attendants in Korean-style mourning cap and robe of untreated hemp.[17] While the procession did retain some Korean elements, it featured many new elements: parades of the Japanese army and navy guards, the firing of a cannon from a Japanese naval vessel in the port of Inch'ŏn, and transporting of the bier by railway. The only part of the rites that observed Chosŏn laws was the send-off ceremony at Hullyŏnwŏn to the burial site, which took place outside of the East Gate, outside of the traditional city limits.[18]

The most significant change was made to the route of the funerary procession. That the point of departure for Kojong's procession was Tŏksu Palace—where Kojong resided and died—is not so important, as the procession for Queen Myŏngsŏng during the Taehan Empire also started from Tŏksu Palace, not Kyŏngbok Palace. Notable, though, were the changes made to the traditional route via Chongno. Chosŏn royal funerals featured two biers—the bier carrying the body of the dead king (*taeyŏ*) and the mock bier meant to carry his spirit (*kyŏnyŏ*)—and never in Chosŏn or modern Korean history had the two biers been separated from each other in the procession. For Kojong, the mock bier went on the traditional route on Chongno with bier carriers in traditional mourning garments. However, the bier carrying Kojong's body took a route south of Chongno via Ŭlchiro, where a Japanese settler community was located, and from there headed to the state funeral site, Hullyŏnwŏn, near the East Gate. Then the two biers united and headed to the burial site. The chief mourner, Sunjong, along with his sons, followed the bier carrying Kojong's corpse on the southern route in a horse carriage to the ceremony site.[19] In this way, the magnificent spectacle staged in front of thousands of spectators, yet with noticeable modifications, presented a complex web of signs to be deciphered in terms of exactly where and how the kingly power was located. In the end, under Japanese control,

the funeral was completed in much less time than the five months usually allocated for a royal funeral.

Funeral as Ritual: Ŭigwe

The importance of rites to the Chosŏn dynasty is well illustrated in the
publication of thousands of documents called *ŭigwe*, which recorded important rites and court ceremonies. These events included royal rituals
around rites of passage such as weddings and funerals, and other court
events such as royal banquets, construction projects, and receptions for
foreign dignitaries. For chronicling how to administer events in detail,
we can think of ŭigwe as a comprehensive set of records and manuals
for rites that included different genres of documents: royal orders, letters
of request from court officials, documents between bureaus and offices,
income and expenditure figures, plans for objects and equipment, and
hierarchically arranged seating charts and diagrams. Therefore, many
ŭigwe were highly visual and offered important sources for understanding the elaborate and extravagant rites of the Chosŏn court.

Typically, royal funerals yielded the publication of three ŭigwe by
three bureaus of *togam*: *Kukchang togam ŭigwe*, *Pinjŏn togam ŭigwe*, and
Sallŭng togam ŭigwe. The most elaborate and labor-intensive production
went into a painting called *panch'ado* depicting a royal procession (figure
2.1). This painting is usually referred to as the flower of ŭigwe and took
up more than fifty pages, becoming longer over time. Panch'ado is an
important visual reference to the formation and composition of the procession. More important, panch'ado, a visual representation of an event,
was a reenactment via a unique temporal experience: reading. Ŭigwe
was published in book form, so each page contained only a partial view
of the procession; thus, as readers turned the page, they could follow
the procession from beginning to end, as it was replicated in the linear
experience of book reading. These fragmented views came together only
through the act of reading the book from cover to cover, which allowed
readers to experience the procession as a moving image. A mural instal-
lation of the royal procession from Chŏngjo's Hwasŏng panch'ado along
the Ch'ŏngyech'ŏn Stream shows what the reading experience may have
been like in its connecting of panch'ado images side by side (figure 2.2).
A passerby can see the whole procession in an undisrupted sequence of
images, one after another, by moving from one end of the mural to the

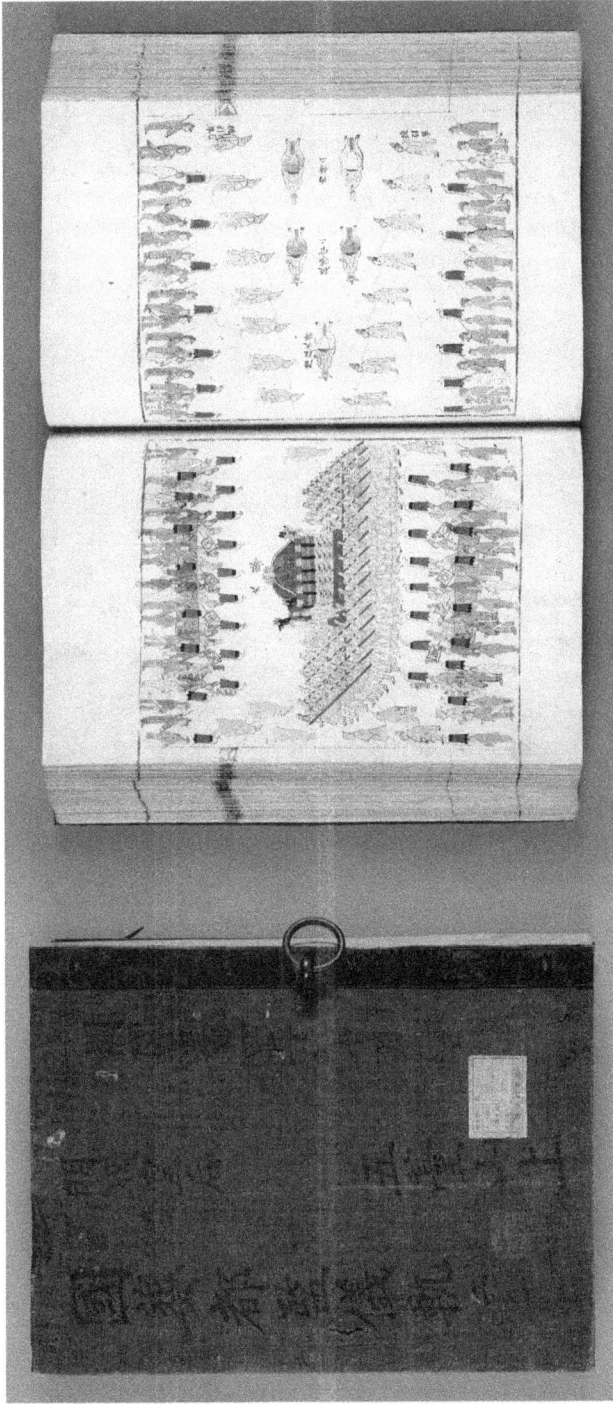

FIGURE 2.1. *Panch'ado* for Queen Myŏngsŏng's funeral procession, from *Royal Protocols for the State Funeral of Empress Myeongseong* (Myŏngsŏng Hwanghu kukchang togam ŭigwe), 1898, 44.6 x 33.1 cm, National Palace Museum of Korea. Reprinted with permission.

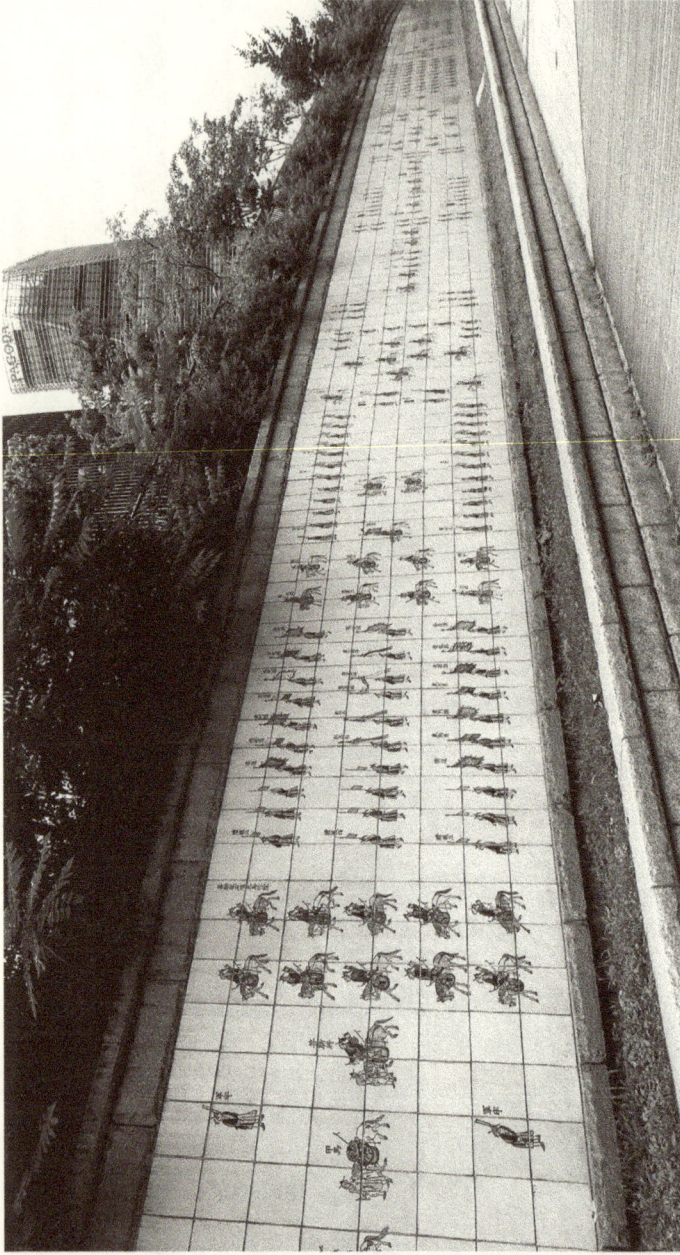

FIGURE 2.2. *Panch'ado* of the journey to Hwasŏng (Hwasŏng wŏnhaeng panch'ado), 2021, Ch'ŏnggyech'ŏn Stream, Seoul. Source: Kaeun Park.

other, simulating the movement of the images in the book. Whereas procession spectators would have stood still, with all movement determined by the procession itself, these visual renditions depend on spectator-readers to create the illusion of movement, either by turning the pages of the book or by physically moving from one end of the mural to the other, thereby recreating a sense of movement, a spatial experience, through the temporal experience of book reading or walking from one place to the next.

This does not mean that panch'ado created a real-time experience. The background of images in panch'ado was left blank; there was no contextual information as to when and where the ritual took place. The contextual void was not simply a stylistic choice; such representation was intended to apply to all places and times—to be universal. In other words, the panch'ado illustrations were intended to be instructive and prescriptive: when preparing for a rite, the planners were supposed to refer to the *Supplementary Treatise on Funerary Rites*, the manual for rituals, and precedents from the previous ŭigwe.[20] Even so, ŭigwe were also historical records that reflected historical changes made over time. For instance, as Yi Sŏng-mi noted, *Kojong Karye Togam Ŭigwe*, which recorded Kojong's wedding to Queen Myŏngsŏng in 1866, contained palanquins for his mother as well as his father Taewŏn'gun. This was unprecedented but not surprising, as Taewŏn'gun was the regent for the young king.[21] Also, the ŭigwe that recorded Sunjong's wedding in 1906 was published after the founding of the Taehan Empire and thus reflected many changes that Kojong put in place to exert Korea's sovereignty.[22] But most rituals followed precedents as rites recurred and were repeated throughout generations. This is well exemplified in the evolution of picture making. Images in early ŭigwe were hand-drawn and painted, but after 1671, printing was used as well. As panch'ado became longer, starting around 1759, printing became more frequent, mostly used for repeated elements, such as the placement and depiction of soldiers, musicians, and horse riders. A woodblock printed the contours of these figures because the same template could be used for multiple events, whereas newly introduced or important elements were still hand painted.[23] This note on their production underscores the role of ŭigwe as protocols for posterity, despite permissible variations, and the fact that, while a ŭigwe was based on a singular event in history, the record keeping and the use of ŭigwe also rendered the event that it depicted to be a

repeatable event—a rite. This notion of repeatability collapsed the temporal boundary between past and future, as the ritual serving as a model
rendered itself an eternal event, however paradoxical that may sound.

During the colonial period, the tradition of ŭigwe continued—there
are thirty-seven books of twenty ŭigwe—but with many of the details
simplified.[24] The three *chugam* established for Kojong's funeral under the
Office of the Yi Dynasty (Yiwangjik) published three volumes of ŭigwe
shortly after the funeral in 1919: *Kojong T'aehwangje ŏjang chugam
ŭigwe* (Ritual Manual for the Bureau of the Imperial Burial of Emperor
Kojong), *Kojong T'aehwangje pinjŏn honjŏn chugam ŭigwe* (Ritual Manual
for the Bureau of the Mortuary Hall for Emperor Kojong), and *Kojong
T'aehwangje sallŭng chugam ŭigwe* (Ritual Manual for the Bureau of the
Burial Mound for Emperor Kojong).[25] These three ŭigwe contained the
usual information about the administrative details of the funeral, some
organized by type and others chronologically in daily logs. However,
as all ŭigwe published during the colonial period, these descriptions
lacked rigorous attention to record keeping, and most importantly the
inclusion of panch'ado, which was so characteristic of previous ŭigwe.
This is quite striking, as other types of images did exist in these ŭigwe.
In place of panch'ado, only the diagrams of participants' placement appeared, with text standing in for images. While the texts gave basic information about the procession, a great deal of detail was missing that could
have been easily transmitted in pictures. The genre of *munbanch'ado,*
or diagrammatic renditions of panch'ado in texts like this, had previously existed but was not in wide use. Kojong's *munbanch'ado* is even
more perplexing because other panch'ado produced during the nineteenth century boasted some of the most artistic and refined productions
of visual rendering in the history of ŭigwe, even though kingly power
had declined gradually during this time.[26] Panch'ado may have been a
labor-intensive process for which the colonial government did not have
a commitment or a budget. However, in considering how a documentary
tradition produced rites and how rites sanctioned and upheld the monarchy and its moral universe, we could also suspect that the omission of a
visual depiction of Kojong's funerary procession was a deliberate choice.
Interestingly, all visual records of the funeral procession for Kojong are
photographs, outside the tradition of ŭigwe, susceptible to narrative production of another kind.

Funeral as Historical Event: Photography and Cinema

Maeil sinbo, the Korean-language official newspaper of the Government-General of Korea, featured articles almost daily with updates on the progress of the funeral preparations. Different from ŭigwe, *Maeil sinbo* reported the day-to-day progress of the funeral preparations, with a great deal of attention to decision-making processes. For example, the initial budget set for the funeral was 60,000 won, but the decision to have a state funeral raised the budget to 100,000 won.[27] In the end, expenses climbed to 250,000 won.[28] Another point of contention was whether the funeral was going to be in the Korean or Japanese style, particularly for the royal family. Sunjong, for example, was reported to be planning to wear either Japanese or modern attire for the procession to the ceremony site at Hullyŏnwŏn (February 7), but later decided to wear Korean mourning attire the entire time (February 25).[29] Those advocating for Ch'ŏngnyangni as a potential grave site proved more vocal at times than those advocating for Kŭmgok Hongnŭng, where Kojong had prepared his burial site while he was alive and where Queen Myŏngsŏng was buried.[30] In this way, the contested decision-making processes added a sense of contingency to an otherwise routine affair for the monarchy and rendered the funeral into an event in real time. The prescriptive aspect of ŭigwe and ritual performance subsided as the representation took on a journalistic dimension.

Interestingly, photography, whose usual task is to capture reality, played a role in authorizing the colonial government and deauthorizing Korean participants, effectually mediating the realism of the newspaper. *Maeil sinbo* made an editorial choice to publish only photographs of the Japanese officials involved in the funeral preparation.[31] These photographs presented a narrative that ran counter to the textual one: with the visually imposing presence of Japanese authorities—the most visible actors—the photographs tempered the sense of contingency in the detailed accounts of the funeral preparation and reverted power to the colonial government as the ultimate decision maker. One photograph that did not feature Japanese officials was the photo of Hullyŏnwŏn that was published on February 4. In this photo, an empty training field was spread behind a figure wearing a *hanbok* and a straw hat (figure 2.3). Instead of looking at the field, the subject is awkwardly turned toward the camera, making himself an object to be viewed, and the face of this unidentified figure was made indistinguishable by shade from his hat, which obscured his returning gaze. Similarly, the members of the royal family never appeared in photographs during the preparation and in the coverage of the funeral. Even when Sunjong paid a visit to the mortuary hall to observe the first anniversary of Kojong's death on January 21, 1920, photos of neither king nor queen appeared. The news appeared in the top-right column of the first page, which was reserved for the most important news of the day. However, a photograph of Yi Kŭn-sang, a former official who had served in the Imperial Household Agency, in a well-decorated military uniform, was published instead in an adjacent article. Also, the biggest visual news was on a fire in Myŏngdong, which was reported in two oversized photographs of a burned building and spectators of the fire at the center of the front page.[32]

In light of the erasure of Korean subjectivity in these photographs, it is curious that extensive coverage of the funeral procession appeared in *Maeil sinbo* on March 4, 1919. The article on an account of the day's events lauded it as the first state funeral ever to be witnessed in its full glory. The headline included a lengthy lamentation song for Kojong:

FIGURE 2.3. View of Hullyŏnwŏn, from *Maeil sinbo*, February 4, 1919, National Library of Korea, Seoul.

"Ah, the third day of March. This is a day filled with grief, inconsolable grief. The funeral of Great King Yi took place today. A state funeral was bestowed by the emperor; the whole country showed respect; and all households lowered the flag to half-staff. On the path of the passing bier, all the people wept. How sorrowful. How sorrowful."[33] It then provided the details of the event chronologically from the preparation inside the palace early in the morning and indicated the exact hour, eight o'clock, as the beginning of the procession. It also gave an hour-by-hour account of the crowd: estimated in tens of thousands, the crowd had gathered since four in the morning on the streets of Chongno and near the East Gate. The mood was described as solemn, but the funeral went on effortlessly: "The funeral proceeded as if water flowed in the midst of moving crowd."[34]

The "flowing" narrative of the article offers a visually evocative experience of watching the procession passing by in front of one's eyes, much like watching a film. Cinema would have been a preferred medium for capturing the funeral procession, with its ability to collapse the motion of the event and the time of the narrative. In fact, in 1919, a film about Kojong's funeral, *A Real View of Kojong's Funeral,* was produced. Not coincidentally, the other film made that year was *A Panoramic View of the City of Kyŏngsŏng.*[35] Neither film survives today, but the fact that both films were produced in that year offers ample clues about the politics behind the sweeping views of the funeral and the city. Even without the film version of the account, we can gain insight into the important role that cinema played in the narration of the article through the accompanying photographs (figure 2.4). In these photographs, at the top is the view of the procession emerging from Taehan Gate, and at the bottom is the bier entering the funeral ceremony site. The top photograph showed movement from left to right, with the participants seen in frontal view. With perspective, the front rows appeared bigger than the back rows, which created a sense of forward movement out of the gate. The bottom photograph was taken from behind the participants, so the front row is smaller and farther from the camera, as if disappearing into the horizon. These two photographs marked the beginning and end of the event, corresponding to the article's linear narrative from morning to night. Together, they created a sense of continuous movement, capturing specific moments in that movement. The cinematic experience of these photographs was, therefore, framed by the only points of the event visually represented, the beginning and the end. The movement that these photographs produced was essentially a panorama of a totalizing view in which all complexities were reduced to the points of departure and arrival within a linear narrative.

What this photo collage produced is, therefore, a kind of history that flows in time, directing the hour-by-hour account toward the determined goal and unable to reposition itself as relevant in the present through repetition. In that regard, this narrative temporality of cinema-photography in *Maeil sinbo* is in contrast to that of ŭigwe. Although reading ŭigwe created a sense of motion-movement, that it functioned as protocol rendered the funeral as ritual, which collapsed the boundary of past and future in the performance of the present and consecrated the subject of the ritual through the transcendence of temporal boundaries. On the contrary, the journalistic account of *Maeil sinbo* rendered the funeral as

FIGURE 2.4. Kojong's funerary procession leaving the Taehan Gate (top) and the bier arriving at the ceremony site (bottom), from *Maeil sinbo*, March 4, 1919, National Library of Korea, Seoul.

a singular event. The funeral was representable reality, simply marking a point in historical time. As the ritualistic aura diminished in creating a panorama cinema-reality, repeatability gave way to singularity, sacredness to secularism, and eternity to presence. In this context, how Jean Baudrillard spoke of photography and cinema as a way of secularizing history is pertinent: "Photography and cinema contributed in large part to the secularization of history, to fixing it in its visible, 'objective' form at the expense of the myths that once traversed it."[36] Similarly, the photojournalism in *Maeil sinbo* created only the effect of secular history in its representation of the funeral; lost therein were mythical properties of the chimerical that could translate the historical event into ritual. In other words, *Maeil sinbo* did not have to negate the history itself—the fact that the funeral took place—but it did have to check the potential power of that history becoming ritual, elevated to the level of myth and possibly endowing the dead king with a passage out of history into the realm of eternity. In that regard, *Maeil sinbo*'s photography desanctified ritual by turning it into a singular event in linear history with relevance only in the then-present, which would create another temporality—the past to which his memory was to be relegated.

History as Collection: The Tŏksu State Funeral Photo Album

Photojournalism as a mode of producing secularized history required controlling many other aspects of photography that transcend temporal and spatial boundaries. Photography is uniquely positioned to overcome singularity by mechanically repeating what can only happen once in reality.[37] The photographs of Kojong's funeral in *Maeil sinbo* controlled this important facet of photography, so it was then taken up by another medium, souvenirs and memorabilia, which gave the photographs a sense of permanence in place of the lost ability to transcend time. Shortly after the funeral, a photo album called *The Tŏksu State Funeral Photo Album* (Tokujukyū kokusō gachō) was published by the Keijō Newspaper Company (figure 2.5).[38] For days, *Maeil sinbo* ran advertisements inviting readers to preorder the limited-edition album of two thousand copies, each beautifully adorned with a silk cover and printed on thick, archival-quality ivory paper. The album was advertised as curating the king's portraits from different years, photographs of commemorative objects and places, and photographs about his death and funeral—all to memorialize (*aedo*) a king who had reigned for sixty-seven turbulent years, to remember (*ch'umo*) his talent, to reflect on (*hoesang*) his life, and to commemorate (*kinyŏm*) the state funeral. The album itself was sold for 3 won, pricy but not so inaccessible, with a special discount reserved for preorders.[39]

The album contained a one-page introduction that offers clues about how its producers framed the following photographs. As in the earlier-mentioned imperial edict, the introduction used the title "King Yi" for Kojong and also referred to him as "King Yi of Tŏksu Palace" (Tŏksugung Yi Wang), as did the title of the album, tying his status to his residence instead of the country he led. It implicitly reserved the highest authority for the Japanese emperor, who was said to have played a key role in issuing the order for the state funeral, for which the parliament unanimously ap-

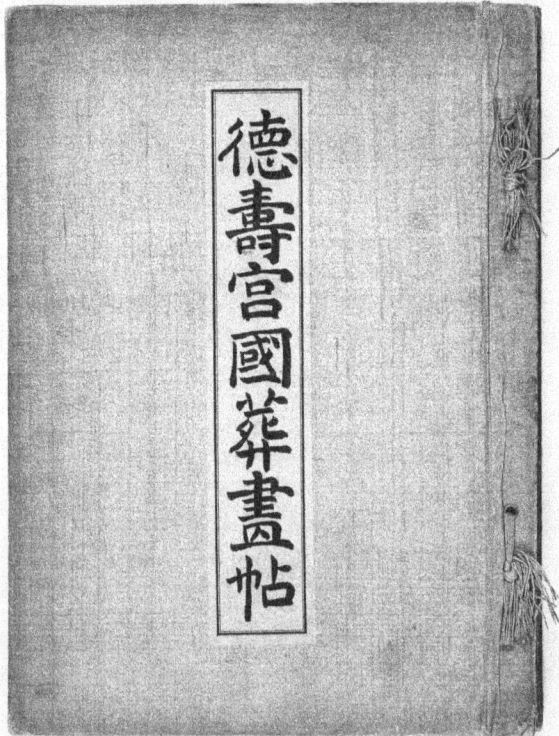

FIGURE 2.5. Cover of *Tŏksu State Funeral Photo Album* (Tokujukyū kokusō gachō), 28.8 x 21.6 cm, 1919, Seoul History Museum.

proved paying for all expenses. Also, the album presented a fuller range of images from the funeral and contained many photographs featuring non-Korean or nontraditional elements, especially of Japanese military and officials. It also included all stages of the funeral, whereas the *Maeil sinbo* article ended with the moment of arrival at the ceremonial site in Hullyŏnwŏn, leaving out the details of Korean-style rituals. This allowed the introduction to the Tŏksu album to praise these Japanese additions as the "modern or new style" (*sinsik*) as opposed to the "traditional or old style" (*kusik*) of Korea. In this way, the short introduction checked the resurrection of Kojong's kingly power, ratified imperial authority, relegated Korea to the past, and repackaged Japanese interference in Korea as modern intervention.

The album's photographs covered Kojong's lifetime, death, and funeral, and the first part about Kojong's life included a portrait of a sitting Kojong in Western clothes with a traditional Korean landscape painting in the backdrop; a Yi family portrait with all members in traditional attire; a portrait collage of Kojong in Western, traditional, and military attire, and one of him on a palanquin wearing a black cape; and another portrait from after he was reported to be sick, seated in full military uniform. Inserted between the portrait photographs were images of Kojong's calligraphy and of different buildings of Tŏksu Palace, including Sŏkchojŏn and its modern interior. Grouped together, the photographs provided a biographical sketch of the king. However, the ordering of these photographs did not point to a particular chronology or any other sequence; they rather resembled flashbacks of memories from his life.

The rest of the album presented photographs of Kojong's death and funeral in a remarkably different way from the part that introduced his life. First, Kojong's death was depicted in photographs of two special editions of *Maeil sinbo*. The first one, from January 21, reported that Kojong was critically ill (figure 2.6): Kojong had appeared to be in good condition when the doctor visited at eleven the previous night, but he suddenly fell ill at 1:45 a.m., prompting Sunjong to bring two doctors to the palace to examine him. The second was from January 22, announcing the death of Kojong, which was reported to have occurred at six in the morning on that day (figure 2.7). The former announcement was accompanied by a photograph of a carefully wrapped package, and the latter by a photograph of a crowd that gathered in front of Taehan Gate. On one level, these special edition inserts offered documentary evidence of Kojong's death through journalistic realism and the use of clock time. On another level, as discussed in the previous section, they contributed to making Kojong's death a singular event—real and historical. This was all the more interesting given that Kojong's life in the previous section was presented as memory in an ahistorical perspective. The portraits, calligraphy, and palace photographs gave a romantic view of Kojong's lifetime, lacking the sense of immediacy evident in the depiction of his death. The result was that, ironically, the photo album endowed his death, not life, with a sense of history.

The accompanying photographs, on the other hand, mediated journalistic realism. The photograph of the crowd gathered in front of the Taehan Gate of Tŏksu Palace was taken after news of Kojong's death, and possibly after publication of the news, but in its place in the album, it seems simultaneous to the news when in fact it was a reaction to it. By reporting two nonsynchronous events side by side, the photos told the story in retrospect, knowing what took place before and after the death announcement, which ultimately points to editorial intervention. Likewise, the wrapped box in the photograph that appeared next to the news-

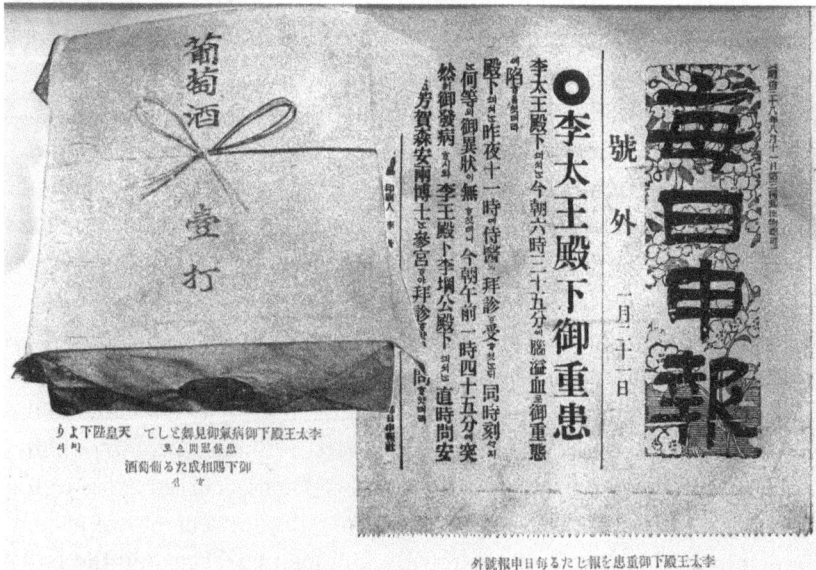

FIGURE 2.6. Announcement of Kojong's illness, from *Tŏksu State Funeral Photo Album* (Tokujukyū kokusō gachō), 1919, 28.8 x 21.6 cm, Seoul History Museum.

FIGURE 2.7. Announcement of Kojong's death, from *Tŏksu State Funeral Photo Album* (Tokujukyū kokusō gachō), 1919, 28.8 × 21.6 cm, Seoul History Museum.

paper's special edition contained a bottle of wine sent by the Japanese emperor. The contents were indicated only on the box's packaging, so the caption explained that the drink was intended to help invigorate Kojong. The wine was presented visually as a gift, in a carefully wrapped box, representing the benevolence of the emperor. This photograph was also displayed differently than the rest of the photographs in the album: the gift box was excised from its original photograph, so it appeared more like an object itself than an image, as if to indicate that the object was too sacred to be photographed or be represented in a photograph. Moreover, the image was superimposed on the newspaper, whereas the newspaper had been superimposed on the image of the crowd on the other page. Decoding this image, then, offers much insight into the production of the complex web of meanings in positioning Kojong vis-à-vis Japan, and the emperor in particular. Notably, when the album was reprinted in 1975 as *The Photo Album of the State Funeral of Emperor Kojong of the Taehan Empire* (Taehan cheguk Kojong Hwangje kukchang hwach'ŏp), the photograph of the wine gift was replaced with one of Sunjong visiting the palace in military uniform.[40]

After the photographs of Kojong's life and death, the album moved on to detail the funeral in the order of mourning by Koreans gathered outside of the palace and Japanese visitors inside the palace, preparation of the funeral by Japanese and Korean officials, honoring Kojong at the mortuary halls (which only showed the Korean-style arrangement before the change into the Japanese style), and a straw hut made for Sunjong for mourning duties. The procession was also depicted in painstaking detail by showing its progression from the bier leaving the palace from inside and coming out of the Taehan Gate, its arrival at the ceremony site, its transport via railway, and its travel along the passage through the East Gate, eventually transitioning to its arrival at the gravesite Hongnŭng as well as the return to the ancestral shrine. As for these photographs, of the procession in particular, analysis of the camera's perspective is critical. Most of the album's photographs were taken from a higher vantage point or a frontal perspective, so the photographer had the best possible view. One photograph of the bier passing through the crowd outside of Taehan Gate stands out as a wide shot that captured the grandeur of the procession (figure 2.8). It presented a detailed view of the bier, the procession, and the crowd surrounding it, and being captured through a

FIGURE 2.8. The funerary procession, from *Tŏksu State Funeral Photo Album* (Tokujukyū kokusō gachō), 1919, 57.6 x 21.6 cm, Seoul History Museum.

camera positioned far away on an elevated plane, it showed a panorama, a surveyor's view—the imperial gaze.[41]

This deliberate positioning of the photographer becomes even more apparent when compared to photographs by, for instance, Albert Taylor, the UPI reporter mentioned at the beginning of this chapter. The photograph in figure 2.9 was taken around the same time as the photo in figure 2.8, but from a different vantage point, near the Keijō Newspaper Building. Taylor was standing behind the military guards when the bier passed, evident in the cropping of the guards in the foreground. The shot almost seems voyeuristic, given its obstructed view and lack of a privileged perspective. However, from this position of disadvantage, the photographer was still situated squarely in the moment of the event, witnessing as it unfolded. Many of Taylor's photographs likewise delivered a sense of accident and revealed unorchestrated moments—hard to find in the Tŏksu album. In one photograph, a bier carrier appeared slightly off balance as he wiped the sweat from his brow (figure 2.10). In this photograph, the procession seems more dynamic, with the bier carriers at right pulling the rope parallel to the streetcar's electrical wire, which

FIGURE 2.9. Photograph of Kojong's funerary procession, Albert W. Taylor, 1919, 8.5 x 14.2 cm, Seoul History Museum.

FIGURE 2.10. Photograph of bier carriers, Albert W. Taylor, 1919, 8.5 x 14.2 cm, Seoul History Museum.

created an effect of forward movement. The bier carrier at center disturbs the procession's rhythm, even momentarily, adding another movement to the already lively representation. Motion connotes the transience of time: a moment that is captured destabilizes the held-together pieces that add up to the whole image.

Taylor's photographs, rather than serve as fixed referents like the other newspaper photos we have discussed, as well as photos from the Tŏksu album, showed reality as undeveloped and unpredictable—following Barthes, they transformed reality without duplicating it or vacillating. Barthes defined this as *punctum,* an unintentional consequence of the photographer's art—a deliberate composition—and an accidental outcome of simply being there: "It says only that the photographer was there, or else, still more simply that he could not photograph the partial object at the same time as the total object. The Photographer's 'second sight' does not consist in 'seeing' but in being there."[42] This sense of being there was shared by the photographer and the people whom Taylor photographed. In his photographs, the crowd's activities were dispersed and diverse: some people stood by the road attentively watching the procession; some looked down from a balcony; some gathered in front of a building; and others walked away leisurely or turned their gaze to others in the crowd (figure 2.11). The crowd lacked a unified identity in Taylor's photographs, in contrast to the Tŏksu album, which featured several photographs of the crowd but deliberately depicted them as mourners, not spectators. Mourners participated in the meaning making that was the photograph's subject. Spectators were simply *there.*

Taylor's presentation of the funeral as partial and incomplete was the camera reality and historical reality. Contingency, randomness, and unpredictability are key features of such photographs. They convey a sense of endless possibilities of an event and testify to the actuality of the event through fragmented views rather than an explanation of the event.[43] In contrast, the purpose of the Tŏksu album was not to record an event but to narrate it. In short, as a collection first and foremost, the album's goal was to weave a coherent, complete narrative in retrospect about Kojong's life and death, which it achieved by presenting individual images in one space and creating relationships among the photographs.[44] Chronology was important to achieve a sense of totality and unity as in the ordering of the life, death, and funeral of Kojong, and most importantly in the sequential descriptions of the funeral. In other words, narrativity was

FIGURE 2.11. Photographs of the crowd, Albert W. Taylor, 1919, 8.5 × 14.2 cm, Seoul History Museum.

not inherent to the event, but a product of editorial intervention. The Tŏksu album constructed reality rather than reflecting it, and so we can understand the Tŏksu album not as a record of history, but as a writing of history, one that collapsed the space-time configuration of photography and history. The reader of the Tŏksu album was to bridge the space continuum of photography and time continuum of history in order to piece together fragments into a new meaningful order: historicism, in which "the complete mirroring of an intertemporal sequence simultaneously contains the meaning of all that within that time."[45]

Then, how do we bridge the tension between the photo album as personal collection and its historicism created by the editorial intervention? Did history writing compete with the production of subjective memory by the collector? A clue is found in the photograph that depicted the burial site of Kŭmgok Hongnŭng (figure 2.12). This is not the last image in the album, but it marked the end of the funerary procession. Instead of a moment of arrival, however, the photograph portrayed a moment of non-activity, evident in the disarray and dispersal of the participants who have suspended their duty. With the gate as its focal point, a sense

FIGURE 2.12. The burial site of Kojong, from *Tŏksu State Funeral Photo Album* (Tokujukyū kokusō gachō), 1919, 28.8 x 21.6 cm, Seoul History Museum.

of time is conspicuously absent in this photograph, as is the sense of movement. The photograph indicated a stage, the end of the procession, only by the virtue of how it followed all previous points of the procession in the album. The photograph in and of itself was void of any narrative impulse, and the scattered participants also seem to yield their narrative agency to the place of the gravesite. The choice to privilege space over time seems to upend the history writing of the album and attest to the tension between teleological history and memory. However, having gained narrativity from the sequential placement in the album, it sanctions history and memory at the same time, or better yet concludes its history writing through memory. The photo album itself was organized in such a way that the ahistorical depiction of Kojong's life at the beginning and the (non)events after the funeral bookended the history writing with photographs about Kojong's death and funeral, which suggests that the goal of this album was to write a history that would overcome the singularity of the event and replace the permanence lost in the secularization by photography with subjective memory.

* * *

This working in tandem with history and memory is most poignant in another photograph of the same gate from *The Photo Album of the Funeral of King Yi* (Ri taiō denka sōgi shashinchō) (figure 2.13). The photo depicts the gate of Hongnŭng, but with no specific reference to the funeral. Rather, it shows four men standing at the gate with the empty ground in the backdrop. In the contextual void, the photograph produces timelessness through the stillness of the landscape. The only sense of time is hinted at in the trees that are lined up toward the vanishing point on the horizon, so Hongnŭng is shown in a recollecting, reminiscent, and reflective mood. This photograph is a memory-image that transcends a fixed moment in time (the time of photography and history) and outlasts the singularity of the moment. The image bearing multiple temporalities of the past relived in the present reinforces the split gaze into the past (the dead king) and future (the path ahead), both with nostalgia, although the yearning for the history that has disappeared makes the future uncertain. In the end, the entwined times create a sense of permanence through timelessness, and history sublimated by memory loses the potential of propelling the dead monarch to be relevant to the nation's future: there simply exists a longing.

FIGURE 2.13. Photograph of Hongnŭng, from *The Photo Album of the Funeral of King Yi* (Ri taiō denka sōgi shashinchō), 28 x 37 cm, Seoul National University Museum. Reprinted with permission.

The fact is, history and memory production went hand in hand in Japanese colonial discourse, subsuming the locality of Korea into the context of the empire, producing the temporal hierarchy between the colonizer and the colonized, and relegating Korea to a timeless past all at the same time. What we see in the various photographs of Kojong's funeral is an attempt to bridge the boundary between memory and history while disaggregating event, history, and memory. This is an attempt to colonize. The funeral itself and the funeral as media event are both strategies of narrative production that checked the power of ritual by controlling both its performance and its documentation. The funerary procession usually celebrates the journey of the dead to a place of eternal rest. As ritual, it consecrates the dead king into eternity. Under the Japanese colonial government, however, this age-old royal ritual was modern spectacle. Any documentary evidence of it rendered the funeral a singular event captured by photographic freeze-frame and cinematic linear, panoramic narrative. It was history writing that disavowed the contingency and incompleteness of the event and replaced the loss of eternality in ritual with that of memory.

If we ask why Japan went ahead with the funeral a mere two days after the outbreak of the March First Movement, we are redirected to the question of how image, historical reality, and history writing intersect. Mary Taylor thought the funeral hardly assuaged Koreans' grief and anger because the primary goal of the funeral lay elsewhere—image politics intended not to deny history but to write a specific kind of history. That history, though, is superficial. As Susan Sontag cautioned us: "The ultimate wisdom of the photographic image is to say: 'This is the surface. Now think—or rather feel, intuit—what is beyond it, what the reality must be if it looks this way.' Photography implies that we know about the world if we accept it as the camera records it. But this is the opposite of understanding, which starts from *not* accepting the world as it looks."[46] Heeding Sontag's call to understand the world by not accepting it as it looks and with the courage to say no, I continue in the following chapters to explore the multiple layers of the city's sedimentary history in search of unexpected fissures and disruptions.

PART TWO

Language, Text, Play

3

Signage and Language

READING HANJA/KANJI

An article appeared in *Tonga ilbo* on March 28, 1929, describing a commotion taking place on a street corner on Chongo as people gathered at a streetcar stop. The crowd, so large that it blocked the sidewalk, fixated on a man painting a signboard across the street. The man, with a topknot and in *hanbok*, was up on a ladder and staring at a section on the sign after having finished painting the *hanja* character *chŏm*. He seemed to be pondering his next move, and as he raised his brush and started painting another stroke, the crowd broke into chatter: "The top-knotted man can write signage," said one. "He is pretty good," marveled a student. Another student agreed. The man went about his task rather slowly, taking his time. Then, all of a sudden, he put his fingers around his nose, blew it, and left paint stains around it. The crowd burst into laughter. Why would someone who was supposedly literate have such poor hygiene? They mocked how he ended up painting the signage on his face. Then one person in the crowd exclaimed, "This was the best advertising tactic I have ever seen!" Suddenly, a police whistle blew, and the crowd dispersed, leaving the man with the topknot alone.[1]

This short episode, called an "urban sketch," is a mundane yet curious story about city life. At a basic level, it calls to mind a predominant surface phenomenon of Seoul that has been largely invisible on a discursive level—signage. On another level, it is filled with nonsynchronous events that take place between medium and script, between script and body, and between spectator and spectacle. The allegedly modern, streetcar-riding crowd, some of whom were students, were confronted by a man in traditional attire and a topknot. He was painting a character in hanja; he was literate enough to write in a script that was difficult to learn, but his slow pace and lack of hygiene undoubtedly cast him as the opposite of modernity and certainly not a member of the literati. The crowd wondered how to comprehend this incongruent match of the premodern, unsanitary, and ill-mannered man with the modern medium of signage. Their answer can be captured in one word: *spectacle*. The role of signage was to draw the attention of passersby, and the old man performed it to perfection through the imperfect display of his body. This chapter takes part in that spectacle—by being amused by the sketch and drawing critical potential from this unlikely source—exploring the vignette's signage and script, and the incongruity between the two.

Signage in Seoul under Japanese colonial rule has rarely received significant attention from historians, partly because there is no archive to make such study possible. However, many photographs of Seoul contain street views showing an abundance of signage; the signs are impossible not to notice.[2] According to a survey, *The Commerce of Koreans*, published in 1925, there were 17,781 Korean shops and 6,270 Japanese shops at that time.[3] The sheer number of shops hints at a sense of what the urban streetscape and commercial clusters might have looked like. The survey's publication date of 1925 is also significant because the word for signage (*kanp'an*) had not been widely used in the Korean context before this point. Kanp'an is a neologism introduced by Japan, and the survey included an explanation that the word *kanp'an* was equivalent to the Korean word *hyŏnp'an*.[4] This translation is anachronistic: *kanp'an* and *hyŏnp'an* were not used interchangeably; rather, the word *hyŏnp'an* gave way to *kanp'an*, which referred to modern signage whose purpose, function, and design differed from those of hyŏnp'an. Hyŏnp'an mostly indicated building or place names as public signage whose role was to articulate power and demarcate boundaries, and in commercial settings, its role was limited to communicating announcements and conveying information. Kanp'an, however, was commercial and created to attract consumers. For this reason, whereas hyŏnp'an usually hung from the roof, kanp'an was placed above the roof or on the outer walls of a building for better visibility; the signs were oftentimes out of proportion to the size of the building but still created an illusion that they were part of the building.[5] This suggests that visuality was the foremost concern of kanp'an, which incorporated elements such as diagrams, trademarks, and illustrations, and paid attention to typeface and graphics.[6] Thus, the distinction between hyŏnp'an and kanp'an marked a shift from text-centered to image-centered design in the mid-1920s.

Although it is tempting to disregard signage (kanp'an) as inferior to architectural ornament because it was added to buildings, separate from their design, this chapter insists that signage be treated as ornament. While *ornament* commonly refers to decorative architectural elements, Kracauer spoke of ornament as something not just on a building's two-dimensional surface but as something that encompasses other meanings and contexts, even a child's scribble, all of which "once interpreted, can become the basis for critical awareness."[7] For this reason, I treat signage as ornament and examine how its vernacular and commercial usage created a semiotics that was decidedly different from architecture's ornaments that seamlessly narrated continuity on the façade of the building.

Signage was essentially a product of capitalism and functioned as an advertisement, as the crowd in the *Tonga ilbo* episode was keenly aware. This means, first of all, that signage always indexed a context beyond its built environment. Second, it was designed to appeal to reflex rather than reflection through writing that functioned also as picture. Yet, unlike architectural ornaments that relied on visual consumption, signage employed linguistic signs that required reading through speech and sound. For this reason, the surface phenomenon of the city as seen through such a vernacular, quotidian lens is no longer simply a matter of phenomenology or ontology; it requires a performative reading. This chapter attempts to take signage as the sign it is and to pay full attention to its multifaceted aspects of writing, picture, and sound.

When considering the script on signage in Seoul, we are forced to look at the city through a multilingual lens. Consider an example of a photograph of the Chosŏn Gramophone Company for how its eclectic signage employed a variety of languages: we see different scripts—han'gŭl, kana, hanja/kanji, and alphabets—written in different orders, from left to right, right to left, and top to bottom, and in calligraphic, typographic, and trademark forms (figure 3.1). The record label Columbia over the second-floor window was written in kana from right to left, and another

FIGURE 3.1. Chosŏn Gramophone Company, from *Chūō jōhō senman shisha*, ed. *Dai-keijō shashinchō* (Keijō: Chūō jōhō senman shisha,1937), p.91, National Library of Korea, Seoul.

vertical sign for the same label was written in han'gŭl underneath the symbol of a gramophone record with the Columbia label in English logotype. Other record labels, Taihei and Chieron, were also transliterated in han'gŭl as "T'aep'yŏng" and "Sieron," the former vertically from top to bottom and the latter horizontally from right to left. Adding to this assemblage were the titles of songs on the signage and flank cards written in han'gŭl and hanja/kanji. Such display of multilingualism and stylistic diversity created a montage supplement to the monumental history of Japanese colonialism. Layered against the cosmopolitan surface of the city, the multilingual signage with predominantly "Asian scripts" created a temporally and spatially disparate sediment. Adding to this visual complexity was the oral rendition of the scripts, evident in multiple iterations of the same name in different languages, which urges us to chart the intersection between visuality and orality and to examine how the production of sound created another layer of sediment atop the signage's surface.

In the image of the Chosŏn Gramophone Company, surrounded by all the assorted signage draping the building, was a sign bearing the name of the gramophone store, written in hanja/kanji, placed just underneath the railing of the second-floor balcony. The chapter thus focuses on this most prominent script in Seoul and examines what kind of soundscape its reading practices created. But first, the term hanja/kanji requires further clarification. It is commonly referred to as "Chinese characters" (the term I also have used previously), but that highlights the foreignness of the script, making it the exclusive property of continental culture. Calling the script "Chinese characters" ignores that the script has been a shared script of a cultural sphere called *Chunghwa* and an integral part of the local histories of diglossic cultures in Korea and Japan for centuries. Therefore, I opt for the term *hanja/kanji* in this chapter, however cumbersome it is to use both the Korean and Japanese renderings. It will become clear that there is no better way to capture the ever-changing practice of reading this script. In taking up the surface of hanja/kanji and signage, this chapter first discusses the liminal space and multiple temporalities of hanja/kanji and then the practice of reading it, and situates reading signage in the urban context of Seoul.

Time and Space of Hanja/Kanji

Speaking of hanja/kanji entails at once acknowledging the script's otherness to modernity and its place in a shared civilizational bloc that destabilizes the boundaries now demarcated by modern nation-states. What it should not do is reinforce the contrast between the putative properties of the Occident and the Orient. At one end of the spectrum, China and its language have served as a reservoir of exoticized imagination, well known in works like the 1919 book *The Chinese Written Character as Medium for Poetry* by Ezra Pound and Ernest Fenollosa. This Orientalizing perspective dehistoricized China and placed it outside of the West as the West's ultimate alterity. Such a tendency was noted even in the poststructuralist thinking that turned to the Chinese language and script as a privileged site for deconstructing language in Western philosophy. Roland Barthes, for example, discussed China as the *chinois*—the bizarre, the complicated, and the incomprehensible—whose semiotic chaos made him declare that there is nothing to interpret in China.[8] Derrida likewise saw the nonphonetic nature of the Chinese language as "the testimony of a powerful movement of civilization developing outside of all logocentrism."[9] This reference to China as the "other" that reflects the utopian fable of the Western system of logic with "a certain charm of another system of thought" is illustrated in Michel Foucault's preface to *The Order of Things*, particularly in his discussion of the strange taxonomy of animals in Jorge Luis Borges's passage on a Chinese encyclopedia.[10] The uncontrollable laughter Foucault broke into upon reading Borges's passage is said to have shattered "all familiar landmarks" of our thought, so he claimed that China is "a kind of thought without space, to word and categories that lack all life and place,"[11] an atopia and aphasia in which correspondence between place and name does not stand.[12] The ways China has become fictionalized as the radical other in Foucault did not go unnoticed by Zhang Longxi, who argued that "the monstrous unreason and its alarming subversion of Western thinking, the unfamiliar and alien space of China as the image of the other threatening to break up ordered surfaces and logical categories, all turn out to be, in the most literal sense, a Western fiction."[13] There is irony in how China had become a myth of difference in itself, argued Zhang, but this served as a reflection of the West's utopian fantasies and dreams.

At the other end of the spectrum, the Chinese script had been criticized as inferior to phonetic scripts, motivated by self-evaluation about how to position oneself in the universalizing discourse of modernity. For instance, inspired by Ferdinand de Saussure, many May Fourth intellectuals in China became proponents of vernacularizing the Chinese script and even proposed a Latinized Chinese script such as Sin Wenz.[14] Lu Xun, among the harshest critics of the Chinese language, saw the script as a major impediment to China's modernization and impassionedly argued for its abolition in a speech in Hong Kong in 1927. In this speech, "Silent China," Lu Xun argued that the language of the Chinese was divorced from the masses and their feelings and thoughts: "Couched in crabbed, archaic language, it describes outmoded, archaic sentiments. All its utterances belong to the past, and therefore amount to nothing."[15] In such a stark and pessimistic tone, he then compared the choices between the Chinese script and a phonetic script, past and future, and death and life: "One is to cling to our classical language and die; the other is to cast that language and live."[16]

In Korea—as in Japan, where debates about recovering sound were led by Kokugaku scholars in the eighteenth century by reinterpreting the language of *Kojiki* as the language to construct the Yamato language[17]—phonocentrism and the unity between writing and speech (*ŏnmun ilch'i*) began to privilege the Korean vernacular script. For instance, Chu Si-gyŏng, the leading scholar of the Korean language, in the 1877 article "A Theory of the Korean Language," published in *Tongnip sinmun*, argued that ideograms like the Chinese script create not a language but a picture, because sound and script do not correspond.[18] He even argued that the use of Chinese script had led to the extinction of many Korean words and the sound of Korean itself.[19] Han'gŭl had been regarded as *ŏnmun* since its promulgation in 1466 while *hanmun*, literary Chinese, had been the high variety. But han'gŭl came to represent the pure and native sound of Korean, casting the script and writing of the diglossia, hanja and hanmun, as the "other" for the purpose of self-articulating Korean nationalism. Vernacularization was an enlightenment project that promoted han'gŭl over the other scripts in use. Yet, hanmun, not han'gŭl, offered the lexicon for understanding modernity and enlightenment ideas through neologisms from Japan, such as society (*sahoe*), individual (*kaein*), being (*chonjae*), nature (*chayŏn*), right (*kwŏlli*), liberty (*chayu*), love (*yŏnae*), novel (*sosŏl*), and modern (*kŭndae*).[20] The script of the "past" universal, then, was ironically what mediated the introduction of modern civilization to Korea. The reality on the ground was, therefore, much more complex, with a tendency for hybridity (*honjong*) and heterogeneity (*chapchong*) of different linguistic practices.[21] Hanmun and *kukhanmun* (mixed script) persisted throughout the colonial period, and even as the debate over vernacularization reached its peak in the 1920s and 1930s, classic scholars like Chŏng In-bo continued writing in hanmun and han'gŭl simultaneously. While Chŏng was a proponent of phonocentricism, believing that han'gŭl was uniquely capable of representing the true voice of Korea, he did not reject hanja/hanmun but rather embraced it as a medium that also could represent the traditions of Korea. He argued that, since a sense of the Korean (*punhyang*) can be found in ideas and emotions as well as in the melody and tone of a language, any language that is capable of representing *punhyang* is "our" language.[22]

In this complex web of debates, discourses, and practices about language regarding vernacularization, translation, loan words, mediation, and hybridity, we are confronted with a set of practical questions about how we should interpret the "peculiar" choice of script that dominated the surface of signs in Seoul, especially given that the debates on language reform were in full force in the 1920s. Does hanja/kanji inevitably point to a lagging culture that still needed to catch up to the modernizing city as it transformed from the top down? Would any attempt to recuperate critical potential from hanja/kanji fall into the pitfall of being antinationalist or, conversely, exoticizing, eventually forcing it out of its historical context and its environment? To pay full attention to the actual usage of the script in the context of the everyday, this chapter decouples letter (*cha*) from writing (*mun*). This is not to disregard the complex language practices discussed above, but to explore how hanja mostly came to be used for names in signage and became vulnerable to different readings, therein hanja/kanji. But first, let's consider the temporality of hanja/kanji.

Most arguments about hanja/kanji have defined it as pictograph or ideograph, privileging the visual form, making it susceptible to criticism as a nonphonetic script, and so inferior to phonetic scripts. So Ha Yŏngsam suggested that *logograph* is a better term for describing hanja/kanji, which consists of morphemes that are wholes in themselves and lend traces of form, meaning, and sound to their very formation. Ha argued that hanja/kanji crystallizes meanings beyond those in circulation, as a living fossil with accumulated thoughts of the past underneath the surface.[23] This model points to temporal totality rather than a sequential process of syntax formation. What can be unearthed from hanja/kanji, therefore, are myths, symbols, images, spirituality, mentality, belief systems, and practices.[24] The case is even richer because of the ways Chinese morphemes were borrowed into the local diglossic contexts of Korea and Japan, in which a single character can end up representing multiple morphemes with similar meanings but different origins in multiple languages.

To read memories of multiple pasts in hanja/kanji is thus to acknowledge a different kind of temporality, for which we can consider Henri Bergson's idea of duration. In pursuit of uncovering the plurality of time, Bergson proposed duration as an alternative to temporal movement that successively replaces one with another. Bergson defined duration as "the continuous progress of the past which gnaws into the future and which swells as it advances."[25] In duration, the past exists alongside the present and contains heterogeneous temporalities. The past may have been suspended or forgotten, like Seoul under erasure, but it persists and stubbornly returns, refusing to be pushed away by the present. For this reason, hanja/kanji—which is at once particular, for containing the accumulative memory of its construction and practice, and universal, for its creation of a totalizing universe in which diglossic cultural differences coexist—can offer us a different tool for recovering what appears to be a relic of the past. For this, the practice of reading hanja/kanji has to be performative. Because hanja/kanji integrated the dialectical and linguistic differences of different locales, the reading of hanja/kanji is a process of excavating the temporal traces of historical practice (sound performed), not the ontological purity of the script (sound written). The "performative" here is akin to Homi Bhabha's definition: something counterpoised to the pedagogical through a repetitive, recursive time that is contiguous rather than continuous, which leads to a dense constellation of pulse and punctuation by mobilizing "the scraps, patches, and rags of daily life" as material correlatives of the gaps and ruptures.[26]

This would also lead to a different spatiality, one that would prove useful for complicating a conventional view of the dichotomous space of Seoul via linguistic distinction. As the spatial boundary between Honmachi and Chongno has dominated studies of Seoul as a sign of political, economic, and cultural disparity between colonizer and colonized, the spatial dichotomy has also been discussed in terms of "bilingual (ijung ŏnŏ)" spaces.[27] However, the demarcation of Honmachi as a "Japanese space" from Chongno as a "Korean space" demands more careful consideration, especially when seen through the lens of hanja/kanji in use in signage across the Honmachi-Chongno border. The 1929 map *The Tour Guide Map of Seoul* (Keijō annaizu) shows how signage in both Honmachi and Chongno would have looked by listing the names of shops placed on all four sides around the map (figure 3.2). Here, the distinction between Honmachi and Chongno becomes ambiguous because the names of shops, as well as of streets, were written in hanja/kanji. The written boundary between North Village and South Village was virtually indistinct, so any difference between the two spaces had to be heard; and the speaker could determine how to read that script differently—either as hanja or kanji. The name, Honmachi, for instance, also written in hanja/kanji, was read as *honmachi* in Japanese or *ponjŏng* in Korean depending on the interlocutor. Many postcards featured the main gate to Honma-

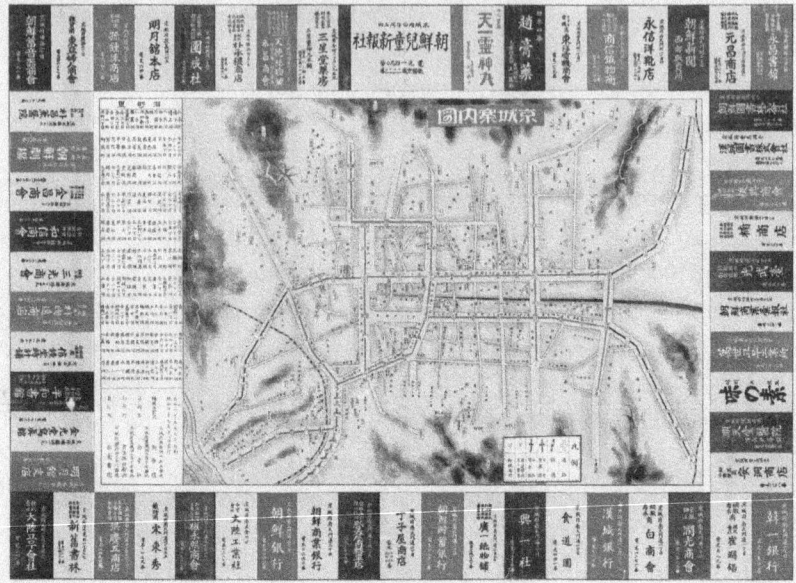

FIGURE 3.2. *Guide Map of Keijō* (Keijō annaizu), 1929, 79.1 x 54.2 cm, Seoul History Museum.

chi, on which its name was written in kanji; the English caption always read, "The street of Honmachi, Keijō," dictating its reading as Honmachi in Japanese and referring to Seoul as Keijō (figure 3.3). However, the characters as written could be read as Ponjŏng by anyone who ignored the caption, and certainly in practice the name Ponjŏng was frequently used and coexisted alongside another commonly used name, Chin'gogae, which can lead to a completely different set of characters, Irhyŏn. Irhyŏn when transcribed means "the muddy pass." This suggests that a boundary between Honmachi and Chongno—be it linguistic, ethnic, cultural, historical, or spatial—cannot be understood solely in terms of Japanese-Korean opposition. The distinction existed, in other words, but not exclusively in spatial terms; nor did linguistic and spatial boundaries neatly coalesce.

Instead, hanja/kanji destabilizes the city's bifurcation by opening itself up to verbal play. In this vein, the difference is not simply a reference to disparate place identities, but names performed through the choice of reading the same script either in Korean or in Japanese. The reading practice of hanja/kanji in these examples forbids one name from

THE MOST BUSTLING STREET OF 1ST. BLOCK, HONMACHI, KEIJO.
目丁一町本る な華繁し最　(城京)

FIGURE 3.3. Postcard of Honmachi, 1910s–1920s, postcard, 9.1 x 14.1 cm, Seoul History Museum.

sticking to a place, harkening back to linguistic practices of diglossia, translation, and everyday practices, and allows for a potential redrawing of the boundary in the soundscape. Capturing this dynamic between Honmachi and Chongno or between Honmachi and Ponjŏng, or a history that charts the change from Chin'gogae to Ponjŏng or Chin'gogae to Honmachi (or Kyŏngsŏng to Keijō for that matter), then would require a different kind of mapping. To further explore the sound production of hanja/kanji that would add dimensions to a flattened map of Seoul and recuperate the time of duration, the next section examines varied practices of reading hanja/kanji by navigating across the boundaries of *langue* and *parole*, reading and speech, and sound and voice.

Hanja/Kanji and the Voice

Important to the discussion of speaking is the question of corporeality, which was brilliantly demonstrated in the *Tonga ilbo* episode. This is pertinent also because hanja/kanji existed in the media space of signage, where it was rendered with typography, which attests to how writing was transformed in this space. With the advent of modern signage, on most signboards in Seoul letters were mechanized, or painted or carved onto a wooden panel, or painted on an enamel plate.[28] The *Tonga ilbo* episode, for this reason, described the old man's "writing" on the signboard with the word *paint* (*kŭrida*). The confluence of writing and painting is intriguing, as there does exist a difference between the two.[29] According to Gerrit Noordzij, writing is an act of brushing a stroke, a product of the body in varied forms depending on tool, surface, speed, and method, and it is performed through control over the medium, through which the time of movement was translated into a line.[30] In contrast, lettering is writing with built-up shapes that replace the single-stroke writing, as multiple strokes are applied. In the process, it buries the traces of time seen in handwriting by allowing for the retouching of strokes.[31] This shows that in letterform and typography, any sense of bodily movement was diminished as the organic traces of time left by the brushstroke were made reproducible.

The modernization of signage in 1920s Seoul made lettering a preferred method, so the subject of writing became removed from its production. Where, then, do we locate the body of the colonial subject when writing no longer contained the traces of the body? An answer to this question can be found in how the poet and artist Henri Michaux described the stroke-by-stroke movement of the brush in calligraphy in terms of recuperating sound.[32] Michaux found his poetic inspiration, visually and verbally, in the continuity and spontaneity of bodily movement, attempting to recapture the corporeal performance of calligraphy that runs against the poetic narrative and passage. More important, Michaux saw this as an intervention that freed the sound that had become buried in the ideograms of the Chinese language: hence, calligraphy enabled the "dead" sign to be a sign, to signify rather than imitate. The transference between the visual and verbal that he made is particularly helpful and allows us to seek corporeal performance, once seen in brushstrokes of calligraphic writing, in sound. With this in mind, this chapter treats the production of sound, the act of speaking, as an important site of corporeality, when writing increasingly precluded spontaneous bodily movement, and examines different practices of reading hanja/kanji.

Although it is not easy to trace phonetic readings of a script, we can rely on a writing practice that accompanied the phonetic reading

alongside the characters known as *t'o* or *furigana*. This annotative practice possibly began in Japan, as t'o was not much in use before the colonial period in Korea; it originated to indicate the correct reading of a
character out of multiple possibilities, which some language reformers
in Japan embraced as a means of promoting literacy. Others, though,
harshly criticized it as a practice unseen in other languages and a trait
of an uncivilized culture.[33] Albeit different perspectives, both positions
defined furigana or t'o as a didactic tool that guided correct reading.
Although writing t'o was rarely done in commercial signage, we have
a few examples from smaller, painted enamel-plate signage. One is for
Nashiyonaru Battery (figure 3.4). This sign contained two rows of words
for the brand name Nashiyonaru and the word *battery*: Nashiyonaru
on the top was written in katakana and accompanied a t'o in han'gŭl
underneath it, transcribing its reading as *nasiyonaru*. The word for battery on the bottom was written in hanja/kanji, for which the t'o wrote its
Japanese reading, *kandenchi*, not the Korean reading, *kŏnjŏnji*. The t'o
likely guided the correct reading of the characters for the word *battery*
in Japanese because the brand name was in Japanese. Other examples
demonstrate how hanja/kanji words were subject to multiple readings in
Korean and Japanese, as seen in a sign for a popular brand of domestic
medicine (figure 3.5). Underneath its trademark featuring the image of
a nobleman, the brand name was written vertically in hanja/kanji, accompanied by three readings in han'gŭl, kana, and rōmaji. The han'gŭl
t'o on the left read the characters as *indan*, and the furigana on the right
as *jintan*. These two readings, one in Korean and the other in Japanese,
occupied equal space on each side of the brand name in hanja/kanji,
but the reading on the top in rōmaji designated a privileged reading in
Japanese: *jintan*. Unlike the Nashiyonaru battery sign, there was no
contextual flow that would guide the reading of the hanja/kanji word
in Japanese, so it was not the context but the interjection by rōmaji that
privileged one reading over the other, which only attests to how unstable
the practice of reading hanja/kanji words was.

   More often than not, writings of the reading of signage showed
highly unsystematic practices. One example can be seen in a commonly
circulated plate signage for cigarettes (figure 3.6): the reading of the characters for "cigarette" as written should be *yŏnch'o* in Korean, but the t'o
read it as *tambae*, a vernacular word for "cigarette." This is due to two different reading practices that existed in Korea's diglossic tradition: a read-

FIGURE 3.4. Signage for Nashiyonaru battery, 1920s, enamel plate, 30 x 45.2 cm. Source: Park Armjong.

FIGURE 3.5. Signage for Jintan, metal plate, 58 x 34 cm, National Folk Museum of Korea, Seoul.

ing that deciphers meaning (*hundok*) and a phonetic reading (*ŭmdok*). The reading "tambae" in this example results from reading the characters for meaning rather than sound and then transcribing that meaning in vernacular expression. The evidence of this sign's use, seen in two photographs of street views, one in Honmachi and the other in front of T'aep'yŏnggwan theater in Pusan, further complicates the story (figures 3.7 and 3.8). The first sign in Honmachi, on the left side above a group of Japanese women, wrote the Korean reading "tambae" as in the previous example and designated it as a reading by writing it in a smaller size than the hanja/kanji characters. The other photograph shows the word *cigarette* (*yŏnch'o*) in hanja/kanji three times on the signboards of a small shop partially shown on the right side of the photograph where one of the enamel plates at the bottom appeared in the same design as the aforementioned plate sign—a red outer layer, an inner white oval-shaped background, and the calligraphic writing of the word for "cigarette" in hanja/kanji (*yŏnch'o*) and a han'gŭl t'o (*tambae*). The key difference is noted, however, in the equal size of the han'gŭl t'o and the hanja/kanji word. In this, the hierarchy between the word designating the reading and the reading itself becomes ambiguous. Also ambiguous is whether *tambae* functioned as a reading, faithful to its written form. Because tambae was a vernacular expression, it could well indicate the residual traces of the everyday practice that called a cigarette tambae without reference to the hanja/kanji word. In other words, it could simply be a result of interjecting orality from the everyday into the textual space. In this case, the reading took place outside of the textual and spatial contexts of the signage and referred to everyday practices—chattering in the alleyway. So, we encounter another version of this sign post-1945 (figure 3.9), on which the word *cigarette* was written in kana and han'gŭl as *tabako* and *tambae*, respectively. The two words appear in equal sizes, making it unclear which is writing and which is reading; they might very well refer to the hanja/kanji word that appeared on the other signs; yet, they simply transcribed vernacular words corresponding to the meaning of the referent word. The absence of the hanja/kanji word on this sign, therefore, suggests the primacy of reading (the sound) dictating the writing on the signage rather than the writing on the signage prescribing the correct sound.

To further examine the multivalent practices of reading hanja/kanji, we can turn to product labels, packaging, and advertisements. The first

FIGURE 3.6. Signage for cigarettes, 1920s, enamel plate, 30.3 x 22.7 cm, National Museum of Korean Contemporary History, Seoul.

FIGURE 3.7. Postcard of the signage for cigarettes, 9.1 x 14.1 cm, National Folk Museum of Korea, Seoul.

FIGURE 3.8. A photograph of the street in front of T'aep'yŏnggwan in 1920s Pusan, from Kim Sŭng and Yang Mi-suk, ed., *Sinp'yŏn pusan taegwan* (Seoul: Sŏnin munhwasa, 2010), p. 586.

FIGURE 3.9. Postwar signage for cigarettes, enamel plate, 30.2 x 22.2 cm. Source: Busan Museum.

example is packaging for a cosmetic facial powder (figure 3.10). The product name, Pakkabun, written in hanja/kanji, was placed inside the black strip set diagonally across the center as each character of the name accompanied a t'o: *pak/ka/pun.* In another example of a label for red pepper powder, this simple and faithful reading of the characters gave way to linguistic chaos (figure 3.11). The product name was written in hanja/kanji in the middle from top to bottom, with han'gŭl t'o on the right and furigana on the left, and yet the neat format balancing the hanja/kanji characters with bilingual readings on each side is misleading, to say the least. The word for "pepper powder" was written in three characters: the first two formed the word for "pepper," and the third referred to the powder form. The t'o at right read as *ko/ch'o/karu,* in which the first two characters were read by sound, but the character for "powder" read *karu* when the same character was read correctly as *pun* by sound in the example of the cosmetic powder Pakkabun. The expression *koch'ubun* was not commonly used, so we can surmise that the reading *koch'u garu* was more faithful to the word in everyday use than to the text that it was supposed to read. This hypothesis becomes even more plausible when

FIGURE 3.10. Pakkabun packaging, 1930s, print on paper, 4.8 x 4.8 cm, National Folk Museum of Korea, Seoul.

FIGURE 3.11. A label for red pepper powder, print on paper, 14.4 x 8.8 cm. Source: Busan Museum.

looking at the furigana written to the left of the hanja/kanji characters, which read as *tōgarashi hu. Tōgarasi*, the Japanese word for "pepper," did not correspond to the hanja/kanji characters for which it was supposed to serve. Instead, the Japanese reading also pointed to the everyday language of Japanese without any reference to the text on the label. In this way, the hierarchy between writing and speech was reversed even though the hanja/kanji name of the product, carefully aestheticized in lettering, was supposed to guide the reading.

The primacy of everyday spoken language is also seen in advertisements. For example, a toothpaste/powder brand called "Lion" was usually written in katakana for "lion" and *ch'ima/ch'imabun* in hanja/kanji.

The first advertisement (figure 3.12) wrote the brand name in this combination of katakana and hanja/kanji words in the heading, in the text, and twice in the images of the product. The heading and text featured t'o for all hanja/kanji words in a conventional layout that wrote the t'o much smaller than the characters. Yet, while the t'o faithfully read the katakana characters for lion, it added another reading, *pun*, for the hanja/kanji characters for *ch'ima* to read *ch'imabun* instead. The earlier version of this product was mostly in powder form, as seen in the advertisement, so the added t'o was a reference to the image of the product in the same textual space and what the product was called in daily practice—a misreading of the hanja/kanji characters in all instances. The same mismatch among the name, product image, and reading also appeared in a second advertisement, which included a negative space of a kitelike black rectangular box containing the Korean word *raion ch'imabun*; the product name shown in the image was *raion ch'ima*, but the same misreading was repeated in this han'gŭl text (figure 3.13). Although this advertisement did not include t'o, the larger text box in the foreground, which partially blocks the view of the product image behind it, indicates that the Korean reading (or misreading) of the product name stood on its own rather than as a reading of hanja/kanji. In all these cases, speech took precedence over writing, either by supplementing a reading that did not derive from the text or by more prominently showcasing the Korean reading. These advertisements' privileging of speech over writing shows that their concern was not the correct reading of the characters. Rather, their reference lay beyond the textual context of the advertisement in the everyday market context where Lion *ch'ima* was called Lion *ch'imabun*.

These examples illustrate that reading hanja/kanji is not simply a matter of recuperating sound buried in memory but of interjecting the everyday—the habitual, hearsay, and orality. They demonstrate a practice that challenged the primacy of writing and created fissures in the unity of writing, speech, and sound. It shows that recovering sound from hanja/kanji was a performative act that privileged the interlocutor over the text, as the reading was ultimately the interlocutor's choice. In this way, the cacophony added another layer to the montage script of the signage, opening up a space of heterolingual possibility. This is significant because such reading practice disaggregated non-disaggregatable proper nouns of brand names, product names, and shop names that could only be quoted. These names had already undergone semantic transformation

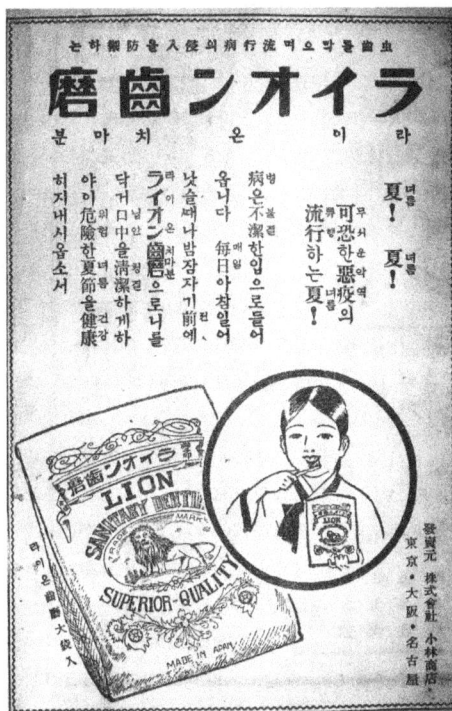

FIGURE 3.12. Lion toothpaste advertisement, from *Pyŏlgŏn'gon*, September 1930, Museum of Magazines, Seoul.

FIGURE 3.13. Lion toothpaste advertisement, from *Tonga ilbo*, January 10, 1933.

as an index sign, so the meaning of individual characters in the name became irrelevant to naming an object, person, or place. In referring to department stores, Hirada was a name, not an open field, and Tonga, the name of a store that sold modern goods, not a geographical location in the East. Therefore, the act of reading proper nouns in multiple ways inevitably destabilized the very identity of the name and challenged the authority that named it. In that process, the hierarchy between the name and its reading might even have been reversed, as in the case of *tambae* and *ch'imabun* standing alone, which freed the reading from its referent and became a name itself.

This was made possible by the text undergoing a process of disaggregation. The text (*mun*) was disaggregated into individual characters (*cha*); as in the example of the pepper powder, the character *pun* was detached from the name *koch'ubun* to be transformed into the vernacular *karu*. The character (*cha*) underwent further disaggregation, and like *pun* in Lion tooth powder lurking in the textual space, was detached from its corresponding character as sound from another context was added to the text. Through decontextualization and fragmentation, speech (*hwa*) itself was disaggregated and there existed only sound (*ŭm*). However, that sound was a product of sounding out, not inherent to the character but added by the interlocutor's voice (*sŏng*). Then, text became characters, characters became sound, and sound became voice; the text eventually returned to the body of the spectator-turned-interlocutor.

Another Haptic: Time and Tempo

How can we understand the visual experience of seeing and reading signage in the context of urban space, and where do we locate the moment of enunciation? To answer these questions, I turn to an article that appeared in *Pyŏlgŏn'gon* on New Year's Day in 1927.[34] Mimicking a product review meeting (*p'ump'yŏnghoe*), it featured one reporter interviewing Kim Pokchin and An Sŏk-chu, who reviewed the signage in Chongno.[35] As they walked along the street, they first encountered signage for Paengmogok Import Goods store. The store's building was rather small and faced southeast, not aligned with the broad intersection where it was located, so the reviewers commented that such a building would have to have signage that was visible from the street and that would help disguise its unimpressive size. This store's signage was quite noticeable from a distance, they noted, thanks to the typesetting, which created the illusion of depth and also made for interesting viewing at close range; moreover, by harmonizing with the rather dim interior of the building, the signage was not separate from the building. Next up was a store specializing in goods for weddings and funerals; its sign was a decorated wooden panel with traditional colors (*tanch'ŏng*). Kim called it "signage without words" that did not live up to the function of signage even though it played to the store's specialty. An agreed and commented that the color and pattern were too familiar to Koreans to make any impact (*kamch'ok*), so it would appeal only to foreign tourists. The unusually large sign for Tonga Women's Store also used Korean style but was commended for its efforts to advertise the products. Aesthetically, however, it was criticized for using too many different colors, which prevented instant contact (*ch'okkam*) with the eyes and bothered onlookers.

One store that sold hats received contentious reviews. The interviewing reporter praised the painting of a Western woman in a silk hat holding a mandolin and a handsome Western man sitting in front of her against a landscape, which he described as arousing emotional responses. An vehemently disagreed, saying that the picture had nothing to do with hats, and even if the store sold only luxurious silk hats, it would make one blush. If the store attracted customers with this kind of sign, An pressed, it would ruin the shop's reputation. He reproached the reporter: "This is like a background that can be found at the theater Kwangmudae. Such marvelous landscapes and elegant taste are so separate from our life and people. What relation does this signage have with us? It has forgotten the meaning of signage and is trying to attract customers with a stimulus so intense and alluring that it seduces like magic. Sellers need to flatter customers and need to invade their lives as if it is a national obligation."[36] Kim replied that too many signs in Korea were like this one, an uninteresting example that turns off the eyes.

In another instance, they introduced an interesting concept in comments on the signage of Ihwa Clothing and Shoes Store. Kim recalled seeing something similar before and quickly added that that was not necessarily a bad thing. Then, he explained that this was what was called *ch'agyŏng*, which refers to the miniaturized reconstruction of natural scenery in a garden to bring an element of nature into the built environment, and defended it as a necessary component in signage and architecture. An, who also remembered seeing a similar design in an advertisement in a Western magazine and later in Honmachi, replied that it was better to imitate something good rather than to create something ugly. This idea was mentioned once again in discussions of the signs of several bookstores in the area, which they remarked were indistinguishable from each other and unremarkable in their shabby attempts to contour the letters. Bookstore owners should be discerning individuals, they lamented, but they were so indiscriminate about signage and, An pointed out, they had to put a stove in front of their signboards. Then, Kim reminded them of what was missing—*ch'agyŏng*, which he explained as borrowing from someone else for one's own advantage because the goal of signage was to wage "urban competition." In this, only the keenest mind would succeed.

As the three reached the intersection near Kwanghwa Gate, they commented on major commercial buildings in the area. The Hwasin Store, which would become a department store in 1931, flaunted a large gold sign that exuded confidence. Kim Hŭng-ho Store, next to Chongno Police Station, was frowned on for its design, no better than the "ornaments of barbarians," but the Taeryuk Rubber Store next to the courthouse was seen favorably for its text that stood out against the wooden and iron sign. The reporters reserved the highest praise for two other stores: the Chosŏn Women's Association, which, despite featuring Western-style painting, created harmony between image and text through its restrained use of monochromatic colors. The Tongyang Medicine Company also caught their eye for its small sign that featured the character *yak* for "medicine." The simple design was tastefully achieved by the outline of the character, embellished in blue, which earned praise as "a sign that is truly a sign." These two choices contrasted sharply with that of the Tonga Football Manufacturer, which put a large flank card of a painting of a football player on the roof, where two oversized signboards featuring more athletes already hung. The pictures were unique, they commented, but hideous—they could not distinguish whether the figures were human or animal.

This article is a rare account that through its vivid descriptions helps us imagine what a passerby at the time might have seen and experienced. It also offers very useful insights into the role of signage in a fiercely competitive urban environment and demonstrates a sophisticated understanding of how visual and verbal signs work. The commentators fundamentally understood signage as an advertisement to catch the passerby's eye: the design could not be too ordinary or familiar, nor too outlandish, in attracting attention; it also had to achieve harmony with the building, because signage was architectural ornament (*chang-sik*). One of the most important criteria was legibility, achieved through choice of lettering and coloring, size of the text and signboard, and the combination of text and image. Their goal was to "invade" people's lives, but they also needed to refrain from enticing viewers with images and ideas that were inaccessible to ordinary Koreans.

Another interesting comment is on the concept of *ch'agyŏng,* which can be interpreted as a metonymic reproduction of landscape in miniaturized form. Here, Susan Stewart's conceptualization of miniature is helpful. Stewart explained that miniaturized objects are not important in and of themselves and do not have narrative capabilities; rather, they refer to the physical world. A miniaturized object, therefore, "resists the interiority of reflexive language in order to interiorize an outside: it is the closest thing we have to a three-dimensional language, for it continually points outside itself, creating a shell-like, or enclosed, exteriority."[37] The imagery of the three-dimensional language is quite striking as *ch'agyŏng,* expressed in the two-dimensional space of signage, continually refers to another dimension and another context. The imagery of enclosed exteriority, refusing the production of subjectivity through narrativity, also contrasts sharply with the inward and emotive experience of urban space discussed in chapter 1. *Ch'agyŏng* thus provides an important analytic tool for reconceptualizing the city that was to be experienced as a *kyŏng* (panorama). Moreover, *ch'agyŏng,* the favored imitation technique, speaks directly to the fabricated nature of urban façade and celebrates its very fakeness. "Copy it if you can" is its message, which carries many implications about the status of the colonized and the city, criticized for being a copy of metropolitan modernity. In the city of Seoul, built on the principle of mimicry, in other words, the signage of *ch'agyŏng* offers a different type of simile that bypasses the construction of interiority and subjectivity and serves as a reference to something else as an index sign.

The signage functioning as an index sign is also attested in the tension between showing and telling in image and text, another aspect to which this article brought attention. As in the case of the Tongyang Medicine Company's sign, in which the character *yak* was applauded for its power to arrest the attention of passersby, successful signage treated verbal signs as visual signs. These were text-images in which the graphic quality of writing was most important. In short, in signage, writing was a picture, but one that was different from the view designating hanja/kanji as a pictograph because it was begotten by the role of signage rather than the ontological status of the script. The evolution of text as picture is evident in the history of signage in Korea. First, without signage, the shops displayed objects they were selling outside the shop. In early signage in modern Korea, these objects appeared in pictures on the signs. By the late 1920s, although there was residual use of pictures in signage, writing had replaced most pictures, at least in the ones that the commentators of the article thought deserved to be called signage. This is a process through which the text-image became an index sign, no longer needing a referent object to be present, physically or visually, for it to signify the product on sale.

The two advertisement pamphlets for the Taeryuk Rubber Company (figures 3.14 and 3.15) illustrate this point. Both advertisements have similar compositions featuring a text box, two different types of trademarks, stylized in a modern, geometrical, streamlined font, placed on four corners of the paper as well as inside the text box, and the company information written in a more traditional calligraphic font at the bottom. Resembling a dialogue bubble in cartoons, the text box contains detailed information about the product, which appears to be an advertisement in and of itself, combining word-images with texts that were to be read more narratively. It is these word-images that attest to the evolution of the text-image into an index sign. In the three different designs of trademarks—vertical writing of the full name of the product in han'gŭl, one writing the brand name in han'gŭl inside a rectangular box, and the other in the circular logo featuring a hanja for land—each one points to an evolution from one to another, from the full product name (*taeryuk komusin*) to the brand name (*taeryuk*) to only one character of the brand name (*ryuk*), each indexing what came before. The difference between the two advertisement pamphlets also indicates this change. The first one displays pictures of various types of footwear with the names of each item written underneath the corresponding image. The second advertisement shows how the trademarks came to function as index for the products without requiring the presence of actual images.

On another level, the replacement of product images by the map of streetcar routes is significant because the moment of index referentiality

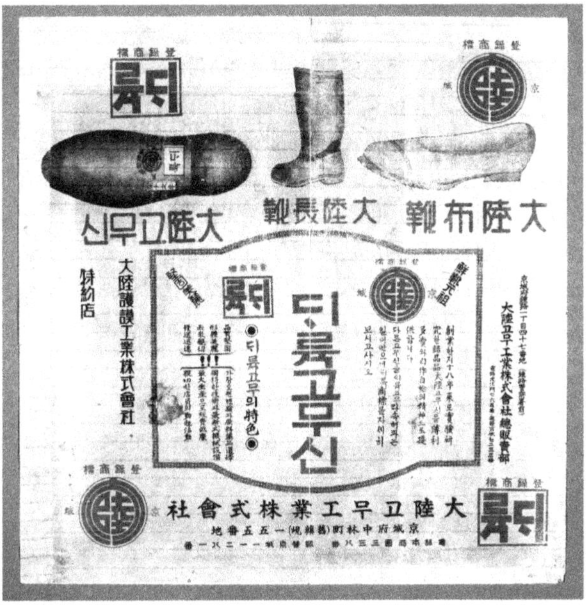

FIGURE 3.14. Taeryuk Rubber Shoes advertisement, 1930s, print on paper, 38.2 x 38.6 cm, National Folk Museum of Korea, Seoul.

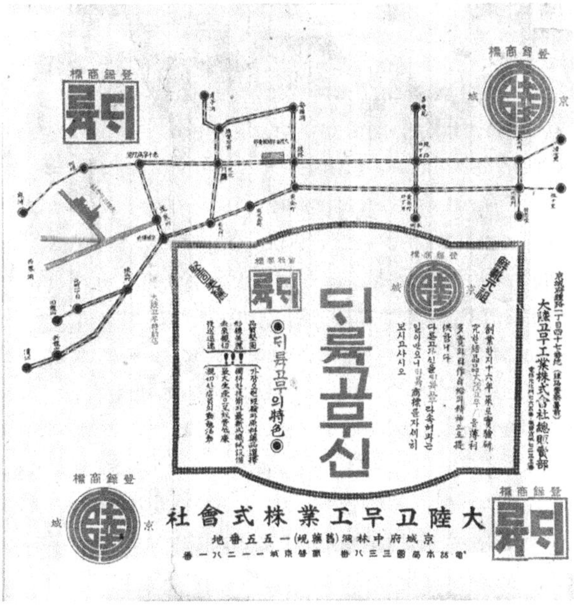

FIGURE 3.15. Taeryuk Rubber Shoes advertisement, 1935, print on paper, 37.3 x 38.1 cm, Seoul History Museum.

takes place in the moving passage and when signage arrests the eyes in that continuous flow of movement. Interestingly, the pointy corner of the text bubble functions like an arrow, pointing at a streetcar stop on the map and making a gesture of saying, "Here it is." In this instance, the text box (and possibly the texts contained within it) came to function as an image and an index sign, saying, "Look! Here it is." According to Peirce, "The index asserts nothing; it only says 'There!' It takes hold of our eyes, as it were, and forcibly directs them to a particular object, and there it stops."[38] In other words, index signs—such as a pointing finger, footprint, demonstrative pronoun, and photographic images—"denote without describing."[39] The index simply points to the object, transporting passengers from their itinerant context into the context of commodity exchange. Because of this, the reading of writing-as-picture in signage always appealed to reflex rather than reflection—one that took place in transience, relying on the eyes coming into contact with the image in the instantaneous moment.

The experience of seeing and "reading" signage in the urban space can be compared to how the textual space of advertisement arranges words, images, and narratives. For one, reading advertisements was a highly fragmented practice—from left to right, right to left, top to bottom. Also, each text and character in different sizes, typefaces, and scripts visualized degrees of volume—how "loudly" they spoke—and the amount of time the eyes were to spend capturing them. The narrative blocks demanded more prolonged attention, but the image-text of brand names halted the continuum of narrative and were read more spontaneously. The narrative blocks that created a continuous movement of the eye in advertisement are comparable to the narrative space of the city created through kinetic motion, such as walking or riding a streetcar. How different images and text-images entailed a highly cacophonous and fragmented reading experience in advertisements can also be seen in the coexistence in the urban space of vertical and horizontal signs, wooden panels, neon signs, flank cards, shop names, product names, and brand names. In the moment of arrested gaze and movement, therefore, the reading of a sign bypassed the hermeneutic reading of text; by fusing the semiotic and mimetic, they were less likely to be read textually and more likely in distraction and transience.

This moment of contact between the eyes and the object was enabled only when the subject had encountered the scene. This was contact between two surfaces, so the *Pyŏlgŏn'gon* article used expressions evoking physical sensations such as a sense of touch (*kamch'ok*) to explain the impact of signage and described the eyes coming into contact with the sign as "the instant sense of touch that the eyes felt" (*sun'ganjŏgin sisŏn e ch'okkam*).[40] Such sensory descriptions combining optic and tactile experience are reminiscent of how Giuliana Bruno talked about the haptic experience of the city (see chapter 1), but the haptic here should be distinguished from the one that constitutes a narrative subject of the cinematic panorama. The haptic on a sign's surface pointed to a moment of decontextualization by index referentiality. It shouted, "There!" and then stopped. It is this forceful imperative with which an index operated, so Miyako Inoue described index as a shock. For Inoue, shock is a sign that bypasses the cognitive or intellectual faculty, "a sensory mode of subject engagement with the world rooted in the mimetic quality, and tactility and immediacy."[41] It is a sign system that celebrates the primacy of tactility and corporeality, which Walter Benjamin described as "prompt language"—"a degeneration of symbols into indexes" because it was "adopted to the speed, rhythm, tactility, affinitive subject-object relations, and other historically emergent dimensions of corporeal being in the modern world."[42] This was the same process that took place when things became commodities. Just like index signs, which emptied out meaning and pointed to something other than themselves, Inoue argued, "the commodity acquires value as the concrete social relations behind its production are hollowed out."[43] In short, signage in Seoul exemplified "a modern capitalist semiosis."[44]

*   *   *

What took place in the moment of the index of signage is that a space opened to multiple temporalities. An index is a sign that indicates a temporal trace and thus a temporal lag because the index points to an image that preceded it.[45] The memory here does not necessarily refer to a time of the past relived in the present, which is vulnerable to political and cultural interventions, as we saw in the previous chapters. Rather, it is a space created by the delay between the index and its referent that coexists in the here and now. Therefore, this space of time lag, decontextualization, and haptic encounter is where I locate the moment of speech. As we navigate the urban space of Seoul, linguistic disorder of what appeared to be the unlearned, vulgar, and persistent practices of the everyday haunts our senses on the surface of signage. We encounter a kind of memory that was epitomized by the delayed indexicality of the signage. In this space of time lag, the seeing subject, through a kind of haptic contact with the object of the gaze, became an interlocutor, not an interpreter, because speech was necessarily fragmented, as sound did not correspond to speech, and writing could not designate the correct sound. Rather, sound was a realm in which heterolingual difference could be found, in which the voice, the body of the sound, marked a moment of enunciation. In this moment, speech was no longer a conduit of meaning or an act of solipsistic subjectivity. Rather, it simply indexed the real world, everyday life, the life of things, and urban subjects in motion and commotion. In this light, what the *Tonga ilbo* episode got right was placing the body of the man with a topknot front and center, whether it was the deliberately slow track of time that his unhurried movement left or the grotesque display of his body. It was a true spectacle, as one observer exclaimed, because in Seoul's signage, even the calligraphic form of hanja/kanji existed in a simulated form in lettering. The old man's body brought to attention the corporeality under erasure by creating a delay and rupture in the repetitive movement of the brushstroke, a reminder of a nonsynchronous time that permeated the everyday in the modern city.

When the ornamentality of architecture in Seoul was to produce discourse recognizable by the self-reflexive subject, the surface matter became a disciplinary space of Japanese colonialism. Thus, when surface matter became speech matter, speech became speaking, and in the cacophony there existed a possibility of difference—and the corporeality of resistance. This corporeality of resistance should not be reliant on a given cultural or linguistic construction. It resisted—or rather, desisted—a move from phonetic to vernacular and from sound to speech, which would control the body of difference and tame performativity in the bilateral interaction between writing and speech. The next chapter further investigates this corporeality in desistance, the body in flux, and the disembodied voice in a genre of *mandam* in the gramophone recording and how this subject performed difference by bringing attention to the body through the laborious production of sound.

4

Oral/Aural Community

SIN PUL-CH'UL'S LANGUAGE PLAY AND DECEPTION

An article in *Maeil sinbo* in January 1935 described a crowd spontaneously breaking into laughter while listening to a famous recording by
Sin Pul-ch'ul called "The Funny Bald Man":

> Several days ago, an old man of roughly sixty years of age was seen
> standing outside of a shop in Chongno. He was attentively listening to
> the song from "The Funny Bald Man" playing from the gramophone
> inside the store. When the actor laughed, the old man burst into loud
> laughter. Everyone who had been listening with him also laughed,
> and then tens of more passersby came to listen and laughed together.[1]

"The Funny Bald Man" was a performance of storytelling called *mandam*,
narrated by an old man, played by Sin, who humorously describes to
his sidekick the kind of trouble he runs into because of his baldness.
His head looks like an ironing stone,[2] so people start beating his head;
his head looks like an octopus, so fishermen plunge a harpoon into it;
his head looks like a soccer ball, so people kick it around; his head looks
like a urinal, so children urinate on it. Each time a painful slapstick is
described, the old man and his sidekick laugh and sing, to which the
crowd responded by also breaking into laughter. "The Funny Bald Man,"

released by Okeh in 1933, was a megahit that, upon its debut, sold more than twenty thousand records in less than two weeks and instantaneously made Sin a household name.[3]

Sin Pul-ch'ul's rise to fame is a story made possible by the improbable partnership of the expanding gramophone industry and a man of genius whose mastery of language, storytelling, and performance created a piece so unforgettable that it changed the recording industry. The gramophone industry in the 1930s in Korea was enabled by the integrated colonial economic structure and global operations of recording labels. Labels from the United Kingdom (Victor), the United States (Columbia and Okeh), and Germany (Polydor) operated through their Japanese branches alongside Japanese labels (Chieron and Taihei), bringing with them resources and industry know-how and allowing Korea access to recording studios and manufacturing facilities in Japan and the United States. The adoption of global labels by Japanese companies was a result of the domestication of the industry in Japan, a combination of the technological knowledge of major labels and the infrastructural support of Japanese companies. This meant a relatively quick take-off for the Korean industry, without the need for huge capital or infrastructural development.

Early labels operating in Korea, such as Columbia and Victor, produced approximately one hundred recordings of traditional Korean, Japanese, and Western music before 1911. In September 1911, the Japan Phonograph Company, under the label Royal Record Nipponophone (simply Nipponophone after 1913), established itself in Korea and produced approximately five hundred recordings before its incorporation into Columbia in 1928 (Nippon Columbia). The year 1928 marked the beginning of a new era for the gramophone industry in Korea with the development of technology for electric recording that replaced cylinder recording. This propelled Columbia to diversify its sublabels and create low-cost records for popular genres. A newcomer, the Japan-East Gramophone Company (Victor), also appeared in the same year. These two pillars of industry were the major producers in Korea, producing 1,470 and 1,005 recordings respectively by 1945,[4] particularly during the industry's exponential growth in the early 1930s. By the year 1932, record sales reached two million, through approximately two hundred retail stores throughout the country.[5]

The number of records also indicates a change toward mass production and the popularization of genres. In earlier recordings, traditional genres such as shamanic chant (*kut*), *p'ansori*, and its operatic adaptation (*ch'anggŭk*) persisted. Beginning in the 1930s, however, thanks to diversification, the gramophone industry underwent intense mass production, and as a result, recordings began to evince increasingly popular flavors, such as the *sinminyo* genre, which featured sentimental and romantic tunes. The turning point, arguably, was Yun Sim-dŏk's "An Ode to Death" (Sa ŭi ch'anmi), released in July 1926, which launched the era of popular music in Korea, fueled by the scandalous double suicide of the singer and her lover.

Alongside the popularization of music genres in the late 1920s was the emergence of a genre of comic skit called *mandam*. One company in particular that changed the industry in favor of this genre was Okeh. A label founded in the United States in 1918, Okeh began business in Korea in 1932 under the leadership of Yi Ch'ŏl, who partnered with Japan's Imperial Phonograph Company (Teichiku). Okeh was a formidable producer of popular genres, with 1,300 recordings in circulation by 1945, a number comparable to the achievements of Columbia and Victor. Okeh's success can be attributed to its marketing strategy of promoting artists such as Sin Pul-ch'ul and aggressively pushing for reduced record prices. In 1933, for instance, "The Funny Bald Man" was sold at mere 50 chŏn through promotions; its competitor sold records between 1 to 2 won and 50 chŏn.[6] The success of "The Funny Bald Man" is also significant because the year 1933, when this record was released, is when the censorship of the recording industry began under a newly established branch specializing in this medium.[7] "The Funny Bald Man" was released shortly before the new censorship law was enacted in May, and Sin's subsequent record, released shortly thereafter, "Seoul Tour," was censored, as were many other recordings.[8]

Sin Pul-ch'ul was a poet, writer, performer, director, and producer who had a prolific career in theater until he began to focus on his recording career. His real name was Sin Yŏng-il (or Sin Hŭng-sik), but much of his life is shrouded in mystery. Almost everything known about him is a brief sketch of his career: Sin was born in Seoul and educated in Kaesŏng. He began his career in Ch'wisŏngjwa, which was founded in 1917 by Kim So-ryang and later reopened as Chosŏn Theatre Company in 1929. The enigma surrounding his personal life and career is not surprising, as Sin elevated his theater persona above his personal life and maintained an aura of mystery. In fact, Sin changed his name a few times. His pseudonym, Pul-ch'ul, as written in hanja, means "not to appear." Although Sin is his family name, that character is used in words describing legal actions of individuals who are summoned by the government, so his full name had a subversive tone of defying an order to appear by not appearing. He is also well known for his later protesting of colonial policy that forced Koreans to adopt Japanese names. He changed his name to Ehara Nohara, which sounds like a Korean expression that means "whatever will be will be," trivializing the impact of colonial policy while acting as if he were unaffected by it.[9]

During his career in theater, he worked as an actor, writer, and producer and became famous for mandam. It was customary to have multiple shows each night for as long as four to five hours. In between plays, performers entertained the crowd with singing and dancing to smooth the transition. Mandam originated as part of these intermission acts but soon surpassed the popularity of the main acts, so many theaters that were struggling financially came to rely on mandam to attract an audience.[10] When the gramophone industry featured mandam as a separate genre, it provided performing artists with a viable alternative to their theater career, and many came to specialize in this genre. Some people speculate that Sin's favoring of mandam was a result of his encounter with censorship. In 1930, Sin was arrested after changing his line in a play, "Dawn Comes to the East," to call for the establishment of more Korean theaters, in defiance of Japanese industry dominance. Throughout his career, he ran into trouble with the police for satirizing the Axis powers and capitalism, and, after liberation, Sin was arrested and jailed in 1946 in what is known as the T'aegŭkki blasphemy incident. After going to North Korea in 1947, he enjoyed success, but the circumstances surrounding his death are unknown, and he is suspected to have been purged in the 1960s.[11]

This chapter looks at the effect of the unlikely collaboration of the highly commercialized industry of gramophone recording and the previously marginal genre of mandam in the recordings of Sin Pul-ch'ul. The impact of this venture was colossal, evident in the changes that took place in the gramophone industry and that reshaped the soundscape of Seoul as a result. In particular, mandam, a genre that celebrated humor and satire, offered Sin a creative space for his defiant spirit. As evident in the language play of his names, Sin excelled in using language as the main source of humor and perfected the genre of mandam. The next section thus discusses the genre in more detail, followed by an exploration of Sin's language play and the popular record "The Funny Bald Man," also situating that language play in the urban space of Seoul.

Mandam, the Art of the Voice

In gramophone recordings, the genre of storytelling was classified into mandam, nonsense, and sketch. The use of the terms did not adhere to a systemic logic, but sketch usually referred to a comical play accompanied by music; mandam was a one-man performance; and nonsense consisted of a two-person dialogue in which each actor ridiculed the other, often of the opposite gender, class, and age. What defined nonsense was the rhythm that moved the dialogue forward rapidly, with repetition of verbal exchanges that featured either a skit of funny situations or language play that usually involved homonyms. This contrasts with mandam, which resorted to the imitation of sounds in onomatopoeia and alliteration. For this reason, fewer recordings were categorized as mandam, as most were labeled as nonsense or sketch or both. However, the distinctions between the genres proved blurry. The three had various commonalities and developed similar repertoires of stories that were not too complicated to tell in the brief three minutes allotted to each side of the record. For instance, "The Funny Bald Man" appeared as nonsense in the Okeh recording and as sketch in the Chieron recording.

I use the term *mandam* to refer to all the genres of humor recorded by Sin Pul-ch'ul because he identified himself as a mandam artist, not a sketch or nonsense artist, and because outside of the records' labeling, his artistry was usually called mandam. Mandam largely referred to a field of humor that approached lighthearted, funny matters with a satirical twist through different mediums such as *mandam*, *manmun*, and *manhwa*. Whereas its cohorts manmun and manhwa utilized writing and pictures, respectively, mandam relied on orality.[12] Sin Pul-ch'ul also emphasized the role of spoken language in mandam by comparing it to oratory (*ungbyŏn*). By tracing the democratic roots of oratory to ancient Greece, Sin advocated oratory as public speech with revolutionary potential. Borrowing the truism that the pen is mightier than the sword, he argued that his weapon of choice was spoken language: "Oratory is a weapon of words under your power. It has power like the sun that can influence the hearts of the people. It can become a comet of revolution that orbits the million years of the universe in one day, or the flood of war that can defeat the power of many generations. There is nothing that surpasses the power of oratory."[13] Sin asserted that mandam cannot exist without oratory, and it differs from other mediums that rely on spoken language such as lecture or speech, as well as from witticism (*chaedam*), because of its forceful use of language with a satirical edge. Sin argued: "Mandam is full of humor and free-spirited in its satire and irony. It is an art of language that works like fire or sharp blades."[14] The potency of mandam, for Sin, stemmed from the strategic use of language: "Mandam has to be premised on fun, but it cannot be achieved simply by uttering eccentric words or repeating elegant expressions. It must have real power that pierces into the heart of the modern people. . . . Today the language tends to be conceptual with heavy focus on meaning. It rings empty when it is not based on the actuality of daily life."[15] Thus, in place of "ideological language," Sin pressed for the use of "everyday language," that is, "candid and realistic expression of thoughts and emotions from daily life."[16]

Well aware of the hierarchy of spoken and written language, Sin often argued against the insufficiency of written language to reflect speech.[17] His privileging of spoken over written language made him subject to harsh criticisms from intellectuals. For instance, Yu Ch'i-jin, a playwright and director, reacted to the proliferation of mandam in the theater, calling it a "phony act."[18] Another playwright, Yi Sŏ-gu, accused mandam recordings of spreading indecent mannerisms through meaningless language play, and Sim Hun criticized the genre's humor for stirring up social disorder and moral degeneration.[19] Sin Pul-ch'ul responded that their criticisms reflected "self-contradiction and lack of consciousness on the part of the intellectuals."[20] He referred to intellectuals as "educated fools" and argued that intellectuals' rebuke of mandam artists as uneducated technicians (*kisulcha*) who engineered vulgar acts stemmed from ignorance about Korea's situation and was damaging to its struggling cultural industries: "Stop being deploring in your argument (*kongnon*). Be rational in acknowledging reality and criticizing the self. Repair your rotten compass and renew your perspective to start afresh. Theory had been your weapon until yesterday, but practice (*silch'ŏn*) is today's weapon."[21] What Sin meant by "practice" was the quest for an art form that was feasible but not complicated, new but still simple and inexpensive for the struggling cultural industries in Korea. Yet Sin's vehement opposition to criticism went beyond defending the integrity of his profession by asserting its political potential to replace the old tactics of theory. In other words, Sin's practice was about turning this disputed taste into a strategy of resistance.

Sin also pointed out that his critics uncritically adopted foreign culture: "Whenever we find the gaunt shadow of our impoverished cultural heritage, we imitate advanced cultures of foreign countries and apply their principles to enrich our own. . . . Today, those who study Western literature create immature works begotten from their uncritical imitation."[22] He did not oppose adoption of foreign culture per se, as he openly talked about tracing the origins of mandam to Japan. Sin credited himself with importing this form of mandam to Korea, but he insisted it was a result of his further experimentation with Western and Chinese comedies. Sin argued that "the value of imitation only lies in making it one's own," in that it needs to "employ the blade of critical thinking and change it into nutritious food."[23] Thus, Sin argued that mandam was a modern phenomenon and a product of the time in which he lived. In the process of being transplanted to the Korean context, it had become something distinctive from its counterparts in Japan or elsewhere.

Sin's defense of mandam speaks volumes about how he prized this form of art. He did not necessarily try to erase the distinction between highbrow art and the lowbrow performance culture of mandam, but he did try to overturn the hierarchy between the two by privileging practice over theory and differentiating critical and creative adaptation from uncritical imitation. The hierarchy that Sin sought to overturn is well represented in how mandam artists are described as *kisulcha*. As technicians or engineers, mandam artists were looked down on as those who operated with skills but without ideology or theory, but perhaps this is where we can also locate the creative power that Sin and others brought to the scene. In his evocative study of the concept and practice of technology in the late-colonial Dutch East Indies, Rudolf Mrázek defined engineers as "a superior class of worker," borrowing from Karl Marx, and spoke about engineers using a metaphor that might lend an unintended insight into understanding Sin's position: "[Engineers] believe in their language as we all believe in ours. More than the rest of us, however, engineers believe that their language and everything else can be taken apart and reassembled (and taken apart again) for the language's and everything's benefit."[24] This metaphor of language likened to machinery is particularly beneficial for understanding Sin's mandam, because Sin, too, de-constructed language by disaggregating its parts—words, characters, consonants, and vowels—rather than treating it as a transparent medium of representation. It is with that engineer's mindset that Sin was able to reassemble already-disassembled parts into an unexpected creation.

Sin saw language as imperfect and mandam as art using that im-perfect means: "Language is a representation of the mind. It is a tool to express one's thought, and yet it is neither effective nor transparent. Even new words cannot perfect its imperfections. In the end, language is not very significant in our world, and mandam is a creation derived from these imperfect and unsatisfactory means."[25] For this reason, Sin described mandam as "a language that is not a language"[26] and played on the ambiguity inherent in language by exposing imperfection and con-tradictions and making them available for creative use. Sin's recording "The Mock Oratory" is a good example.[27] He started the act by saying he had heard about an orator who excelled in giving speeches in English, but he found out that the person merely put syllabaries into an alphabet and pretended to be speaking in English. Sin mocked the orator's cun-ning artistry by giving a speech of his own in which he repeated the syllabaries in Korean and formed nonsensical sounds. Sin deliberately enunciated each syllabary while pretending to speak about serious mat-ters such as materialism, spiritualism, and social justice. The prolonged and measured emphasis on the syllabary had the effect of delaying the enunciation of the word that came before or after it, or disrupting the sentence's flow through repeated consonants. The original Korean words in the following translation are put in parentheses where the sound is relevant and are written in dictionary forms:

> Where are you going (*kada*)? There are many places to go (*kada*). *Kag-yagŏgyŏgogyogugyu*, the more we go (*kada*) the more motionless we become over there (*kŏgi*). This and that, this and that (*kogo, kugu*), only through me (*na*), we debate between you (*nŏ*) and me (*na*). In the end, who would say, instead of *na'nya, tadyadŏdyŏdodyodudyudŭdi*? Wouldn't it be fortunate (*tahyaeng*) if we all (*tagach'i*) help each other? *Raryarŏryŏruryurŭri* you cannot resort to play (*noljap'an*) because there happened (*nada*) a disaster (*nalli*). *Mamyamŏmyŏmo-myomumyumŭmi*, what is language (*mal*), and what is body (*mom*)? What is spiritualism (*yusimnon*)? What is materialism (*yumullon*)?

Why continue to debate? *Pabyabŏbyŏbobyobubyubŭbi*, day and night (*pam*) you run busily (*pujirŏnhada*) to earn (*pŏlda*) the bread (*pap*).

Sin deliberately composed each sentence with words that began with the same consonants and inserted nonsensical words made up of the same consonant with varying combination of vowels. In this way, Sin's exaggerated sound interfered with achieving a coherent meaning, creating gibberish. Nonsense is funny because it does not make sense, but Sin did not merely refer to the irrational nature already inherent in words or situations; he made art about the act of revealing it. The amplification of sound in "The Mock Oratory" served as a process of emptying the meaning of language to redeploy the power of oratory when the language had been deconstructed. He accomplished this not by assuming a philosophical stance from an ivory tower. Rather, Sin assumed a position of coming belatedly but "proceed[ed] differently from the one who goes ahead."[28] In his mockery and mimicry, he revealed the pretense of the one who wanted to appear to be intelligent by imitating and repeating what the other did, and in doing so he destabilized the coherence of language to be deployed for creative and critical purposes.

Language Play: Kyŏnmal and Kŏjinmal

Language play in Sin's mandam was called *kyŏnmal*, which usually refers to argot or slang, an allusive substitution of words that can be understood only by a particular group. Kyŏnmal operated on the affinity of sounds between two or more words and duplicated the sound in another language or usage to change the meaning of the original word. In the process, the sound was separated from the word to transform its definition or usage or to arrive at a different word. Most of the time, kyŏnmal relied on the pairing of two homonyms of two different hanja words or hanja and han'gŭl words, as in the following example from Sin's "The Comic Story of Ch'unhyang":

Yi: Bring me some wine (*sul*).
Pangja: Yes, there are many kinds. There is statecraft (*kwansul*), witchcraft (*chapsul*), technology (*kisul*), magic (*yosul* and *masul*), Taoist magic (*tosul*), painting (*misul*), and art (*yesul*). What shall I bring out?
Yi: Look at this clown. Not those kinds. Bring the kind that I can drink.[29]

In this mandam, the servant Pangja performs language play by substituting *sul*, a Korean word for wine, with a homonym in hanja that means "skill," comically reversing the hierarchy between master and servant in terms of taste and knowledge.

Examples of more complicated kyŏnmal appeared in a recording called "The Lock of Kyŏnmal,"[30] featuring a modern boy and modern girl conversing with each other in dizzying combinations of different techniques of language play. In this excerpt, the modern boy (MB) replies to the modern girl (MG)'s greeting. The translation includes the reading of the words when relevant and hanja words as they appeared in the lyric sheet in parentheses:

MB: Do not mention it. I am overwhelmed by the palace (*taegwŏl*).

MG: What do you mean by palace?

MB: I mean the palace (*kung* 宮). Indeed, the half of it (十錢 折半 read as *chisen chŏlban*) is in bad shape.

MG: Oh, the suffering (五錢 read as *kosaeng*) has shrunk your face (*soban* 床).

. . . .

MB: Look at the chaff (*yŏmul*), how I patched up my clothes.

MG: I see, the chaff (*kkol*). Look at your appearance (*kkol*). Why do you not lick (*halt'a*) your clothes?

MB: I see, wash (*ppalda*) my clothes. My thoughts make my liver cut off.

MG: Oh, you long for it (*kanjŏl*)

MB: I wear this because of my wife's drum (*yŏp'yŏnne changgu*).

MG: What do you mean?

MB: I mean my wife's drum (*yŏbuk* 女鼓).

MG: Why do you not ask your wife to wash your clothes?

MB: It has been a while since we became green (*ch'orok*).

MG: Green, oh, you have become estranged (*nam*).

. . . .

MB: Loss of love is neither her fault nor mine. There is only one place where the blame can go. I need to cool off. Why don't you hand me a cigarette?

MG: This cigarette is not very good.

MB: It is carelessly made (*hamburuk'o*).

MG: It is carelessly made (*hamburuk'o*).

MB: Robe (*turumagi*) around the cigarette.

MG: Oh, the robe (*turumagi*). It is the robe (*chuŭi* 周衣).

On the basic level, language play occurred by pairing similarly sounding words and expressions: the modern boy expresses his disapproval of the cigarette's quality as that it was made in Hamburg, whose pronunciation is modified as *hamburuk'o* to approximate the sound of *hamburohada*, meaning "carelessly do something" in Korean. Most of the language play here, however, added another step to arrive at the pairing of homonyms. Sometimes, the transition involved pairing of Korean homonyms and a detour through another synonym: a destitute situation is called the chaff (*yŏmul*), which has a synonym (*kkol*) that refers to a homonym meaning "appearance" (*kkol*); and the verb "to lick" (*halt'a*) has a synonym, *ppalda*, which has a homonym that means "to launder." At other times, the detour involved a translation of Korean vernacular expressions into their written forms in hanja whose reading for sound (*ŭmdok*) allowed it to refer to its homonyms. For example, the modern boy tells the modern girl to be careful with the cigarette by using a Korean vernacular expression for robe (*turumagi*). The modern girl translates it into its written form in hanja, *chuŭi* (周衣) to mean "carefulness" (*chuŭi* 注意), which has the same reading. Similarly, "a liver cut off," whose hanja expression, *kanjŏl* (肝切), has a homonym meaning "earnest emotion" (懇切); the color "green" (*ch'orok*) has a synonym, *nam* (藍), which has a homonym, "the other" (*nam*). In another instance, the modern boy describes his worn-out clothes by comparing them to his wife's drum (*yŏp'yŏnne changgu*). He explains this again in hanja as *yŏbuk* (女鼓), which the transcript of the recording makes clear by adding the characters in parentheses next to the Korean reading. His counterpart uses its reading as the stem word for the Korean verb *yŏbukhada*, which refers to the extremity of a situation: in this, the transition occurred from a Korean expression to its written form in hanja, and then to its sound alone.

The beginning of the excerpt shows all these examples in a short exchange by navigating between different languages and between spoken and written language. In replying to the modern girl's greeting, the modern boy explains his impoverished condition by saying that he is overwhelmed by the palace using a more colloquial expression, *taegwŏl* (大闕). The modern girl asks, "What do you mean by palace?" to which the modern boy replies, using the written expression for palace (*kung* 宮) to refer to the verb "to lack" (*kung* 窮). This exchange is followed by the modern boy and modern girl playing on the Japanese reading of hanja to mimic Korean words. The modern boy (mis)reads *jissen* (ten cents) as *chisen*, to mean "topography" (*chise* 地勢) in Korean, and the modern girl reads *gosen* (five cents) as *kosaeng* (suffering) and said that his face had shrunk in half (*soan*) through the metaphor of a meager meal (*soban* 蔬飯), and the lyric sheet added a hanja for table (床) to ensure this transition. In doing so, they managed to express a condition of poverty on multiple levels. While the conceptual understanding of suffering was achieved mainly through metonymy of language and sound, the dialogue also yielded metaphorical examples that visualized poverty through the poor condition of the palace, a skimpy meal and famished-looking face, and meager monetary figures.[31]

Because this exchange, packed with difficult transitions between spoken and written language, Japanese and Korean, and metonymy and metaphor, came at the very beginning of the play, it required that performers explain; they often asked each other to clarify, proving that language play was indeed a kind of code to be unlocked. However, once the rules of kyŏnmal were established and understood, the dialogue proceeded at a faster pace as the two performers effortlessly moved back and forth with kyŏnmal. What is more interesting is that, as noted, the transcript of this recording contained some hanja characters in parentheses next to the transcribed words in Korean. Here, the difference between the words is visible only in writing and so could only be read. This means that for the humor to succeed, listeners had to decode the words they heard to arrive at the text, fluidly maneuvering between orality and text, as did the mandam performers. The performativity of mandam was, therefore, premised on shared knowledge between performers and listeners, with humor strengthening that bond. Moreover, membership in that community was not inclusive but exclusive, limited to those who had the tool of decoding kyŏnmal.

For those who did not share that code language, kyŏnmal was a trickery that confounded them. A story about a confusing situation involving café waitresses from the popular magazine *Yŏsŏng* illustrates this point. The writer inquired into common names among the café waitresses and to his astonishment discovered that the names Anna (안나) and Aira (아이라) referred to the same person. He explained how the name Anna [ɒn na] was the Korean reading of the name in English, Anna. When Anna ['ænə] was pronounced with the stress on the *A*, unlike the short sound of the *A* in the Korean reading, it was written in hanja characters as Aena (愛羅), which the Japanese read as Aira [aira].[32] For the names Anna and Aira to refer to the same person, they had to undergo a translation back to the original in English, be transcribed in hanja/kanji, and then read in Japanese. The metamorphosis of the name Anna can be best described as the "alchemy of the word," in the words of the poet Arthur Rimbaud.[33] Through metamorphosis—the alchemy of the word—things look like "one thing and another at the same time."[34] Yet, prefiguring surrealism, Rimbaud's poetry was more about changing reality through language so that things "*become* something else" through metamorphosis.[35] In the piece in *Yŏsŏng*, the café waitress created a hallucinatory effect by deploying pseudonyms so she appeared as one thing to one person and as another thing to another person. What this revealed is an element of passing, both linguistic and physical, making it difficult to pinpoint the real identity of the café waitress by playfully reenacting the bilateral relationship between signifier and signified and moving between different languages. In doing so, it celebrated ever-changing forms through language play, thereby making things unclear and rendering the identity of the named person fluid, unstable, and elusive—that is, to allow the café waitress Anna to *become* someone else named Aira.

Language play was a deconstructive process that dismembered the signifier. It refused to accept language as a system of representation and rejected its regime of knowledge by dismantling the unity between signifier and signified. It did not merely rely on exposing that disunity. It went a step further to actively bring the ambiguities of language to the surface by moving between spoken language and written language and between Korean and other languages. In doing so, it produced an effect of passing—a disguise—that would appear as one thing to some people and as something else to other people. In other words, deception was the centerpiece of Sin's art: "The Lock of Kyŏnmal" is filled with dialogues with elusive (and evasive) references about the livelihood of the modern boy and modern girl; "The Dog-Shit Grandmother," a reprise of a traditional joke about a woman in search of a son-in-law who excelled in telling lies (*kŏjinmal*), recasts the son-in-law as the one who excelled in language play (kyŏnmal)[36]; in another mandam, "The Lilies of the Battlefield,"[37] Sin's character, in an attempt to coax affection from a woman, pretends to be a soldier dying on the battlefield and claims that his honesty would not allow him to lie (kŏjinmal), which is a lie, but he excels in language play (kyŏnmal). The pairing of language play and lies was based on the similarity of sound between kyŏnmal and kŏjinmal, but the affinity between the two proved more than that, as the principal method of kyŏnmal was to evade recognition by making things unclear through deception, forgery, and imposture.

Sin offered some clues, albeit enigmatic ones, as to what he meant by deception in the poem "The Lie": "It is said that the bird cries, but how could there not be times when it smiles? / Why would a flower only smile when there must be a time it cries / Man just lies, and he is the only one who doesn't know it."[38] In this short poem, the natural elements have two dialectical sides: smiles and cries are the same. However, man lies because he is ignorant of the other side of the thing. In the theory of negativity, the other is not external to the subject but already integral to it. Therefore, the subject is in truth only insofar as it is in the movement of positioning itself through the mediation of self-othering. It implies a differencing or moving away from itself, not just through opposition to external alterity but through internal alterity. Negativity, in sum, is a self-related difference in which subjectivity arises by negotiating sameness and difference.[39] Therefore, the man who lies is not only ignorant of the negativity within himself; he is unable to complete the subjective process. In this, the "lies" that Sin performed can be seen as a process of self-differencing in disguise: by moving about in the dialectics of things that are opposite but the same, Sin created a deception of his own to mock the true lies of those who abandoned the subjective process: Sin exposed the phony speech by the person who pretended to speak English by performing a sham of his own. In this regard, Sin's artistry of language play, as if playing on his name—which referred simultaneously to appearing and disappearing—was indeed a subjective formation through negativity. This was also the foundation of "The Funny Bald Man" and the body in metamorphosis that it featured.

"The Funny Bald Man": Metamorphosis,
the Carnivalesque, the Acousmatic

The single most popular recording by Sin Pul-ch'ul, "The Funny Bald Man," utilized the same technique as language play for visual signifiers.[40] The interchangeability between verbal and visual signs is inferred at the beginning of the act when the woman calls out in a screeching voice to the old man, to which the old man comments, "Is your voice a pickax? Why is it so sharp? If you pierce someone with that voice you would cause instant death." With the transference of speech to visual imagery, the pair proceeds to ridicule the old man's bald head by separating the image (signifier) from the object (signified) and finding metonymic pairings. In the following excerpt, the young woman follows the old man's self-deprecating jokes and laughter with singing:

M: I am worried that people would mistake my head as an ironing block and start beating on my head while I am asleep. Hahahaha.

W: The old man's head is a fulling-block head. He cannot fall asleep in front of careless women. (*Singing.*)

M: That is not the only thing. When I bathe in the sea, the fisherman would mistake it for an octopus's head and plunge a harpoon into it. This is dreadful. Hahahaha.

W: The old man's head is an octopus head. He cannot even bathe in the sea. (*Singing.*)

M: Here's another one. I cannot go to a soccer game without my hat. I would be baptized with kicks because my head looks like a ball. Hahahaha.

W: The old man's head is a soccer head. He cannot go to a soccer game without a hat. (*Singing.*)

M: I cannot sleep in the same room with children. They would mistake my head as a urinal and urinate on my head. Hahahaha.

W: The old man's head is a urinal head. He fears that the urine would splash on his head. (*Singing.*)

Just like language play, visual language play created a humorous effect by juxtaposing unlikely images. In that process, the body underwent a kind of deformation as if the effect of physical violence was displaced onto the body of the old man.[41] The intense metamorphosis of the body is a reminder of the mutating forms of language, which similarly feature disembodiment and realignment. José Gil explained this as a kind of exfoliation, the operational logic of infralanguage, which is "multiple at the same time as one, in each individual exfoliation, letting each come into operation according to the specificity of each space of the body."[42] The fundamental properties of infralanguage are, therefore, found in its capacity to disappear, multiplying in each exfoliation but retaining its singularity. This ability to be "absorbed in each exfoliation" defines the metamorphosis of the body.[43] In this, there is no whole or unified body, only a partial body, a disembodied body part breathing a life of its own and changing constantly. At the beginning of the act, the woman asks about the old man's age, with the colloquial "How many are you?" (*myŏch'iisyu*) rather than "How old are you?" The old man replies: "Two. Me and my shadow." This encapsulates a body performing as infralanguage—in self-negation and one and many at the same time. This simple and nonsensical comment resonates profoundly because this was the body in partial form and metamorphosis—the body of multiplicity and disappearance at once.

The display of the body of infralanguage becomes even more intensified during the old man's laughter. Listening to this record is truly an unforgettable experience because of the varying techniques of amplifying the voice. It begins with the woman's shriek, followed by nonsensical language play, and then the old man concludes each instance of his self-mockery with loud laughter that is followed by the woman's singing.[44] The resounding laughter of the old man is especially remarkable. He sounds nearly hysterical, unable to contain himself and hardly able to breathe. His laughter reverberates, creating vivid imagery of the distorted body, twisting and turning as he laughs. The effect of laughter encompasses a whole range of bodily mobilizations and disturbances. A mandam recording by Pak Chae-gyŏng titled "Twelve Kinds of Laughter" thus described the physiology of laughter in imageries such as a disjointed jaw, aching stomach, bending of the body, ejection of body fluids, and even gas puncturing a hole in one's clothes.[45] Laughter was no marginal act for Sin, and he recorded a mandam called "Laugh This Way."[46] Neither the record nor the lyric sheet survives, but we can imagine from the performed laughter in "The Funny Bald Man" that this also mobilized the whole body.

The vulgarity (and forcefulness) of the old man's laughter called to mind the obscene image of the distorted body, which demonstrates the subversive side of laughter that produced the unfinished effect of which Mikhail Bakhtin spoke. For Bakhtin, the extravagant and grotesque body in carnival is the antithesis of the complete man of the classical age because it is "the ever unfinished, ever creating body."[47] The body of the carnival undergoes a process of copulation, pregnancy, birth, growth, old age, disintegration, and dismemberment, and through this, the carnivalesque body becomes "the people's second life, organized on the basis of laughter" and "a parody of the extracarnival life, a 'world inside out.'"[48] This idea of death giving way to rebirth is a fitting description of how language play worked as a kind of death through metamorphosis. Language, too, underwent a grotesque transformation and deconstruction, and through disaggregation and assemblage, resulted in an unexpected creation. Likewise, the visual language play through which the old man's body transformed transgressed the boundary between organic and inorganic as each gave birth to the other.

The question of death and rebirth is even more pressing when considering the medium of the gramophone. That is, the voice in the gramophone recording existed as a disembodied voice, which R. Murray Schafer described as "schizophonia"—a split and dislocation of sound from its original context through electroacoustic reproduction.[49] It refers to the event of the body heard but not seen, which creates haunting acousmatic imagery. Curiously enough, when the young woman asked the old man where he is at the beginning of "The Funny Bald Man," he replied, "I am inside the Okeh record right now." Sin's joke is cunning because the old man was indeed always inside the Okeh record, not in the studio or on the stage, and not in the past, but always in the present of electronic reproduction. The old man existed as a voice stored and reproduced, as if he had entered a grave to be reborn just as transducers turned sound into the spiral groove on the shellac surface (death) and then generated it as sound again (rebirth). Having undergone a sort of death, the acousmatic voice made a ghostly reappearance but was free of spatial constraints; it could reemerge apart from its original context of utterance.

This notion of the disembodied voice poses a problem, however, if we are to speak of any liberating potential of the ever-generating carnivalesque body, because sound no longer existed in the face-to-face interpersonal context, the primary mode of communication. Walter Ong also described the electronically reproduced voice as the secondary orality, where the senses are mediated by the machinery between the subjects.[50]

Then, is the disembodied and decontextualized voice produced through the commodification of sound necessarily inauthentic and fraudulent? When the old man was already out of place, decontextualized, as a figure of the past in the modern city, how should we think about the impact of his disembodied voice?

An answer to this question might be found in a story "Four Scenes of the Spring in the Department Store" by Han In-t'aek, which appeared in *Chogwang* in 1938.[51] In the first vignette, "A City That Does Not Know Warmth," Han set out on a quest to find scenery that reminded him of spring warmth in a department store. He first found an old man from the countryside standing in front of a mannequin on display while being perplexed by its likeness to life. To Han, the mannequin looked like "a woman who had forgotten how to smile or how to move," "a flower unable to attract butterflies because it had lost its fragrance." The old man, however, could not tell the difference between a lifeless figurine and a real person, so he mistakenly identified a store clerk as a mannequin and pinched her cheeks. In the second vignette, Han described the soft and refreshing clerk's voice. When she shouted, "Welcome!" she brightened up the mood and relieved the minds of the customers who suffered from the burdens of daily life. However, as Han quickly pointed out, her friendliness was a result of surveillance: "The gaze of surveillance is present at all times, watching the service of smile and thanks, but the guests do not know that this regulates hundreds of clerks." So, Han confessed that he would rather stare at the mannequin and her blazing red lips. In the last vignette, Han found a pair of old rubber shoes that the old man mistakenly left at the escalator, thinking he was entering an interior on another floor. He exclaimed: "In a department store adorned like a park in the middle of the city, this is the scene of the spring. I would like to embrace (*saranghada*) the heart of the old man." For Han, the old man represented humanity in a world of artificiality and personal encounters in a world ridden with impersonal relationships. In contrast, the department store where the exchange value of commodity trumped all is where Han found plasticity and artificiality in the guise of life and nature.[52] In these stories, only through the old man's ignorance was the fakeness of the mannequin's life brought to the surface; also by confusing the clerk with the mannequin, the old man exposed the mechanical reproduction of service, in which the smile on a real person was no different from the fake smile of a mannequin.

The effigies in the department store contrast with the electronically reproduced body (voice) of the old man in "The Funny Bald Man." Both were ingenuous copies of life reborn—or rather, reproduced—as mechanical beings that had undergone death. However, unlike the mannequin's perfect simulation, the body of the funny bald man was subject to metamorphosis and deconstruction. One remained in death as a perfect, finished body of lifelessness; the other generated life through death, disembodiment, and decontextualization. Furthermore, the disembodied voice generated laughter (life) in others when it was electronically resurrected, as we saw in the *Maeil sinbo* article describing an old man on the street and passersby spontaneously bursting into laughter upon listening to "The Funny Bald Man." This oral/aural community existed in multiple spaces of the urbanscape and soundscape, also constantly shifting its site and delaying any attempt to trace the origin.

This is where we can revisit the question of deception, the modus operandi for Sin's language play, to view it as a tactic of the colonial subject pitting its own "lies" against the fakeness of urban space. The lies of the modern city were about what was on its surface—the blazing lips of the mannequin and the clerk's makeup. Just like the things on display in the department store, the city surface masked, rather than revealed, the oppressive power of modernity—phantasmagoria. Sin pitted his deception against the deception of the modern city and offered a cunning but honest commentary, all the while loosening the lock between signifier and signified and putting language, as well as his own body, into metamorphosis—transient and elusive, and ever more multiplying. Moreover, through laughter, Sin affirmed his existence only in the here and now because, as Simon Critchley explained: "Humour does not redeem us from this world, but returns us to it ineluctably by showing that there is no alternative. The consolations of humour come from acknowledging that this is the only world and, imperfect as it is and we are, it is only here that we can make a difference."[53] This echoes Sin Pul-ch'ul's argument that Korean intellectuals did not confront the situation of colonialism and that practice through jokes was the only viable resistance. For Sin, mandam was an instrument for the weak to intervene in the present by relying on the hearing subject who inhabited the soundscape along with the disembodied voice of the performer. As with orality, hearing was a preferred mode that immersed the subject in the world, unlike vision, which removed the subject from the world.[54] Therefore, the subjects of mandam ceased to be seeing, a subjectivity preferred by the colonial, modern city of Seoul, and seceded from historical time by reaffirming its being in the present. Through the replay of the sound recording—death and rebirth—they lived in the now-time (*Jetztzeit*), a messianic time that is experienced as a kind of inner loop within historical time, breaking themselves from the linear continuum of history and its process of becoming.[55]

* * *

When reflecting on Sin Pul-ch'ul's artistry, a question remains about how Sin might have viewed the city of Seoul and how his language play, art of deception, and privileged subject of the old man would play out in the urban context. Unfortunately, recordings that Sin produced about Seoul do not survive today. As mentioned, "Seoul Tour," released in the same year as "The Funny Bald Man," was censored for inciting public disorder.[56] However, since most recordings about Seoul have the same repertoire of sightseeing (*kugyŏng*), reprised in many different versions across the print and sound media, we can rely on other recordings to get a sense of what Sin's recording might have been like.[57] A good example is a recording called "The Idiot Tours Seoul" by Kim Sŏng-un.[58] In this piece, an old man from the countryside makes his way to Seoul with his daughter; as expected, his unfamiliarity with modern city life causes him to misidentify things. On the train, the old man hears the steam whistle and thinks it is the sound of thunder. When the train passes through a tunnel, he cannot understand the darkness. When the daughter explains that they are inside a tunnel (*kol*), he asks which village (*kol*) he is in. In the city, he continues to confuse artificial things with nature: when he hears the noon alarm blasting in the city, he mistakes it for the sound of a calf. In the department store, he mistakes a mannequin on display for the female clerk. Later, when the old man arrives at the South Gate, he asks the daughter whose house has a gate so impressive. The daughter says it is the South Gate (*namdaemun*), to which the old man replies, how gracious the writing of *namdaemun* is on the signage: the name as written was another name *sungnaemun*. A sequel to this recording, "The Idiot's Sightseeing in the Zoo,"[59] similarly consists of the old man's confusion about animal names in different languages, but confusion about verbal signs extends to visual signs, which leads him to conflate the animals caged behind the bars at a zoo with the prison system, so he asks why the cashier at the admission booth is not wearing a sword. He also comments that the zoo and the botanical garden look like a palace, to which the daughter replies nonchalantly that they are in the palace.

Whereas the old man in "The Funny Bald Man" was a subject of infralanguage undergoing metamorphosis of his own, these recordings recast the figure of the old man, as seen in the above episode about the old man in the department store, in a rather passive light through his misrecognition of things. This was a feigned passivity, however, because it was through the old man's misrecognition that the language underwent deconstruction. In the old man's misreading of the signage of the South Gate, his incorrect reading was not a matter of illiteracy but a result of his reliance on hearsay (orality) rather than seeing (visuality). More important, it was a refusal to recognize the writing as a signifier and endow it with the meaning it seeks, which was the central method of language play. For his daughter, the palace's transformation into a recreational space (Ch'anggyŏnggung to Ch'anggyŏngwŏn) through the colonial government's erasure had already been naturalized. For the old man, his constant mix-up between nature and artifice, the "confusion" over signifiers, led him to a defamiliarizing gaze that questioned the authentication of representation: it was only through the old man's estranging gaze that the artifice of colonial power was revealed.

The old man was a popular trope across the sound and print media, as seen in the few examples in this book, whether touring Seoul, listening to the recording on Chongno, painting the sign in the previous chapter, or the funny bald man. The old man in the city was a figure outmoded and out of place, the antithesis of the rationality and technology of modernity. The temporal and spatial heterogeneity of his body was out of sync with the modern city and represented a time lag. However, he was not disavowed from the space of urban modernity. Rather, he persisted as a reminder of stubborn elements that could not be absorbed into the visual regime of colonial power. More importantly, he was the subject of knowledge who insisted on his understanding of the world based on orality rather than visuality. Therefore, he was always a subject of misrecognition who questioned the power of the surface and its process of authentication, revealing fissures between signifier and signified through verbal and visual language play. This means that, only after having undergone disaggregation, disembodiment, and decontextualization himself, the subject of language play was reborn as the subject of the defamiliarizing gaze, forcing his sight to undergo its own deconstruction. Therefore, his misrecognition, or even "confusion," makes him a subject of deception who tackled the fundamentals of colonial discourse, modernity, and its visual regime of power head-on by feigning ignorance and illiteracy. The next chapters explore other examples involving such tactics of reconstituting the sight in the form of montage in print media and further examine the notion of deception as well as of communality introduced here.

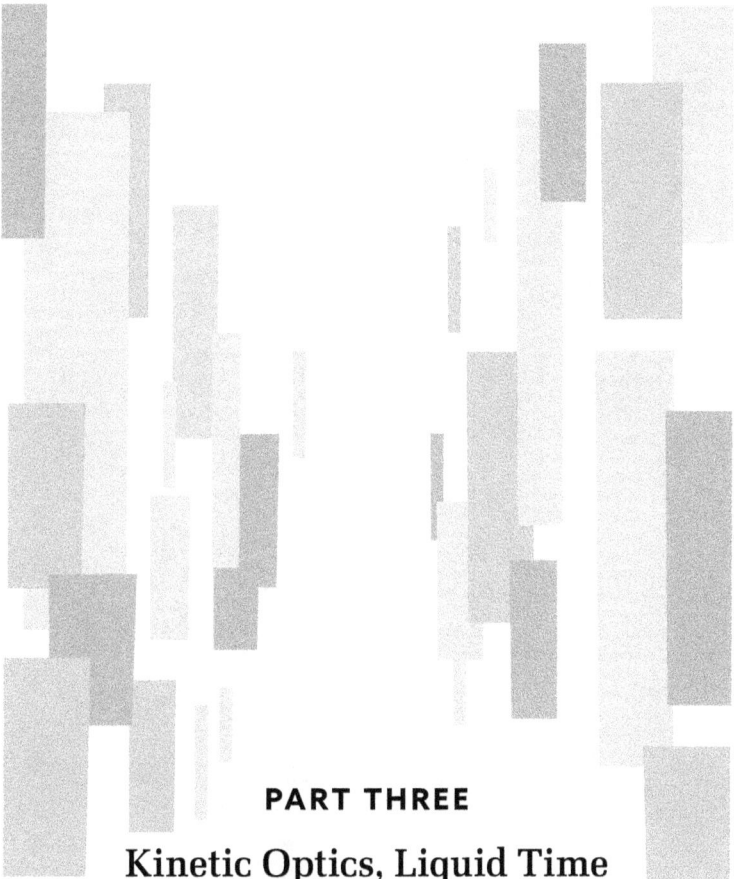

PART THREE

Kinetic Optics, Liquid Time

5

The City on the Move

THE ORDINARY AND THE INFRAORDINARY

On November 15, 1926, a group of reporters from the magazine *Pyŏl-gŏn'gon* was dispatched with a command from the editor's desk to "capture the phenomena of the city on the move."[1] Between two and three o'clock in the afternoon, five reporters scattered around the city to collect stories and report how the "society moves minute by minute."[2] The first reporter, grumbling about the short one-hour limit, found himself in front of the courthouse. The typically crowded courthouse was not too busy in the afternoon hours, but he saw two Japanese men selling bread, a banker registering for an auction, two men playing go, and a woman from the countryside whose son had been arrested for being a bystander to gambling—she pleaded with him, thinking that he was a court clerk. The second reporter aimlessly wandered the streets and witnessed what he called three big events (*taesagŏn*): a man from the countryside splashed by a sprinkler truck, a rooster spilling a basket full of hundreds of dry peppers, and a medicine seller advertising to spellbound spectators a panacea made from manure. The third reporter surveyed the famous bookstores along the road between Pagoda Park and An'guk-dong to find out what people were reading. To his disappointment, the stores were largely empty, but he was told about the popularity of certain magazines by the clerks. The fourth reporter went to the editorial room of the Tonga

Newspaper Company, where reporters were struggling to come up with what to print—"70 lines, 80 lines" and "300 more words"—but there were still not enough events to write about, and discarded papers piled up on top of the desks, reporters' knees, and the floor. The fifth reporter ended up at the city's busiest intersection on Chongno Street and reported in detail about different kinds of fresh produce at a market and the eclectic fashions of people on the street. Then, he encountered a tall, red electric signpost being installed, which prompted him to daydream about erecting a pavilion seventy or eighty stories high from which he could look down and examine all human affairs: "Wouldn't it be great if I could sit on top of the pavilion and put a light and a bell there? I could light up the whole earth and make the entire world tremble with one ring of the bell. I would be able to survey the entire world."[3] His reverie abruptly ended when he realized it was one minute past three o'clock and his time was up.

However fleeting, the last reporter's fantasy of being able to see a panoramic view of the world reflects the desire of the colonized wanting to overcome their position of being seen and observed, which also attests to their awareness of the panoptic gaze. The stories that these reporters collected did not resemble anything close to such power. They were filled with insignificant details about people and events in the city that may not be regarded as newsworthy by any standard. What this collection of mundane reports showed instead was a multiperspectival view of the city on the ground, one that unwittingly exposed the panoptic gaze and how vision was an integral part of colonial power. This report belonged to a genre of reportage called "urban investigative reports," a popular trope for narrating urban life in Seoul, particularly between 1926 and 1929. This chapter and the next take a close look at these reports and examine how they reimagined the urban space through different modes of experiencing the city, challenged the disciplinary mechanisms of Japanese colonialism, and in turn created a sense of individuals and community rooted in the genre and medium in which they appeared.

This reportage represents a genre specific to leisure magazines (*ch'wimi chapchi*) of the mid- to late 1920s, whose emergence is noted in the publication of the *Pyŏlgŏn'gon* magazine in November 1926.[4] *Pyŏlgŏn'gon* replaced the iconic *Kaebyŏk* after its discontinuation in August 1926, as well as *Sinyŏsŏng* from the same publisher, which had suspended publication from November 1926 to January 1931, and became one of the most widely read magazines in Korea, with a readership of more than two hundred thousand.[5] The launch of *Pyŏlgŏn'gon* also signaled a turning point for the publishing industry: the end of general-interest magazines (*chonghap chapchi*) like *Kaebyŏk* and the beginning of leisure magazines (*ch'wimi chjapchi*), which mediated the emergence of popular magazines (*taejung chapchi*) in the 1930s.[6] *Pyŏlgŏn'gon* was a transitional magazine, and it experimented with various strategies to build readership among the masses through popular journalism that blended social obligation with stories to stimulate their curiosity.[7]

A closer look at the circumstances surrounding the rise of *Pyŏlgŏn'gon* also offers an interesting insight into the limitations posed by colonial censorship. The publishing industry grew exponentially in the first half of the 1920s. But the effect of censorship was apparent, as noted by Chŏng Kŭnsik and Kyeong-Hee Choi, in the decreased number of publications that dealt with topics of politics, ideology, and scholarship, so they characterize the publishing trend during this time in terms of quantitative growth but qualitative decline.[8] In the case of *Kaebyŏk*, it frequently ran into trouble with censorship, famously seen in its articles published in the issue of August 1925, for which the magazine was accused of showing sympathy toward socialist ideology and resulted in its eventual closure, citing ideological subversiveness.[9] The year 1926, when *Kaebyŏk* discontinued and *Pyŏlgŏn'gon* began, was also the year when an independent branch of publication censorship was established. The Newspaper and Magazine Law (*sinmunjibŏp*) had been in place since 1907, which was followed by the Publication Law (*ch'ulp'anbŏp*) in 1909. On April 26, 1926, *tosŏgwa*, a separate unit that oversaw publications of print media as well as films, was established and expanded its power by standardizing the criteria for censorship.

In this context, *ch'wimi* can offer an understanding of how this blended-genre magazine negotiated the earlier legacy of *Kaebyŏk* with more popular appeal.[10] For Ch'ŏn Chŏng-hwan and Yi Yong-nam, *ch'wimi* is a term that lies between culture (*kyoyang*) and entertainment (*orak*), indicative of a popularization of modern knowledge that results in the production of individuals, identified as the masses.[11] It is not a lowly pleasure for the sake of pleasure but a hybrid adaptation of culture with a drastically different stance toward readers. *Ch'wimi*, then, accompanied the birth of modern life and a new subjectivity. So, where *Kaebyŏk*'s posture was one of enlightenment from the standpoint of a pioneer attempting to reestablish political consciousness, *Pyŏlgŏn'gon* transferred the masses to "the center of history as its motor," no longer treating them as the object of didactic discourses.[12]

Therefore, through the label *ch'wimi chapchi* in the inaugural issue, *Pyŏlgŏn'gon* claimed to be a magazine equipped with science (*kwahak*) and leisure (*ch'wimi*). *Ch'wimi*, the issue argued, was an expression of human nature in the form of sociability: "Humans are social animals. They have a natural propensity for social life. . . . It is not confined to the tendency for social gathering but depends on having leisure. . . . Living does not mean merely sustaining one's life. Rather, leisure (*ch'wimi*) makes life truly meaningful."[13] The proletariat masses in Korea had been denied ways to fulfill this basic human desire because leisure had become exclusive to the few. It was the duty of the magazine to promote *ch'wimi* among those who had been deprived of this right: "Only when written in lowly language in cheap print mediums, will the leisurely pleasure that the few enjoy in deep mountains be made available in pictures and words to hundreds and thousands of masses [*taejung*]."[14] The goal of *Pyŏlgŏn'gon*, then, was to "create a mood of collective playing, eating, drinking, singing, conversing, and dancing, and thereby satisfy the common desire for leisure."[15] Given this populist sentiment, leisure magazines were often cast as lowbrow, In actuality, they mediated highbrow culture by transforming print media into an affordable leisure medium for those of limited means. In this way, *Pyŏlgŏn'gon* could reflect readers' interests and stimulate curiosity about new things—all to enrich the lives of the masses.

The use of "lowly language" underscores the question of accessibility. *Pyŏlgŏn'gon* used everyday language, not that of the old literati; it was easy to read and aligned with popular taste. The name *pyŏlgŏn'gon* means "a world that cannot be thought of as inhabited by human beings," connoting fascination and curiosity, as well as anxiety and confusion.[16] Thus, the topsy-turvy world of *Pyŏlgŏn'gon* created incongruous relationships between the new, crooked, and bizarre; showed the city's highs and lows; and turned isolated occurrences that appeared arbitrary and historically unmediated into commentary on the urban life of Seoul. The magazine thus featured eclectic types of writing such as jokes, reviews, surveys, tales, and more. These writing types roughly fall into the categories of *ki* (記), *hwa* (談), and *tam* (話).[17] Experience (*kyŏnghŏm*) was the central component of these writings, which *Pyŏlgŏn'gon* rapidly diversified into *sirhwa* (stories based on hearsay), *sugi* (reports of one's own experience through first-person narrative), and *chŏngt'amgi* (investigative reportage); all emphasized the experience of reality by using conventions outside any narrative taken up in literature.[18]

Investigative reportage in particular proved to be quite popular. *Pyŏlgŏn'gon* had picked up this genre from *Sinyŏsong*, which popularized genres of home interview and detective stories like "Ŭnp'ari."[19] Yet *Pyŏlgŏn'gon* developed investigative reportage better than any other mediums and differed from its predecessors. In short, the *Pyŏlgŏn'gon* investigative reports were social investigations (*t'ambang* or *t'amsa*) to expose (*sin'go*) society.[20] Such a commitment allowed these investigations to have a sense of urgency needed to capture the ever-moving plateau of urban life. As seen at the opening of this chapter, reporters needed to be at the site of their investigation for a firsthand experience of the city. The reporters' job was to jot down details of their findings, including every seemingly inconsequential dialogue and description of people and places. Reports varied in length, subject matter, and writing style, but they were all relatively short and unpolished, written in a style that was colloquial, irreverent, and even nonsensical at times. Their minute and mundane details created a view of the city that did not adhere to the identity of place as defined by famous landmarks.[21] Rather, the urban investigative reports mapped the city in new ways anywhere their journey took them as they zigzagged across the city. The places themselves did not attract the reporters, in other words. They became sites of investigation by virtue of the reporters' presence as they wandered around the city hoping for a chance discovery of an event that was at once ubiquitous and unique in its presentation of city life.

Another feature unique to *Pyŏlgŏn'gon* reportage is how they presented fragmented views of city life through the collective ventures of several reporters. So this chapter takes a closer look at two other reports in the same magazine, one from February 1927 and another from April 1929, which both featured special coverage by a group of dispatched reporters.[22] It is precisely this collective aspect of the reports from which this chapter draws a critical possibility: in collective play, the question was no longer about individual existence but social practice. The way each reporter contributed to this reportage and presented fragments of urban life is best described as montage, a key process of experiencing modernity.[23] This chapter presses further, too, to argue that montage, as it appeared in these reports, was not merely symptomatic of modernity but a strategy to produce a different mode of being and of being modern. In this regard, modernity is not the condition but the method of a subject engaging with the world and producing a mode of being. To further explore this, the chapter creates a montage of its own, discussing the investigative reports in tandem with the surrealist game of the exquisite corpse and the Situationist International technique of *dérive*. The goal is to create a chance encounter and experiment with the idea of montage as a method for practice. The first section discusses the surrealist montage and situationist free-flowing passages around the city, which work together to reveal fragments of the city through a collective voice. The second explores situation-making in these reports against the disciplinary mechanisms in the city, namely chronometry. The third section pulls this together into the "infraordinary," the social unconsciousness, to explore how the investigative reports revealed Seoul's substratum.

By Chance: Exquisite Corpse and Dérive

The game exquisite corpse (*cadavre exquis*) originated around 1925 in the old house at 54 rue du Château in Paris, with invitees such as Yves Tanguy, Benjamin Péret, and André Breton. Similar to the parlor game known as consequences, in exquisite corpse, players wrote words on a sheet of paper, folded the paper to conceal the writing, and then passed it around. The result was a collective word collage of nonsensical and irrational phrases that often revealed an unexpected truth in the innermost thoughts of players. The game's name came from the first assemblage: "the exquisite corpse will drink the new wine" (*le cadavre exquis boira le vin nouveau*). Exquisite corpse later became the basis of surrealism, which Breton defined as the "psychic automatism in its pure state, by which one proposes to express—verbally, by means of the written word, or in any other manner—the actual functioning of thought."[24] Surrealism relied on neglected associations through automation and sought to free the subject from the control of reason and any aesthetic or moral concern. Surrealism thus redefined the marvelous as a kind of shock that disorients senses, presented the world through a fissure that reordered a semblance of rationality into the surreal, and turned the subconscious into a superior reality. The surrealist automation was to recover *pensée parlée*, in which language has the power to transfigure reality through the estrangement created by the joining of incongruent realities.

Dérive, the Situationist International method that espoused rapid passage through the city, was also a mode of experimental behavior, which Guy Debord described as the "ludic-constructive behavior."[25] Dérive intentionally disordered the rational plan of the city and "alert[ed] people to their imprisonment by routine."[26] In disrupting the unifying order of urbanity and the totalizing view of the city, dérive radically reordered the city through a revolutionary perception of it, much like what Michel de Certeau called "a pedestrian speech act."[27] The montage-like view of the city produced through dérive is also characteristic of Debord's psychogeography map, "The Naked City" (1957), which presented a collage of Paris in nineteen cutout map sections scattered across the page and linked by directional arrows. This was an imaginary cartography of the city that "set in motion a surrealist experiment with the city."[28] The key difference between the two, however, lay in how the situationists located automation in free-flowing movement in the city, whereas the surrealists relied on dreams merging with the consciousness. The goal of the situationists was not liberation of consciousness, in other words, but transformation of urban space itself.[29]

This transformative aspect of dérive is explained as situation-making, which refers to an experimental mapping of a situation as an end in itself. Situation-making operates by a sort of paradox because it takes place in a space produced by another power rather than having created a space of its own.[30] As de Certeau declared that "the space of a tactic is the space of the other," in that overlapping space, a tactic "must play on and with a terrain imposed on it and organized by the law of a foreign power."[31] This was enemy territory, where the participants were already out of place, because of their marginalized position, and were positioned "within the enemy's field of vision," alienated from the imaginary totality of the city.[32] Reminiscent of *détournement*, which utilizes a given form of art and media of the past and present, dérive is more like a guerrilla tactic—an art of the powerless and a game of the unprivileged—that turned the dominant power of the urban space against itself while staying firmly rooted there through tactical use of the space.

The schismatic view of the city in dérive was essentially a product of, like the automation of thoughts, movement in constant flux. Whether on the road to a faraway place, in a garden of meditation, or among crowds in the city streets, walking has been an important way of connecting the subject to the world and translating that sense of being in the world into a subjectivity. In the modern city, walking was also a reaction against the speed of modernity and the alienation of modern beings. The figure of the flâneur—the possessor of a detached, observing gaze, simultaneously enchanted and disenchanted by life in the city—is a good example of such a reaction. However, the flâneur's gaze and position in the crowd connotes "the privilege or freedom to move about the public arenas of the city observing but never interacting, consuming the sights through a controlling but rarely acknowledged gaze," ultimately embodying "the gaze of modernity which is both covetous and erotic."[33] In dérive, in contrast, walking was not a transitory mode of a voyeur, but a primary mode of inhabiting the urban space so that seeing was no longer privileged. In dérive, walking simply meant being in space; it was a practice and method of being that intentionally charted a new map while drifting around the city. Therefore, Debord defined dérive as "a technique of swift passage through varied environments," in which "one or more persons, indulging in dérive give up, for a greater or lesser duration, their familiar reasons for movement and action, their own acquaintances, jobs, and forms of leisure, to release themselves to the solicitations of the site and of the encounters suiting it."[34] First, dérive was a collective venture, like exquisite corpse, because play was at best a communal expression. Second, the main principle that guided collective play was chance. A chance encounter in dérive was not an expectation of something that would be conjured but, according to McKenzie Wark, a "chance procedure" that produced accidents at will.[35] For this reason, dérive is more than a mode of being; it is a critical social practice that creates a reality more real than the real, the lived reality.

The intent behind exquisite corpse and dérive guides my analysis of the investigative reports of the city in *Pyŏlgŏn'gon*. Accordingly, I highlight the willful maneuvering of the reporters in inhabiting the city in a way that can be characterized only as a critical practice—neither meaningless nor meaning-making, but one to dismantle the dominant discourse of the urban space. The command from the editorial desk for the 1926 issue was this: "Exactly within one hour, go to any places you would like and bring the picture (*p'yŏnyŏng*) of Seoul on the move." As the word *p'yŏnyŏng*, which refers to a small shadow, fragment, or speck, indicates, the reporters were interested in capturing lived experiences of the city that were unseen, uncommunicable, and unrepresentable. They made their aleatory existence in the city a procedure in their practice, wandering and drifting around the city with no purpose other than finding that otherness. Many reporters described receiving their dispatch as "unexpected" and "sudden." They were jolted out of the office and into the city, commanded to drop their usual tasks to seek out the unknown and unexpected. There was always a sense of the game, of something outside the ordinary routine and filled with unexpected encounters. They hurriedly moved and drifted around the city with nothing guiding their movement but movement itself. The city was on the move, therefore, not through teleology, but because of the unpredictability of events, which came alive only through the reporters' willingness to experience the city through chance encounters. Along their way, they peeked into shadowy alleyway corners and empty streets, all the while celebrating the transient city experience and making even famous monuments and landmarks appear mundane in comparison to all the peculiar things they described. The result was heterogeneous and manifold views of the city. In dérive, the landmark gave way to the labyrinth; the sensorium of memory became an exquisite corpse. It was strange, crooked, unforeseen, and marvelous in its own way.

Situation-Making: Overtime, at the Same Time, in Time

"The story is a map, the landscape a narrative," declared Rebecca Solnit in the articulation of walking as narrative and narrative as walking—the intertwining of movement of time and movement in time.[36] If movement is measured by time and time is measured by movement, what happens when rapid and automated movement disrupts and delays the constant flow of time-movement? This is what the time of dérive was all about. It was not a way to unfold stories but a free-flowing movement that went along, against, and ahead of time-movement. There were plenty of turns and pauses as chance encounters disrupted the colonial authority's emplotted routes of movement, and in the rapid passage through the city, every space became temporary, mutable, transient, and disorienting. When the continuous flow of time-movement was disrupted, the singularity of the event in relation to what came before and after also came into question. This is humorously illustrated in the story by the second

reporter in the December 1926 issue. The reporter was unable to decide
how to proceed when he accidentally witnessed three "big events" (*tae-sagŏn*). The first was the soaking of the robe of a man from the countryside by water spraying from a sprinkler truck near Kyodong. Later, near
Tongmyo outside the East Gate, he peeked into a house's gate and discovered the second event, a boy chasing a rooster, exclaiming, "Ah, the
major outbreak of an unforeseen event!" Right then the rooster tossed
a basket full of dry peppers in the air, scattering them on the ground.[37]
As he arrived at Chaegyo near the East Gate, he witnessed his third big
event: a crowd of forty to fifty people gathered in an empty lot amusingly
watching a sales pitch about medicines made from all kinds of manure.
Afterward, he found himself in Ch'angsin-dong in front of a huge gate
of a house belonging to a famous rich man with the surname Im, but he
was unable to do anything because of the sternness of the mood, so he
simply stared agape at the gate. The way this reporter claimed to have
found big, significant events makes readers anticipate some explanation
of how they were related to one another. However, even after recounting the events chronologically, the reporter failed to establish any causal
relation among them. The individual events did not have meaning or
illuminate any context. The events simply happened, and the reporter
simply pointed to an event, saying, "This happened." The movement in
time failed to give any causal narrative to these events because of the
way the reporter drifted from one place to another—from Kyodong to
Tongmyo, to Chaegyo, and later to Ch'angsin-dong. In his drifting, the reporter amplified speed and movement by moving at the speed of the city,
and his hurried crisscrossing around the city privileged moment over
time, which is a characteristic of situation-making that prefers "direct
experience of multiplicitous complexity over the singular simplicity of
distanced reflection."[38]

 In lieu of a narrative structure that could order these separate events,
there was something else that organized the reporters' journey in the
city—clock time: "Exactly within one hour, go to any places you would
like and bring the picture of Seoul on the move."[39] This section thus takes
a close look at how clock time framed the movement and narratives of
the reporters and how reporters in turn negotiated its notion of punctuality, singularity, and productivity through three temporal modalities of
their own.

Overtime

Because the report was conducted over *exactly* one hour in the afternoon, reporters were obsessed with the minute-by-minute passing of time while they drifted around the city. They might have dropped their usual concerns, but their keen awareness of clock time framed their otherwise free movement. Their heightened sense of time might be a testament to their occupation of journalism, which operates through a strict unit of clock and calendar time to meet deadlines for the regular intervals of printing newspapers and magazines. More important, the chronometric intervention in these reports shows keen awareness of the disciplinary power of modernity on the part of reporters and magazine editors. The modern notion of time as measure changed the world. Lewis Mumford argued that "the clock, not the steam-engine, is the key-machine of the modern industrial age" that is "a piece of power-machinery whose 'product' is seconds and minutes."[40] Karl Marx also remarked on how machines and the chronometer came to structure people's daily lives: "Through the subordination of man to the machine the situation arises in which men are effaced by their labour; in which the pendulum of the clock has become as accurate a measure of the relative activity of two workers as it is of the speed of two locomotives."[41] The imagery of people synchronized to the rhythm of chronotechnology is a powerful one, also evident in how the clock's mechanical arithmetic framed the reporters' movement. The reporters did not always specify how they knew the time, but they were extremely aware of its passing, as if the spatialized, measured time of the clock were ticking inside their ears despite the invisibility of any number lines or pendulum.

Nevertheless, their activities could not be contained by the arithmetic of clock time. Without exception, the reporters exceeded the one-hour limit because their experiences did not conclude at the exact moment of the deadline. The following is an example from the reportage in the March 1929 issue:

It's already 2:31! Hopping onto the streetcar, I headed toward the West Gate . . . It's already 2:54! "I heard you were hiring." "We only hire females." "Oh, really?" "Do you employ males at all?" I asked. "Yes . . . but not this time, we are hiring females only." "I see." "How much is the starting pay for women?" "That's confidential, but roughly from 30 won to 100 won." . . . It's 2:57. "I am sorry to have bothered you.

When would you be hiring males?" "We don't know yet." I bid a short
farewell and came out of the store. The clock was already at 3:05.[42]

Punctuality was of great concern for this reporter, but in transgressing
the time limit, he also revealed the unnatural impulse to divide time
into days, hours, minutes, and seconds. The transgression was not an
intentional violation, however. It was because human activities spilled
over the artificial measurement of time. Evident in the several instances
of recounting time in a precise manner is how vigilant this reporter was
about keeping time, but his faithfulness to the witnessed event, not to
clock time, eventually caused him to exceed the time limit. Unlike machines in a factory that came to a halt or schools that adjourned at a certain hour, the situations in these reports had a temporality of their own
that did not correspond to the clock's abstracted time. Because human
activity could not be bracketed off according to clock time, the notion of
"overtime" is a testament to the lived time that spilled over, a transgressive act made possible only through the arbitrariness of clock time. Only
through adherence to clock time, in other words, could one talk about
the notion of being late, making visible the excess of human activity.

At the Same Time

Whereas the notion of overtime played with the diachrony of events that
takes place over time, the synchrony of events paused and delayed the
movement of time. A report about the employment office in the February 1927 issue is a good example, narrating the simultaneity of different
events taking place in one space with no particular order to what happened before and after:

> I entered from the front gate and saw two signs on the doors to the
> left of the hallway that said "male employment" and "female employ-
> ment." Without hesitation I let myself into the office for male employ-
> ment. The time was 1:20! Contrary to how it appeared from outside,
> the room was tiny divided by a board fence in the middle of the room.
> On each side men looking for employment stood huddled among
> themselves one in front of the other. . . . They resembled people at a
> station, all different kinds of people gathered and mumbling among
> each other while on the other side people who just entered the room
> were busily filling out the application forms. Inside the office for

clerks, Korean men along with three Japanese men were busy writing down something on their desks while at another corner of the office five women ranging from 24 or 25 years of age to middle age were sitting down, some in arm in arm and some resting their chins on their hands. Then, the telephone rang, and everyone paused and listened. The room became quiet momentarily. The clerk jotted down something. It must have been a phone call from a Korean shop looking to hire someone. The clerk put down the phone, and the chatter and noise began again.[43]

This report began with a step-by-step account of what the reporter saw from the moment he entered the employment office, but it quickly transitioned into describing simultaneous events inside the employment office. The reporter's eyes hurriedly traveled from the divide in the middle of the room to the men standing in line one after another on each side of the divide, to the opposite side of the room where people were filling out the applications, to the inside of the clerks' office, and to another corner of the room where women were waiting. Although these activities were described one after another, they were simultaneous events taking place in the same space, evident in the momentary freeze caused by the telephone's ring and the individuals' subsequent dispersal to varied activities.

Because of the simultaneity of these activities, the narrative features long and unpunctuated sentences, often missing conjunctions and articles. Reading it, therefore, seems more like watching a montage film scene. It shows the painstaking effort on the part of the reporter to arrest the images from the transient activities, which was not an easy task. The "problem" of arresting an image, according to Ernst Gombrich, can be likened to an artist "trying to make a truthful record of the flashes of lightning which race across the sky."[44] Referring to a cartoon published in *Punch*, in which the painter was trying to paint lightning through the window during a thunderstorm, Gombrich discussed the impossible task of "representing movement in a 'still.'"[45] Because the problem lay in the stationary position that created perspective, Gombrich asked, "What happens when we move, as we normally do?"[46] Movement, which can be as small as a turn of the head, creates different vistas and "infringes on the eye-witness principle by showing us things we could not see from one point."[47] The reporter in the employment office was unmistakably *not* stationary. Looking straight ahead, sideways, beyond, and behind, the reporter presented multiple vistas of the room. The reporter's "eye-witnessing" was a refusal to stand still, instead moving from one corner of the room to another. He moved because of his faithfulness to the observed objects and people even to the extent that his sense of subjectivity dissolved as his perspective multiplied and transferred to the objects he was "witnessing."

The above passage, therefore, would be difficult to translate into a perspectival image, which would inevitably privilege the position of the artist. Rather, the moving eyes of the reporter functioned more like a camera-eye, passively receiving images. The camera-eye is a technique through which events are conveyed, just as they happen before a mechanical eye that does not interpret but simply transmits the image.[48] Interestingly, for the shutter of the camera-eye that is wide open without buffer or filter, André Breton used the metaphor of blindness to describe the camera's defenseless quality. For Breton, blindness—also the operating logic of exquisite corpse—is what enabled access to the unconscious. Blindness was also a choice for situationist practice, turning a blind eye toward the spectacular display of the city.[49] In this regard, we can understand the reporters' passivity as a result of strategic blindness, or a "tactical practice," as McDonough described, which "was consciously adopted in order to subvert the rational city of pure visuality."[50] In that sense, the reporters indeed *captured* how the city moved, as the above dispatch order stated, letting go of their perspectival view and turning their camera-eye on what they witnessed.

In Time

"Waiting" is another position of passivity imbued with tactical possibility. The reporters often described people idly waiting—in front of the courthouse, at the employment office, in the bookstore, in the streets, and at a streetcar stop. The reporters also spent a great deal of time waiting for something to happen, which was turned into a story in and of itself. This was made worse because the sudden dispatch order always came in the afternoon—from 2 to 3, from 1 to 2, and from 2:30 to 3:30—when the movement of the city seemed to have slowed after lunch. One reporter complained about the inappropriate timing when he arrived at an empty courthouse: "Even the military command of Zhang Fei had three days, but our editor's command gives us only one hour. And this hour has to be between 2 and 3. The timing is not very good."[51] Another reporter who failed to witness anyone buying a book in the bookstores on Chongno commented, "Things might have been different before and might be different later, but I only saw two clerks waiting for time to pass while sitting lethargically in front of the abacus and scratching their heads. Once in a while, a student would visit but leave only after glancing at the table of contents of new magazines. A man from the countryside turned away after asking the price of a novel. There is no one here to purchase a book."[52]

The irony is not lost here that the city that promised grand spectacle and rapid movement was depicted as a space of ennui. However, it could be a more accurate representation of reality, understood as Maurice Blanchot's "stationary movement," because the everyday has no events per se: "Nothing happens: this is the everyday."[53] However, nothingness is "not the 'null moment' that would await the 'splendid moment' so that the latter would give a meaning, suppress or suspend it."[54] Rather, nothingness is a position of neither-nor: "What is proper to the everyday is that it designate for us a region, a speech, where the determinations true and false, like the oppositions yes and no, do not apply—it being always before what affirms it and yet incessantly reconstituting itself beyond all that negates it."[55] The spatial metaphor of the everyday thus presents a different kind of temporality that turns a temporal void into a force that resists an anticipatory mode of time and any attempt to define it as either productive or unproductive. Though it may appear passive, Kracauer also called waiting "hesitating openness," in which passivity is replaced with the "ability to hold on" and requires "far more an intense activity and an industrious self-preparation."[56] In that regard, the moment of eruption that the reporters were waiting for was not an extraordinary event that would end or pause stationary movement but the bizarre, crooked, and incomprehensible of what is called nothingness.

Similarly, idleness is not a sign of indolence, but also a liminal position of neither here nor there.[57] It is noted in "part-time spaces," where social groups and individuals are "in a generalized waiting position."[58] The employment office, like the one seen in the aforementioned report, exemplifies a part-time space. When nothingness negates any anticipatory logic that will turn into an extraordinary eruption of event, waiting can also be characterized spatially, not temporally, as a different kind of position in withdrawal, hiding, and still under construction. As Blanchot said: "People waiting, either actively or passively, unconsciously or consciously, are precisely those who are not characterized by a manifest community."[59] This introduces an important concept for talking about the general position of people whom the reporters reported on and the reporters themselves. The individuals in these reports could appear as isolated and unrelated to each other as the random events that these reports described. However, even their unstructured copresence can offer a possibility of collectivity in terms of its disavowal of the manifest community.

Blanchot described this "unavowable community," in which the waiting-by can be seen as neither active nor passive but as a sign of their general position outside of the dominant structure of society. It could be located in latent spaces, indistinguishable and unidentifiable, but nonetheless momentarily free from the usual workings of authority. The courtyard in front of the courthouse occupied by bread sellers and people playing go, the corners of the employment office filled with indistinct chatter, and the sound of abacus beads replacing the sound of clock hands in the bookstore all point to this "empty" or emptied space, a space in which its usual functions have receded. What filled in that emptiness were incoherent and insignificant acts that did not amount to a political manifesto articulating a sense of historical becoming. Instead, the "community" of the polyvocal reportage of urban investigation was already out of place, out of a routine, and on the go (neither here nor there). Therefore, the community in question was not intended for the recovery of intimacy that had been lost in modern society. Rather, it was begotten from the general position of waiting that they shared in the empty place allowed also by their conscious withdrawal. This community was "not namable, avowable, or presentable as such," and was always-already outside of history.[60]

"The Beach beneath the Street": The Infraordinary

Upon a closer look at these latent spaces, the question has become, What happens when nothing happens? Or, how does nothingness manifest as narrative when there is no sense of becoming? The answer might lie in the ways every moment of the reporters' journeys was described in minute detail. Whether a description of people, place, event, or conversation, the urban investigative reports were filled with such detail that one must surmise that they wrote down and reported everything that came to pass in front of them without filter or editorial intervention. An example from the April 1929 issue describes a scene in Pagoda Park where, according to the reporter's estimate, roughly two hundred people gathered:

An old man wearing a *kat*, children in colorful clothes, middle-school students, workers, beggars, peddlers, mochi sellers, men in Western clothes. Some squatting and some walking around, people from all backgrounds are moving about slowly, in no hurry. Around the pavilion, some are sleeping with their heads on the cold stone steps, some are chatting in groups of two or three, and some are loitering. And the biggest attraction around the old, dilapidated pavilion is a fortune-teller surrounded by a large crowd. Nearby, a crowd of sixty or seventy people has gathered. The attraction is none other than an old man seated with his glasses awkwardly slanted to one side and delightfully reciting *Chŏkpyŏkka* in a loud, clear voice. A group of old men is engrossed in listening while a group of unemployed sits next to them . . . Near the rear exit of the park is the 13-story pagoda, whose top three stories are broken. Underneath, a fortune-teller is reading a fortune for a peanut seller, who asks, "I got married at the age of nineteen, but only a few months later my debaucherous wife ran away. How can I find her?" "Go southwest," replies the fortune-teller. "That is the direction to Inchŏn," the crowd speculates. "Unless you find your wife by April or May, you will marry again," adds the fortune-teller, making up stories to soothe this man's feelings. For that, the man takes ten coins from his pocket that he had carefully saved. There are seven to eight fortune-tellers in this small park. This one is in his twenties, possibly from the countryside. How astounding is it that he does forty to fifty readings a day? A group of middle-school students passes by right then, teasing the fortune-teller with questions such as "When do you think I will get married?" and "Is there a way to eternal life?" . . . Near the main entrance, two middle-aged women with thickly powdered faces warily watch people going in and out of the park. A female student who seems to have just arrived from the countryside marvels at the pagoda. It makes me feel uneasy that a delinquent-looking young man in a beret keeps eyeing her. The servants at the restaurant Victory and Jochu entertain each other. A guy coming out of the restroom says, "Why are there several

people in the bathroom when there are only two toilets?" Near the
rotten muddy pond, an A-frame peddler is catching lice.[61]

In this long passage, part of an even longer report, the reporter is unwill-
ing to omit or edit anything. It is akin to the kind of realism with which
an urban ethnographer might treat the city as archive. However, rather
than turning that collecting gaze into an instrument for the system of
knowledge, this reporter intervened in the narrative time through his
faithfulness to another "realism" filled with instances of simultaneity
and waiting. What is more, this report made the stillness of time its
subject—inactivity, nothingness of events, and immobility of time. When
time is being measured second by second and minute by minute, such
plenitude of description was a matter of arresting time. It put a pause on
the progression of narrative and the linear progression of time, and it
did so by stopping movement without stopping moving and through the
reconfiguration of time, movement, and narrative.

The detailing of the banality in this report is reminiscent of the clinical and encyclopedic approach by George Perec, who described the
style as "exhausting" a place. In *An Attempt at Exhausting a Place in
Paris*, Perec recorded every detail of Saint-Sulpice at a specific time over
three days in search of "what happens when nothing happens."[62] What
lies underneath Perec's encyclopedic documentation is a dry sense of
humor that turned science against itself. He wrote in an almost clinical
manner, cataloging colors, the movement and number of people, words
on signage, types of animals—all in a frozen moment. Perec famously
said that the daily newspapers did not interest him because the stories
were ruptures of extraordinary events—unnatural and abnormal.[63] He
appropriately turned his attention to things that did not amount to events
in the news. The insignificant, excessive, and forgotten with which Perec
wanted to occupy himself was not a spectacular rupture of events but a
constant stream of things that would typically escape attention. Here,
the term I rely on is "infraordinary,"[64] which refers to a substratum of
experience. Ben Highmore described this as "neither ordinary nor extraordinary, neither banal nor exotic," as it demands "a kind of quixotic
or excessive attention."[65] It is "a kind of surreal 'take' on the social sci-
ences" or a psychogeography of the situationists that played with the
form of social science but dug deep into the system of knowledge to
recuperate what they deemed insignificant.[66] This is where the time at

a standstill in Perec's "exhausting" of a place can be complemented by a metaphor of space. What was revealed was the substratum of experience, the infraordinary—that is, the constant current underneath the surface, articulated in terms of the subconscious by the surrealists and the social unconscious by the situationists. This is where time becomes liquefied, all-pervasive and unmeasurable. The metaphor that McKenzie Wark offers is "the beach beneath the street," based on graffiti art by the situationists, which compares dérive to the flowing movement of water that turns the city into a space and time of liquid movement.[67] This was a new kind of practice, a new way of being in a place and of experiencing and writing time. Therefore, rather than being measured by the division of clock time and the division of space by urban design, the drifting of the urban investigative reporters charted a new way of experiencing time and space through their own course of movement and own sense of time. What broke the surface was another kind of kinetic optics of the camera-eye that allowed access to unconscious optics. It broke open the undercurrents of the city, not to puncture the continuum of time through an extraordinary event, but to articulate the perpetual through the momentary and a sense of place through dislocation.

* * *

Dislocation in the investigative reports was, therefore, a tactic of engaging with place that was decidedly different from the ways the city was mapped through its famous landmarks and sites. This engagement was not site-specific but situation-specific. Rather than reiterating the meaning of place as something fixed and stable, the reporters destabilized constructed identities, whether constructed by colonial authority or otherwise, through their position of being out of place and out of sync with time. The sense of place and time was being constituted and reconstituted through their practice, which was neither a replication of the tourist gaze of desire nor a feeling of displacement experienced by the colonized. Rather, it was through tactical location and dislocation through rapid, free-flowing movement that they challenged the political, social, economic, and material relations that had defined the place. What they revealed by disturbing the surface was the unseen that could be articulated only by "blindness" and a tactical position of nothingness that nonetheless required mental alertness in waiting and a sense of game and play. The reverie of the fifth reporter in the December 1926 issue, with his tall tower from which he could watch over the world, might have to remain a dream, but the ways the report described people in nonfunctional spaces presented a reality of Seoul that is more real than that of any panoptical gaze. The reporters in the *Tonga ilbo* editing room were struggling to come up with spectacular events to fill in the pages of the day's paper, but the *Pyŏlgŏn'gon* reporters reported on them and the paper trash piling up in the room—the insignificant, banal, and mundane that made up the lived experience of the city and the beach beneath the street. In doing so, they not only turned the city inside out, revealing hidden folds and cracks; they also turned the science of journalism into a marvelously strange form. The next chapter further discusses this genre of reportage in reports that took place in the dark of night.

6

Nightly Reports

PLAYING UNDER SURVEILLANCE

In the September 1929 issue of *Pyŏlgŏn'gon*, the full-page photomontage "Three Movements of Symphony of Great Kyŏngsŏng" showed the varied activities of the city throughout the day—female students at their school, a woman carrying a bucket on her head, a man with an A-frame carrier, two men in *hanbok* and *kat* walking side by side into a store, a rickshaw driver, and crowds gathered on the street and at a market (figure 6.1). The accompanying caption organized the day's activities around the clock by morning, afternoon, and night. In the morning, movement rushed into the city as students, salarymen, and factory workers emerged from streetcars. Machines started spinning, pens and abacuses began racing in offices, and students marched full speed to school. The morning's bustle "moved the city," but morning was hardly when the day's activity began:

Do you know that morning is prepared in the darkness before dawn? It is prepared by the hard work of water bucket carriers and the hurried steps of salt dealers and fish-sauce peddlers. I am searching for poor, moneyless workers in the narrow alleyways. They have gathered at the market since four in the morning. Those who supply the goods to the market came even earlier around one or two in the morning. Some others have waited since the night before. The movement of the day starts the night before.[1]

What abruptly stopped the day's busyness was the noon alarm. When the siren blazed, everything came to a halt. Factories, government offices, and banks stopped their work; workers at a construction site took a seat under shade trees for lunch. Soon, other movements invaded the streets: delivery bicycles came and went "like a bullet," carrying *pibimbap* and bean-paste and rice-cake soups to hungry workers at newspaper companies and printing offices, but the store owners in Chongno unhurriedly ate freshly cooked warm meals fetched by servant women. After sunset, young workers flooded into the streets from the factory and enjoyed their freedom from the brick-wall fortifications, but next to the gate of the factory a child sat begging for money. Some were lucky enough to return home with a bag of beans or rice for their day's labor. Others were not as fortunate and returned with tears in their eyes. Others headed directly

FIGURE 6.1. Photo essay of Kyŏngsŏng, from *Pyŏlgŏn'gon*, September 1929, Hongik University Library, Seoul.

to *kisaeng* quarters. Then it was time for the dusty, noisy night market, filled with old and useless things—everyone came for a good bargain.

"This is the city of Kyŏngsŏng," repeated the texts, neither glorifying nor deriding it, and including those who were privileged and those who were not. Most notably, the texts described continuous movement from morning to night and from night to morning. The day "began" in the morning with workers and students rushing to work and school, but there were people hard at work while others rested at night. Similarly, the noon alarm—though it stopped machines and workers—generated another energy flow. All waking and resting hours were filled with activities and busyness. Like a symphony in which a melody gives way to another melody, a movement to another movement, the photo essay blurred boundaries between activity and nonactivity, work and leisure, and labor and rest, each leading to the next so that the day's movement always started the night before.

This continuous wave of movement is in sharp contrast to another photograph of the Seoul morning in *Nobiyuku Keijō Denki*, published by the Keijō Electricity Company in 1935. This photo shows a tranquil bird's-eye view of the city from Nam Mountain. The dark silhouette of a pine tree occupies the foreground, and behind it, the city is serene and quiet under the fog. The farther from view, the blurrier the buildings are—the hazy contour of the cathedral and its spire emerge against the foggy mountains (figure 6.2). The accompanying poem, "The Morning in Keijō," reads: "Thin fog trailing from Mt. Samugaku. Pale yellow buildings in bold relief. A church spire—High and low, near and far, the siren sounds."[2] Reminiscent of the postcard images discussed in chapter 1, the poem describes a panoramic view of the city in a nostalgic, romantic tone. However, erasure is also evident in the photograph, which hides North Village under the fog and makes visible only an intersection near the cathedral. More important, unlike the around-the-clock activities in the *Pyŏlgŏn'gon* photomontage, the poem and photograph depict night as a time of stillness and inactivity by foretelling the impending activities of the city being awakened by the roaring siren. The double erasure of North Village and nighttime by the wistful, natural atmosphere subtly but inevitably points to colonial violence.

This photograph is a curious choice. One might expect the publication by an electricity company to celebrate bustling nighttime aided by their service lighting up the darkness. Yet the section "Famous Illumi-

FIGURE 6.2. Morning in Seoul, from Keijō Denki Kabushiki Kaisha, *Nobiyuku Keijō Denki* (Keijō-fu: Keijō Denki Kabushiki Kaisha, 1935), 59, University of Pennsylvania Library, Philadelphia.

nated Places of Keijō" has a title image across two facing pages, a panoramic view of Seoul at night in which the buildings' flickering lights dotted across the motionless city. The subsequent pages similarly show photographs of a beautifully illuminated pond at Ch'anggyŏng Palace and the bridge over the Han River, adorned with electric lights and garlands (figure 6.3). The most dynamic image was of Honmachi, filled with streetlights, neon signs, and lights from buildings, all creating a dizzying, dreamlike view (figure 6.4). However, this photograph also showed streets empty of pedestrians.[3] All the photographs show a view of night best summed up as *the nocturnal*, one in which the dreams of lonely souls are reflected onto the urbanscape in the most romanticized way possible. The effects of the lights created a melancholic and romantic mood. All was quiet at night, and only the famous architectural monuments stood illuminated, dotted with light bulbs, to present a different identity, one evocative of a fantasy land. As silence and melancholia draped the city, it became a blank canvas onto which subjective sentimentality was projected, and that nostalgia defined the nocturnal. The city through the lens of the nocturnal was a world apart from reality. This was not a city that harbored the bustle and chatter of the night market. The images of

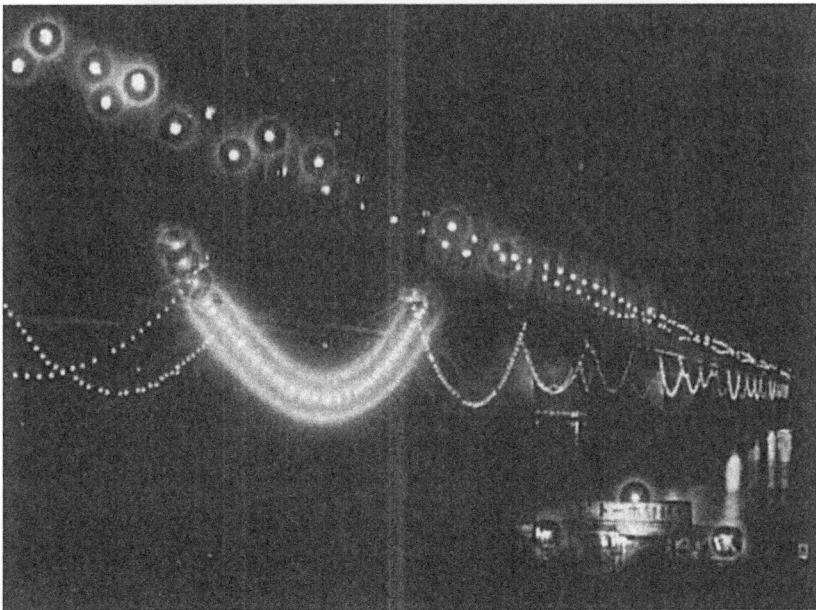

FIGURES 6.3. Views of illumination, from Keijō Denki Kabushiki Kaisha, *Nobiyuku Keijō Denki* (Keijō: Keijō Denki Kabushiki Kaisha, 1935), 108, University of Pennsylvania Library, Philadelphia.

FIGURE 6.4. View of Honmachi at night, from Keijō Denki Kabushiki Kaisha, *Nobiyuku Keijō Denki* (Keijō: Keijō Denki Kabushiki Kaisha, 1935), 109, University of Pennsylvania Library, Philadelphia.

the nocturnal images were not simply an expression of the picturesque; they masked uncertainty and unease about what lay beneath the blanket of darkness, strategic illumination, and nostalgia.

Where did this unease about nighttime, this need for the city to be empty and silent, stem from? What went on at night that could not possibly be part of the aestheticized landscape of the nocturnal? This chapter probes these questions by continuing the discussion about the investigative reportage of *Pyŏlgŏn'gon* but this time, through a type of report I call "nightly report." Nightly reports differed from daytime urban investigative reports in their quest for uncovering the truth—what was going on beneath the surface appearance of a thing or an event. Their concern was with "suspicious" people and events, behind the walls, away from colonial surveillance, which made reporters employ covert strategies to investigate illicit nighttime activities and even disguised themselves to gain access. They spent the night in search of sensational stories of hedonism, gambling, and rendezvous, and ventured through the streets, alleyways, cafés, and boardinghouses to find out how people spent time away from their regimented work hours. While roaming around places that were not immediately visible, the reporters became fascinated with suspenseful and erotic tales of the night. They exposed how an ordinary-looking house in actuality hosted a roomful of men who drank and exchanged jokes with prostitutes. The boarding houses were usually filled with female students—many with the popular chignon hairstyle and red fox fur—gambling with male students. The nighttime brought alive in these magazine pages was filled with vice.

This chapter follows these reporters' inexhaustible journey through the night and takes a closer look at places of gathering and hiding as revealed by their investigation. Because many investigations took reporters inside people's homes, the chapter pays attention to the tactics reporters used to gain access, which was a play on colonial surveillance. It then examines the notion of communality, introduced in previous chapters, with a focus on the practice of reading magazines. But first, the following section compares the investigative reports of *Pyŏlgŏn'gon* to another reportage called "home interviews" to distinguish the notion of nightly reports' domesticity from their counterparts.

Probing the "Private": Empty Time

In a nightly report in the February 1928 issue of *Pyŏlgŏn'gon,* three groups of reporters in disguise set out to different parts of North Village.[4] The first group was disguised as fruit sellers and students selling medicine; the second group carried mandarin oranges to act as fruit sellers; the third group, with the help of dumpling sellers in the neighborhood who loaned them supplies, headed to An'guk-dong and Hwa-dong. The third group then found empty a famous bar run by a person of the surname Yun in North Village that night, so they headed to an alleyway nearby and spent about an hour investigating forty-five houses and selling 95 chŏn worth of dumplings. They heard a young woman giggling from a house nearby and entered the house without invitation, calling out, "Buy some dumplings." Upon entering, they noticed a pair of men's boots and two pairs of yellow women's shoes. Their hunch paid off, and they saw a scene of gambling inside through a door left open a crack. They also noticed a student's coat and red fur scarf on a desk. They picked up a name of a woman, "Sukja," from their conversation, and then the door opened, and a man shouted, "Give us 30 chŏn worth of dumplings."

One reporter handed him twelve dumplings and quickly glanced at the school emblem on a student's shirt—this was later described simply as pink to not reveal the name.

Other investigations happened similarly. First, reporters took cues from sound—a woman's voice, laughter, music—and decided to investigate. They gave details about the house from the outside first, at times offering clues about location and appearance, as well as the address plate, although they never gave full information. They also gave a detailed description of the people, what they were wearing and what other clothing items were hung on the wall, and guesses as to age, occupation, and school (if students). They also noted dialects if the people did not seem to be locals, but some remained simply unidentifiable. They eavesdropped on conversations among the people and at times engaged in casual dialogues with them, all of which were described meticulously.

At around eleven at night, all the reporters gathered in front of the Chosŏn Theater. Each group picked a "suspicious" person to follow from the wave of people flooding out of the theater. They described this investigation as *yosich'alin*, an act of surveilling people of criminal intent. One group saw a tall female student accompanied by a cheeky-looking man in a round fedora who they discovered upon closer look was well known for his skills in scat singing; they censored his name and occupation by saying, "His name was xx, specializing in xx." The woman and the man hesitated in front of the streetcar stop near the Tonga women's store and headed toward Chongno; then they turned toward the West Gate. When other pedestrians had become scarce, they locked their arms together and turned to T'aep'yŏng Avenue, passed a bathhouse, stopped momentarily in front of a Chinese restaurant, identified as "xx-ru" across from the Kikura photoshop, and turned into an alleyway. There the woman whispered to the man: "I'll go in first and see if everyone is asleep. If I do not come out soon, just go home." The woman came out shortly after she went inside, and the two dashed into the house together. Reporters stared at the door plate: "Street number xx, name of street xx, surname xx." Nearby, they met a delivery man from the Chinese restaurant; they learned that the woman was engaged to a schoolteacher. "How can a woman engaged to someone take another man to her house!" one reporter exclaimed. Seven minutes had passed, and twelve minutes since the lovers went inside. Then the man emerged from the house. After smoking a cigarette, he took off toward the South Gate.

Another group spotted a "seriously suspicious woman" in the crowd, a student wearing a purple *chŏgori*, black skirt, and green scarf. She kept looking at the reporters as if she wanted a conversation, so the reporters took a different path. Then, they saw two women in black robes and black scarves; they had their heads lowered and were whispering to each other. The reporters realized that these women had been followed by a delinquent-looking student in Western clothes and a fedora near the intersection at the zoo. The two women burst into laughter and ran into a house nearby; the man followed them into the house. The reporters were aghast. They decided to probe further by putting their ears on the door, to the sound of loud laughter. The sign next to the house said, "School supplies and Japanese and Western General Goods Store x and x Store." A boy came out of the house and went to a nearby restaurant, where he ordered a beef soup for two. Suspicious, one reporter went to question people while the other stood guard. It turned out that the owner was a divorcée living with a younger sister who went to "xx Women's School" in the city. No man lived in the house, he was told, nor had she male relatives. "You can arrive at your conclusion with this much information," reporters wrote. The man still had not come outside at thirty minutes past midnight. Afterward, the reporters regrouped and followed night patrol until 1:30, when they met another group of reporters. "Have you any results?" asked a reporter from the other group. "My feet are freezing, but nothing," answered one in the group. "There is truly nothing happening where the night patrol goes."

What these reporters discovered in the deep of night was "free love" (*yŏnae*) unfolding behind the doors of ordinary homes and boardinghouses, so at times they exclaimed: "This is what truly goes on in the city of Kyŏngsŏng!" "Should the free love of female students be like this!" and "Alas, Kyŏngsŏng at night is hell. Every night after sunset, the city bears sins." However, despite their disdain for immoral lifestyles, their reports were not meant to serve as didactic tales. Instead, reporters filled their stories with anticipation, suspense, and thrill of the discovery of events. The earlier example took up nearly ten pages of the magazine. The title of the report, "Striking Delinquent Men and Women: Nightly Undercover Report," used a classical idiom, *ilmangt'ajin*, which means "catch all the fish in the pond with a single throw of the net." The word *striking* (*t'ajin*) has a reproachful tone and yet refers more to reporters' ability to successfully uncover the real identities of suspicious-looking people: excitement about the hunt for stories became a story in itself.

For this reason, despite their fascination with the "private" realm, nightly reports differed from another type of reportage, home interviews (*pangmun'gi*), also concerned with domestic life and popularized by the predecessor magazine *Sinyŏsŏng*. These interviews reported on home visits to well-known figures, but they were mainly concerned with topics of daily life (*saenghwal*). The idea behind home interviews was "sweet home" (*sŭwit'ŭ ho-m*), a buzzword of the time describing the happy atmosphere of an ideal home. A good example of this is a report in *Pyŏlgŏn'gon* about Yi Kwang-su's home, which featured an interview with Yi's wife Hŏ Yŏng-suk on the first birthday of their second son.[5] Despite the hectic mood, the reporter described the affairs at Yi's house as orderly and—interestingly—healthy, because Hŏ was a medical doctor. She enforced a healthy diet and prescribed medicine for her children and husband, who was reluctant to take orders from his wife. She spent her free time for personal enrichment, such as reading. Another example is the home interview with Yi Kap-se, also a doctor, in which the report described his house as an urban sanctuary where lush trees and a vegetable garden provided a place to "rejuvenate mind and soul."[6] However, the greenery in the house was not simply a gift of nature, as his house was located in the center of Seoul, but the fruit of Yi's hard labor during his leisure time; tending the garden, feeding the chickens, and petting the dog each morning and evening before and after work. For Hŏ and Yi, the freedom of leisure was not to be squandered and had to be channeled productively.

The narratives of home interviews tended to be confessional, offering a source of truth into one's private life, and the insight gained from the interviewee's testimony was complemented by the reporter's description of the person and their home. Hŏ's account of her daily life and relationship with her family was reflected in the orderly atmosphere of her house, just as Yi's daily routine of tending to the garden was noted in the lushness and plentifulness of his house. What is also notable is the position of the reporters as spectators reinforcing the status of the interviewee as a celebrity. Reporters were fascinated with modern artifacts, such as gramophones, pianos, and books, all of which were material requirements of a "sweet home." Their gaze so resembled looking at a window display of a department store that another home interview with the composer Hong Nan-p'a's wife, Yi T'ae-hyang, was fittingly titled "Looking at the Sweet Home through the Window": "Mrs. Yi is beautiful and young like a French doll. She tells a story and now and then smiles elegantly, showing her bright white teeth."[7]

Nightly reports also were fascinated with what happened in private spaces, but the notion of the private contrasted sharply with home interviews. Nightly reports concerned themselves not with the question of daily life away from work but with a time that had no relation to work, one that was filled with unproductive activities. In this light, workers and students who detoured into a drinking establishment or played games in a boardinghouse engaged in subversive acts, because these pleasure-seeking activities did not qualify as leisure.[8] The private space and time after work deviated from how work time and non–work time were divided and complemented each other. The subjects of nightly reports fell somewhere in between leisure, family, and private life, and rarely into only one category.

The different notion of the private in nightly reports partly has to do with the time of the investigation—the deep of night, from midnight to dawn, and the favorite time being two or three in the morning. This was a time no longer regulated by clock time—it was an empty time. The question of morality is important in this context. According to Alain Corbin, at the end of the nineteenth century, the impulse to master time resulted in anxiety over (lost) time and obsessive control over time by the individuals who exercised self-control.[9] This was most acutely applied to the night, a prime symbol of individual time, and this resulted in an emphasis on somatic discipline; sleep was a means of regenerating for the day ahead.[10] When the fear of empty night hours discouraged activities devoid of social function, the nightly reports' fascination with decadent behaviors made visible and celebrated the ways time was being "wasted." Instead of regenerating body and mind for the coming day, nighttime was filled with insignificant acts of play, erotic desire, and gambling. What these "immoral" acts amounted to was a manifestation of freedom itself. Herbert Marcuse declared: "Play is unproductive and useless because it cancels the repressive and exploitive traits of labor and leisure; it 'just plays' with reality."[11] Therefore, play, by male and female students and by young men and women, as well as by nightly reporters, revealed the artificiality of the division of work and leisure and trivialized the authority that controlled time and relied on the ability to enact self-control. On the pages where decadence and erotica were celebrated, colonial control was under attack.

Playing under Colonial Surveillance: Toward Anonymity

The empty time of the night was also the time of surveillance, and the fear of the empty time was the reason for heightened surveillance. Night patrol was ubiquitous, and patrolmen (*sunsa*) walked around slowly, inspecting people and their activities in the streets and alleyways.[12] While night patrols lurked in the street, they often blended into the dark, thanks to their black uniform, making them barely visible. Pedestrians were alerted to them up close either by their "sparkling" eyes or the shiny blade of the sword they carried.[13] The ability to police while being undetected could be an advantage, but not so if the patrol aimed to put people into self-discipline. Thus, when darkness hampered visual detection, the presence of patrolmen was made known through sound. They were well known for carrying two long wooden batons that they beat against each other, which gave them the nickname *ttakttagi*, an onomatopoeia for the clapping sound of the batons. As the clap echoed through the street, it made the night patrol seem omnipresent. People at home could hear a patrolman but not pinpoint his position. Rather, his conspicuous auditory presence was a constant reminder of being watched—the better to prompt people into self-discipline. The sound of a patrolman's baton was a metaphorical panoptic gaze, a symbol of authority visible to the eyes of those who disciplined themselves, made audible through the batons. Just as clock time regimented and disciplined colonial subjects during the day, night patrols' wooden claps permeated the dark and quiet of the night, inciting fear of the all-pervasive but invisible presence of the police, who could be recognized from the security of one's own home.

Nightly reports were written in this context and tense mood of colonial surveillance, but the reporters playfully mimicked such oppressive measures. Reporters even occasionally accompanied willing night patrols. This ubiquitous fixture of the night then became part of the reports, and reporters at times pointedly joked about, as previously noted, how they could not get anywhere near interesting events because the streets were empty wherever the patrols went. Even in their excursion without a patrolman, they replicated the general strategy of the police—the detective gaze—and followed people who appeared "suspicious" to further investigate. So, shadowing, often in disguise, was a favored technique, but curiously, the people whom the reporters followed turned out to be performing masquerades. Nightly reports were thus filled with

amusing details about men tailing café waitresses, *kisaeng* accompanying wealthy men, and gangsters following other gangsters. An intricate
choreography was being performed on the streets at night as all acknowledged one another, though not in direct interaction, watching and following others for their own purposes: the night patrol roamed the streets
and enforced surveillance; the reporters mimicked the night patrol and
followed people in disguise; people on the street also used the strategy of
shadowing to evade surveillance.

Because outer appearance had little currency in the street, nightly reports had to take their doctrine from questioning the one-dimensionality
of truth and the very logic of representation. Suspicion, in this context,
epitomizes the attitude of never trusting surface representation. Some
people were deemed "suspicious" because they were believed to be har-
boring "secrets" behind the veneer of ordinariness. And yet, suspicion is
also a signifier more complex than the dichotomy of outer appearance
and inner truth. Suspicion is located somewhere at the borderline of nor-
malcy, strangeness, and criminality—always an unstable signifier, with
deep roots in urban modernity and the relationship it produced between
individual and crowd. Based on Walter Benjamin's observation about
how the modern city caused "the obliteration of the individual's traces in
the big city crowd," Tom Gunning explained it as "the mobile transformation of identity,"[14] which occurred within modern systems of circulation and mobility such as the railway and the cinema; both of which led
to the birth of the modern detective. The anonymity of the crowd and
fast circulation offered a possibility for the "criminal" to hide, not only in
dark corners but also in plain sight. The criminal's ability to be nowhere
and everywhere at the same time led to the detective in policing and literature as an attempt to restore the social order by identifying "the criminal, who preys on the very complexity of the system of circulation."[15] In
this, the detective is usually the possessor of knowledge and rationality who can offer a lucid explanation via mastery of evidence and clues.
Nightly reporters, on the contrary, investigated from an unprivileged
position: they gathered visual and auditory clues, seldom with complete
access to their subjects; they eavesdropped and rarely questioned their
subjects directly, and often relied on hearsay and gossip. Therefore, their
investigation always remained as such, simply capturing the traces of
a criminal without an anticipated revelation of a true identity accompanied by a satisfying explanation. From this position of disprivilege,

reporters often appropriated the very mobility and instability of signs as a means to disguise the criminality of their own nightly adventures.

An exchange noted in a report in the 1932 issue of *Pyŏlgŏn'gon* illustrates this: a reporter disguised himself as an innocent stroller with the help of a café waitress who accompanied him; they were stopped by a night patrolman who began questioning them. The night patrolman asked where they were going, to which the couple answered that they were heading home. The night patrolman asked about their address and names. The reporter gave a fake address and name for himself, Pak Ch'un-gwŏn, and introduced the café waitress as his sister. Nervous about the situation, the café waitress said her real name, "Chŏn Yŏng-sil." The reporter cringed: "How can she be a Chŏn when her brother is a Pak?" He quickly corrected himself, saying that she was his cousin. Tangled in one lie after another, they saw the night patrolman stepping toward them with a grin on his face. The reporter, with quick wit, revised the story all over again and "confessed" to the night patrol that they were coming from ancestral worship at his house, and because it was late he was escorting his sister to her home. The night patrol asked more questions: "Where is her home?" "What is your occupation?" "Do you have an identification card?" The reporter answered each question, with another made-up address and job title. Then, he told the night patrolman, "I do not have the identification card with me right now, but I am telling you the truth."[16] In lieu of the paper proof of his identity, all the patrolman had to go by were their words. He let them go, and the two imposters giggled and poked fun at each other.

What we see in this episode is a cunning masquerade, a performance of identity. Names, addresses, and workplaces all gave a sense of lawfulness to these "criminals," who doubled themselves like counterfeits.[17] Reporters occupied a space somewhere between the two poles of detective and forger—seeing and being seen, and seen differently. Disguise, for this reason, was a preferred technique for reporters to evade the suspecting gaze of night patrol as well as that of their subjects of investigation. They disguised themselves as students selling magazines, delivery men, or peddlers to claim a noncriminal space in the city and pass through the streets and alleyways incognito. Local delivery men and peddlers often happily became their co-conspirators, helping reporters by providing the right disguise and gossip about which houses harbored suspicious activities. Because most of their investigations dealt with students, reporters regularly disguised themselves as students. For easier access to female students, female reporters joined the team.

For nightly reporters, no elaborate costumes or masks were required, except a simple prop and a name change, because their disguise was a camouflage. They were not just appearing to be someone else (to gain identity); they also were to disappear in the crowd (to gain anonymity). In this context, it is worth noting that nightly reports were often published along with photographs. Yet the nighttime photographs were rarely intelligible, making reporters appear as shadowy figures. Even photography, a medium used to identify a criminal, failed in these instances, as nightly reporters dissolved into the crowd, flowing into the dark alleyways and boardinghouses along with it. This ability to disappear was a kind of freedom in anonymity, which allowed reporters to cross various boundaries of society and upset the normal order of things. Then, the question becomes one of sociability: how to characterize interactions between reporters and their subjects of investigation. The next section explores this question.

Community in Question: Strangers, the Oppressed, the Secretive

In the modern city, where isolation, solitude, and anonymity were symptoms of degrading social ties, speaking of community poses many challenges. In his seminal essay "The Metropolis and Mental Life," Georg Simmel talked about the defensive posturing of the modern individual against the overwhelming stimulus in the city as that of "a slight aversion, a mutual strangeness and repulsion."[18] The modern city forced individuals to be instrumental and rational, lacking the emotional and personal ties of small communities. Therefore, the metropolitan mentality is evident in the "blasé" attitude of the individual. Conversely, the individualized and rationalized city also offered a place of liberation from the binding character of the feudal, rural community. Community here connotes a reversion to another place (the rural) and another time (the premodern), to a more organic, in-person form of sociability characteristic of "the slower, more habitual, more smoothly flowing rhythm of the sensory-mental phase."[19] Regarding community as a largely anti-urban phenomenon, however, risks disregarding intricate social relations being formed as individuals came into coexistence with strangers in close proximity. The question, then, is what form of community or sociability might be possible in the largely anonymous modern city. Nightly reports were a celebration of such a modern mentality, as evident in the description of the transient occupancy of the street by mobile subjects of modernity. When the crowd dispersed at night, the city's spatial dynamics also changed, as people were no longer pressed up against one another. The emptied-out streets of Seoul in turn became an informal meeting place for people in search of a momentary connection with one another, who would extend seemingly transactional but not completely impersonal interactions to other informal meeting places behind the doors of drinking establishments, gambling quarters, and boardinghouses. Dating, rendezvous, and love were all indications of the temporary coming together of individuals to overcome solitary urban existence without recourse to a more intimate, organic community. Away from the hustle and bustle of the daytime, therefore, an inquiry into a new kind of sociality is called for.

One possibility for this new sociality is a model of affective community bound by a sense of belonging, which is an imaginary social tie among strangers. The advantage of being disguised as students, and female students in particular, was that reporters could appeal to empathy from fellow students. Some people responded with generosity, paying more than what they owed and inviting them in to take shelter from the bitter cold of the winter. The bond was over how they identified the other as one of them, rather than as a "criminal" or social outsider. One student who opened his door to the disguised female reporter-student said, "Who would empathize (*tongjŏng*) with us if we the white-clad folk (*paegŭimin*) did not look out for each other?"[20] The "white-clad folk," a term often used to describe the Korean ethno-nation, is recast here as a community bound by emotions (*tongjŏng*). Reporters and students were seeing each other as similarly positioned alienated modern souls and oppressed subjects of colonialism. Through empathy, anonymity ceased to be threatening and had the potential to find a home in the primordial identity of the nation, where individuality was sublimated through a collective bond.

However, this gesture to overcome the alienation of the modern, colonial city proves more precarious because of the position reporters occupied in this possible communion of the nation. The following excerpt shows how the rest of the encounter unfolded between the female reporter and the male students above:

"Is Chŏlla your hometown?" "Yes, I am from Naju, Chŏlla Province,"
I answered right away. The students seemed pleased to meet someone from the same hometown. They tried to appear like they cared
(*tongjŏng*) about me and said, "We are from Naju, Chŏlla Province."
They took turns trying to impress me. As if there was nothing more
to say, the three students began to reach for their books. I used that as
an opportunity to scan the room carefully. On the desk there weren't
any other books besides textbooks. Seeing that there were only two
clothes boxes, one seemed to be a guest. Traditional Korean clothes
and school uniforms were hanging in the room. The hats were too
far away to tell which school they went to. One student purchased
a volume of *Ŏrini* and another purchased paper and an envelope. I
asked them then, "Which school do you go to?" They without hesitation answered that they were first-year students at Chungang. These
students' friendliness to a struggling student must be out of genuine feelings of empathy (*tongjŏng*), but it was amusing to think that,
if I were just one of boys, they wouldn't have purchased anything.
But I offered them my gratitude repeatedly. As I was about to open
the door, one said, "Please visit us again some time." Another said, "I
wish you success!" and closed the door. I was so happy about being
successful at negotiating on my first try that I felt more courageous
going to the next house.[21]

Evidently, the reporter did not trust the intent of the male students, and
thus never became part of that affective community the students thought
should be the norm. Success for her was measured not by the bond with
her subjects but by her ability to convince (or deceive) them that she was
one of them. The reporter without hesitation answered that she was from
the town that they mentioned and took advantage of a moment of pause
to do her visual detective work. She even came across as callous, printing
the name of the school that the students trustingly provided when this
was rarely done in other reports. The failure of the bond underscores
that trickery was the mode of operation for nightly reporters. Nightly
reporters occupied a liminal space between identifiable and unidentifiable, and through their purposeful concealment of identity, they were
turned into "criminals" who could betray the trust of their counterparts
at any moment. Due to the inability of reporters to reciprocate in transac-

tions of affective community, a search for sociability between reporters and the subjects of their investigation must be located elsewhere.

Another kind of community can be based on location, mapped around places and more physically bound than the affective community. Nightly reporters spent a great deal of time describing the neighborhoods where they were located. Although they seldom spelled out the names of streets or neighborhoods, their detailed description of buildings and streets demonstrated the reporters' familiarity with the place they visited and also how they became familiar with that place. Through their regular and repetitive walking in the streets (location), they turned the space they occupied into place (locality). The homes they visited, alleyways through which they traveled, and shops where they were based can all amount to a place identity called "neighborhood," which Michel de Certeau described as a place that is formed and claimed through habituation, either by dwelling or by strolling.[22] This notion of neighborhood, which differs from the functional use of urban space, can be useful in grounding the reporters and the people they reported on as "inhabitants" of the neighborhood. However, we run into several limitations of such locally grounded identity. For one, the "inhabitants" in nightly reports were largely temporary residents—students in boardinghouses, visitors staying for the night or part of it, and even deliverymen and peddlers. Transient itinerants formed gatherings among the "outsiders" who were invited into homes, transforming the neighborhood into a place of "guests." Moreover, the masquerade and secrecy of these guests hindered "the process of recognition—of identification—that are created thanks to proximity, to concrete coexistence in the same urban territory."[23] The instability of identity, as well as the impossibility of intimacy by virtue of occupying space together, was compounded by colonial surveillance that constantly criminalized activities on the street, which forced the community into hiding in "domesticity." Because people had to retreat into the "private" space, the neighborhood could no longer function as a place where the communion between public and private occurs to form a community.[24] Instead, any form of "public" must be located within the "private" space.

In lieu of a plausible articulation of community through affective bond or locality, we have to turn to this liminal space of "home" and search for a kind of sociability forged by an interaction on a level other than the face-to-face—namely, the practice of reading magazines. For this, I draw on Michael Warner's discussion of public and counterpublic in which he points to a kind of public that exists only by virtue of imagining, not physical contact, and whose participants come into relation with one another through texts and their circulation.[25] He contrasts his notion of public to that of *the* public, "a kind of social totality," like the nation, which "is thought to include everyone within the field in question."[26] *A* public, in contrast, refers to "a concrete audience, a crowd witnessing itself in visible space," which also has "a sense of totality, bounded by the event or by the shared physical space."[27] For Warner, a third public exists, one bound by imaginary relationships among strangers. This notion of public is distinguished from the identity politics enabled by longing for unity and public intimacy in solidarity. Instead, Warner's public refers to a relation that unites strangers by participation alone. The possibility of knowing others is not a precondition of a public anymore, because unlike the premodern notion of strangers, who were foreign, alien, out of place, and exotic, disturbing the social order, strangers always-already belong to the world.[28] This public is, therefore, self-creating and self-organizing, created by its own discourse: "The notion of a public enables a reflexivity in the circulation of texts among strangers who become, by virtue of their reflexively circulating discourse, a social entity."[29]

This notion of public is helpful in illuminating sociability among reporters, their subjects of investigation, and their readers—all bound by self-created circulation of discourse—and highlights the participatory nature of nightly reports. The editors of *Pyŏlgŏn'gon* were cognizant of readers and openly solicited them to provide "secret" tips about suspicious places, people, or events. They pledged to dispatch reporters specializing in secret investigation immediately upon the "order" from readers and to publish.[30] *Pyŏlgŏn'gon* had other special series and features that welcomed readers' contributions, one of which involved quizzes where readers had to guess the identity of a photographed individual—age, occupation, and so forth—for a cash prize; at times these attracted thousands of submissions.[31] Nightly reports also included reporters' dialogues with people almost verbatim, allowing their subjects of investigation to coauthor the reports through their interactions with the reporters. For this, Chŏn Ŭn-gyŏng described the language of *Pyŏlgŏn'gon* not as a text to be read but as one to be written, an open and incomplete text because readership was created through participation.[32] In fact, the readership created by *Pyŏlgŏn'gon*, as mentioned in chapter 5, differed from the one targeted by its predecessor. They were the masses (*taejung*), an individualized collective that did not necessarily assume a meta-identity such as nation. Kim Chil-lyang argued that whereas *Kaebyŏk* turned anonymous readers into *tongp'o* or brothers, *Pyŏlgŏn'gon*'s readership was more interested in individuality. This individuality was not an abstract identity realized in the metadiscourses of the nation or nation-state, however. It was an identity based on specific situations in everyday life.[33] Practice preceded the identity, in other words, of those who willingly participated in it, and the magazines provided a participatory space for those pleasure seekers who willingly entered.

These participants were at once subjects and readers of reports; they read about people just like themselves—and possibly even about themselves. The triangular relationship between reporters, their subjects of investigation, and readers created a complicated meeting space that coexisted on physical, textual, and imaginary levels. A humorous episode involving a photograph contest illustrates the complex web of relations among all participants. A female reporter, who had disguised herself as a student selling magazines, encountered a group of students chatting over a photograph contest that featured her. One of the students, holding the previous issue of *Pyŏlgŏn'gon* in his hand and looking at her photograph, said, "This girl is the girl I see on the street day and night. But isn't it too difficult to guess the age from this photo?" The reporter's heart raced. "Why not pay a visit and hear what she has to say?" replied the other. Feeling apprehensive, the reporter moved on and knocked at another room; she ran into the same situation:

> One of them looked for something, then picked up the December issue of *Pyŏlgŏn'gon*, looked at the photo contest of the photograph of me and Mr. Pak and said, "Who could guess the age? So, that's why she should come and pay us a visit." The other said, "You need the address to pay her a visit." Another person in the corner of the room who remained silent the whole time looked at the photo of Mr. Pak and said, "Hey, is this guy wearing a Western suit inside out?" Their words were rough. I couldn't stop laughing and said, "If you guess it right, you get a bag of rice."[34]

The reporter's laughter is warranted given the spectacular failure of visual signs of photography and eyewitness. The fact that guesswork—

decoding an image—was what enlivened the chatter is noteworthy. Warner argued that this participatory public is demarcated from totality because it is bound by a language that is not readily accessible but is more poetic.[35] The language of this public is therefore a kind of "double-voicing of speech," which "denote[s] and express[es] directly and fully" among the participants but does not include others.[36] In cases of nightly reports, their "specialized" language operated through the code-language of the detective. Reporters rarely gave complete information about the place or people about whom they were reporting, but instead supplied just enough details for readers to do their own guesswork. When names were mentioned (unless they were fake), they were written with Xs, allowing a name to appear on the pages but also making it unidentifiable. The censored names preserved anonymity, but never completely, because there were enough clues provided for readers to do their own detective work. The locations of their investigations were, likewise, never fully revealed, but reporters always detailed routes of movement through "landmarks." As reporters put signposts along the way, "right turn here, left turn here, four steps from there, next door from here," readers gathered their own clues by following in their footsteps. Upon a close encounter, reporters also provided ample, mostly visual clues to key pieces of information, such as the pink color of the school badge on a student's jacket. Reporters were extremely aware that they were laying the ground for readers, at times saying that readers should arrive on their own at the conclusion they could not print. In sum, the language of nightly reports was a code language that depended on readers' ability to decode it, which privileged context over text and signaled an existence and coming together of a group that shared knowledge of that context. Moreover, code language never granted closure to the story by way of identifying the criminal but rather perpetuated mystery, thereby supplying endless suspense, thrills, and excitement.

Readers' participation in this mystery making and solving is what allows me to speak of the nightly report's "public" as a kind of community. As in the case of students at a boardinghouse squabbling about the identity of a reporter in the photograph, uncertainty over the identity of places and people was sure to continue the conversation in gossip and rumors (the guesswork would not end unless readers had a face-to-face meeting with the person to ask directly); and the abounding chatter was the only instance of a successful sociability (the presence of the reporter in the photograph among them went unnoticed). Here, we can treat gossip and rumor as a public discourse as Warner did: it circulates widely among the social network beyond private individuals and "sets norms of membership in diffused ways that cannot be controlled by the central authority."[37] Moreover, gossip and rumor are never generated among strangers; rather they affirm personal ties of those bound by shared secrecy.[38] And because secrecy always presumes awareness of the others from whom the meaning of the discourse is kept hidden, it is always self-generating through the demarcation of boundaries. To sum up, the boundless chatter created on the pages of magazines and behind the doors of gatherings is a marker of a community that celebrates the unknowable and proliferates such "discourses," all through a language that allows participation by some but not by others. For this reason, the word *community*, despite all its baggage, might be a better term to describe the sociability of nightly reports for their tendency to withdraw from visibility to the colonial oppressor while at the same time planting secrecy at the heart of the colonial, modern city of Seoul.

At this point, we can turn to Maurice Blanchot's commentary on nighttime to reanchor our investigation into nightly reports in terms of their position within the visual regime of colonialism: "Perhaps there is an invisibility that is still a manner of something letting itself be seen, and then another that turns aside from everything visible and everything invisible. Night is the presence of this detour, particularly the night that is pain and the night that is waiting."[39] Then, he takes an interesting turn to pivot this description of the night to speech: "Speaking is the speech of the waiting wherein things are turned back toward latency."[40] The nocturnal of Seoul in the colonial representation was a way of controlling seeing when the visual regime of power could no longer reproduce itself in the void of the dark. Nightly reports seized on that void and filled it with inconsequential details of vice while playing with colonial surveillance. The night in the nightly reports was a night in waiting, invisible but still visible, and visible yet still unidentifiable. Moreover, this is where speech was also in waiting. In the community created among strangers, rumor, gossip, and chatter continued throughout the night on the pages of magazines, behind closed doors, and in the alleyways, all under the blanket of the dark. This speech act is transgressive because it "seize[d] the thing from a direction from which it is not taken, not seen, and will never be seen."[41] It had an untraceable origin and defied the optical orientation of the subject and its ability to see. Speech haunted senses, especially of sight, so in challenging seeing, the transgressive speech also had to be a transcendence of sight: "Language acts as though we were able to see the things from all sides. . . . Speech no longer presents itself as speech, but as sight freed from the limitations of sight. Not a way of saying, but a transcendent way of seeing."[42]

*   *   *

It might be fitting to conclude this chapter with a description of the deity Fama, who is connected to rumor in ancient literature. She is described by Virgil as having many tongues and many mouths in search of many ears in the *Aeneid*:

> Rumour, compared with other evils is as swift. She flourishes by speed, and gains strength as she goes: at first limited by fear, she soon reaches into the sky, walks on the ground, and hides her head in the clouds. . . .
>
> At night she flies, screeching, in the shadow between earth and sky, never closing her eyelids in sweet sleep: by day she sits on guard on tall roof-tops or high towers, and scares great cities, as tenacious messenger of the evil and the truth.[43]

I end with this ominous imagery of rumor, personified, sitting atop a high tower, haunting a great city after its swift movement in and through the city at night, so that we can revisit the photograph from *Nobiyuku Keijō Denki* along with the poem "The Morning in Keijō," introduced earlier. But this time, we can defamiliarize the image of the serene city. The church spire emerging out of the fog, a metaphor for the quietness of the night and muteness of its subjects, is now seen in a different light; instead of disappearing into a shady corner to await another night, rumor sits high on the spire, paralleling the panoramic and panoptical view of the photographer and the interlocutor of the poem. She is invisible but insurmountable, empowered by whispers from person to person that kept the night awake to claim a truth of their own, "the evil and the truth." This passage from the *Aeneid* was introduced by Francesco Careri in his discussion of the artist Francis Alÿs, who transformed from architect into storyteller of the city in fragments, episodes, fables, and parables that gathered residues of the urban space. A "creator of rumors and urban myth,"[44] Alÿs relied on rumor's ability to circulate a story, making it open to reconfiguration in a new situation by one piece leading to another piece, "echoing" as if "they were clues for each other."[45] This "oral and mythical dimension" of storytelling in Alÿs's works was "perhaps the most 'architectonic' aspect of his practice"; he was an "immaterial architect." [46] Audible or not, speech was the weapon of the secretive community of nightly reports. With shared code language, it generated its own truth by revealing what lay beyond the concealment of the nocturnal and redrawing boundaries with shapeshifting walks through dark corners of the city. Strangerhood was the operational logic of this community, and chatter across the physical, textual, and imaginary spaces among those who freely entered and exited it made its existence visible but never knowable. With no closure in sight, these strangers' "discourse" transgressed boundaries and created oral traces, always incomplete and undeveloped but always pregnant with creativity: they too were creators of myth and fables—we can also call them immaterial architects.

Epilogue
A Time of Rehearsal

The sedimentary history of Seoul I have explored in this book takes as its bedrock the year when the new insignia was adopted: 1926. The mid-1920s in Korea is an interesting period from a historiographical point of view because of the way the emerging forces of architecture, material culture, and visual and sound media changed the way the city was experienced. Although this period is not the most consequential time from the standpoint of urban planning, the year 1926, with the completion of the Government-General Building, marks an important point for the construction of colonial monumental architecture in Seoul.[1] The enhancement of the north-south axis along T'aep'yŏng Avenue, connecting political, economic, and military centers in one sweep, thus altered the form and function of the city and also paved the way for the expansion of Japanese commercial ventures out of South Village to North Village. The growth in commerce, also aided by the opportunities opened by the Cultural Rule, and the integration of the colonial economy had a profound impact on the industries and mediums covered in the preceding chapters: the era of modern signage began in 1925, the gramophone industry began to release popular genres of songs around 1927, and a new breed of leisure magazine *Pyŏlgŏn'gon* was inaugurated in 1926. All this development attests to the establishment of commercial infrastructure and the beginning of a vibrant culture oriented toward the masses. Also evident around this time is the emergence of new ways of understanding the function of text and image (in signage), storytelling (in gramophone recordings), and reading (in leisure magazines). Yet it is not easy to explain such prolific print and sound media during this time through a single metastructure or particular identifiable factor. For instance, "The Funny Bald Man," a product of both the global operation of recording labels and a theater culture particular to Korea, was made in a vacuum created by the absence of colonial censorship specializing in this medium. *Pyŏlgŏn'gon* was a reaction to the censorship law that put an end to generalist magazines like *Kaebyŏk*. If anything, this decade is best characterized as a period of heterogeneity, much like the varied reading practices of signage.

As a practical intervention in writing a history of Seoul that pays due attention to possibilities that cannot be explained in neatly formulated causal relationships, this book treated Seoul in the mid-1920s as the liminal space to allow room for historical contingencies. Particularly helpful in illuminating the collisions of many forces in the urban space was the exploration of the visual dimension of the city: surface matters. That Seoul was a colonial city with similar expressions of modernity as the metropole on surface levels does not make it less modern—all modernity is a copy. What is important is that visuality, particularly in architectural practices, was the main mode behind the textualization of the city by Japanese colonialism. For this reason, architecture became the starting point of investigation for this book. Colonial monumental architecture in Seoul flattened multiple temporalities into a narrative and turned the city of Seoul into a discursive space. To unmask the discursive power of Japanese colonialism that operated through a specific mode of narrative—time—this book built a spatial model of history called sedimentary history. This model allows for a new map of Seoul to emerge, a map on which the material traces of the city are overlapping rather than linked in a sequence of discrete events. The surfaces that make up the layers of the sedimentary history are where the colonial subject inhabited through ever-multiplying sensory experiences—material, visual, oral, auditory, and imaginary—and produced a different spatiotemporal logic that would destabilize the forward progression of historical time. Modernity was the mode of operation for Japanese colonialism, in other words, and modernity was also the mode of practice for colonial subjects. Seoul was modern because of the ways colonial subjects engaged with the language of modernity to defy and desist colonial visual discourse of power.

These overlapping contexts of colonial power and resistance might seem strange, especially if we take resistance to mean being "against" something. It might lead us to characterize Seoul as antimodern or anticolonial if we envision the possibility of an a priori identity before modernity and most certainly outside of the colonial context. However, when we conceptualize colonial power and discourse as rooted in the urban space and its surface-level manifestations, a different picture emerges to reveal the intricacies of the mundane practices that produced a discourse of its own engaging with the logic of the visual regime of Japanese colonialism. For this reason, the methodology of sedimentary history is one of deconstruction; it brings to the fore the energy that quotidian practices generated in order to unthink and unfix the grip of the visual language of colonial power. Such practices that did not amount to a national or anticolonial force might have escaped an inquiry that largely concerned itself with the question of resistance, perhaps because it is not easy to disentangle something that does not present itself as antithetical to the power within which it operates: listening to a gramophone record might appear to be a consumption-oriented act that simply facilitates the market expansion of the industry. However, deconstruction is, to borrow Derrida's words, "always already at work in the work" and "always already contained within the architecture of the work," simultaneously participating in constructing and deconstructing the system within which it is located.[2] For this reason, I started with the assumption that everything is text and took up surface matters as an important analytical site. Such a methodology goes beyond simply pointing to contradictions, elisions, and tensions, but becomes subject to unraveling and in that process is also useful for revealing the entangled relationship between the language of modernity and the experience of colonial subjects. In the following sections, I recap this method of deconstruction and how it can be mobilized toward a different mode of history writing.

The Art of Deception and Deconstruction

The story of surface matters in Seoul is one of deception, not just because the city's architecture assembled different traditions of the West from different periods, creating a sort of kitsch, but because the architectural surface was presented as a moral and aesthetic concept through a semiosis of its own. "Buildings lie," said Keith Mitnick, "by staging deceptions about everything from their materiality, their age and manner of construction, to the ideological messages that they embody."[3] Architecture deceives by bridging abstraction in meaning with physical form, so surface—ornamentality in particular—becomes an important component that arranges disparate images into a coherent concept, dressing up architecture "in the costumes of *authenticity, coherence*, and *nature*."[4] Architecture in Seoul was intended to create a historical myth upon which colonial discourse could naturalize Japanese colonialism as agent of modernization. As a result, Seoul became a phantasmagoria, not just magical in its fetishistic presentation of modernity, but in the way that it masked its actual operation.[5] It concealed more than it revealed, in other words, and mystified even in its efforts to rationalize. Therefore, the truth claim of architecture through a semblance of reality was the ultimate falsification that tricked us to continue mistaking sensory experience for cognitive knowledge. Because the discursive production of architecture relied on our inability to recognize architecture as staging and to effectually link the materiality of architecture to concepts and ideas rooted in a historical stage, any attempt to criticize colonial discourse in Seoul would have to involve setting in motion the staging of architecture (and of modernity, as Timothy Mitchell urged) to reveal its fakeness by privileging a subject who vacillates between reality and fable and between knowledge and experience.

The practices discussed show how the denaturalization of architectural surface and its discursive power was done in the everyday. Signage in Seoul, for instance, draped the cosmopolitan surface of architecture with linguistic diversity and disrupted the visual and conceptual coherence of architectural ornament. More important, regarded as ornament itself and elevated from a utilitarian, communicative device to picture writing, it brought together visual and verbal signs to decontextualize the reading of the sign from its immediate physical environment into the commodity circulation wherein meaning was emptied via its index referentiality. The performative aspect of reading signage also demonstrates how language became vulnerable to interruption by the quotidian, hearsay, and orality. In this process, language was freed from the solipsistic monologue and the bilateral relationship of interlocutor and listener. Rather, it brought the focus to the moment of enunciation and recuperated the voice—the corporeality of the speaking subject—from the context in which subjects encountered others; it did not recover the "correct" sound nor what had been lost that could be "spectacularized as the singularly representative voice of the nation-culture."[6]

In this context, rather than choosing between Japanese and Korean, between monolingual and multilingual, colonial subjects in Seoul resorted to a play with signifiers: they disaggregated names that cannot be disaggregated and unhinged the correspondence between name and object, the very link that made representation possible. The playful misreading of the signifier could become a tactic of deception. This is most explicitly seen in Sin Pul-ch'ul, who turned his language play into an art of deception, setting verbal and visual signs as well as the body of the interlocutor into a constant state of metamorphosis. Such tactics of deconstruction were also a source of disguise in investigative reports, a trickery performed to confound, conceal, and construct an identity, ultimately leading practitioners to assume anonymity in place of a name. The cunning charade of signifiers was also incarnate in the notion of suspicion, which epitomized an untrusting attitude toward the surface representation, continuously seeking doubling images behind the façade. Seizing on the symptom of the modern city that was the anonymous crowd, investigative reporters participated in "criminal" activities hidden in plain sight and enlivened the energy to multiply and copy without designating a proper point of return—a name.

All these practices enabled critical commentary on the deceptive power of colonial visuality, and through mimicry, they all took place within the purview of the system they criticized: the genre of *mandam* is a creative adaptation of storytelling from Japan and elsewhere; *ch'agyŏng* was the principle of good design in modern signage, borrowing elements from other environments; investigative reports mimicked the modern detective and appropriated colonial surveillance. "Copy it if you can" was the message at the core of these rather unremarkable visual, sound, and print mediums. While transferring a signifier from one context to their own, they imitated with no origin in mind. There was only copy after copy, with no closure in sight. A formalistic analysis could not pinpoint the unbounded energy of these practices. What elides our attention is the semblance of the forms, but what demands our attention is the willful and playful engagement of those who set the objects in motion.

Seeing, Misrecognition, Blindness, Speech:
The Question of Corporeality

The myth of Seoul relied on the false objectivity of the senses, especially sight, and the panorama saliently demonstrates how ways of seeing were mobilized to create a sense of spectacular reality. As seen in the evolution of panorama in postcards and travel maps, and the photography of Kojong's funeral, the panorama sanctioned the surveyor's point of view through seemingly self-evident wholeness. However, the panorama also revealed a contradiction in the mastery of position through an imperial gaze because a panoramic view must be consumed as fragments and then reimagined as whole through the observer's cognitive ability. Moreover, the spatial dimension of the panorama also extended to temporal ordering through which an unfolding scene was translated into unfolding narrative, specifically in cinema. This is why photography, a preferred medium for such narrative production, always appeared within a narrative structure (collection) in which fragments could be pieced together into a new meaningful order. The reliance on the subjective memory production in these narratives also made nostalgia a predominant trope of the history writing of Seoul. In the anticipatory logic of teleology where the future was already known, Korea's past became the anterior time of the Japanese empire.[7] For that, the history writing of Seoul was also colonizing at its core.

The colonial subject, in gazing, interpreting, and looking away from the colonial language of power, could disrupt that sequential link that holds together the panorama's narrative. As corporeality (the gaze) became a conduit for organizing image fragments into formulable thinking, corporeal performance through different sensory registers could loosen the grip of knowledge production. The rescuing of the seeing subject from the intellectualizing demand placed on it begins with questioning the objectivity of the senses. It requires a kind of purposeful disordering and disorienting of the senses, not just to disturb but to deconstruct. Misrecognition, for this reason, was not a result of the premodern subject's unfamiliarity with modern semiosis—a sign of lagging—but a strategic position assumed to change reality by forcing language and image to undergo metamorphosis: the old man's bald head looks like an octopus, and in the eyes of the old man in the city, nature and artifice are not only alike but also the same. Despite the image of the old man, outmoded and out of place, the subject of misrecognition was always already in the modern city because semiotic deconstruction and physical disembodiment always presupposed the logic that naturalized artifice.

Disordering of the senses was also amplified by intentionally setting the body in motion at the speed of the city. The urban synesthesia gave way to disorienting views in urban investigative reports as the reporter-drifters interacted and interfered with their environment. The result was a revolutionary perception of the city—a disentanglement from the imagined totality of the city—though one produced through a guerrilla tactic. As they explored the forgotten corners of the vista, seams and folds hidden from plain view, and transitory in-between spaces, they discovered simultaneities of nonsynchronous events—time spilled over, emptied out, and awaiting. This was a social practice that rewrote the sense of place through dislocation and intervened in the moment via situation making. It brought forward the lived experience of the city, pitted against the chronometric—a social mode of time as measure that produced a codified experience. When the clock time and calendar time of journalism provided a reality effect and served as an instrument in history writing for Kojong's funeral, the intentional misalignment with this time of synchrony created a nonhistorical time. Also under attack was the documentary impulse of arduous fact gathering by the imperial subject. In drifting, they created their own "science" of exhausting a place by turning their eyes into a camera-eye—a position of blindness. Doing so turned a posture of passivity, defenseless from the onslaught of visual stimuli, into a position of possibility to disavow the spectacular consumption of the city. The body in motion was no longer a conduit of emotive subjective processes; it wielded a new tactical position of displacing the positivist hold of the modern subject by shifting the focus from interiority to outward exploration. It was a willful act filled with a sense of game and play because play was about deconstructing received categories for apprehending modernity. In doing so, it looked neither back nor forward but only celebrated multiple presents. It was this grounding in the present that unearthed undercurrents of the city, more real than any feigned realism.

What these practices entailed were new configurations of the private and public, individual and communal, and communal and national. The subject desisting from any form of metanarrative, colonial or national, was no longer part of a manifest community, or even an affective community where longing and belonging were the same. The practices discussed in the book point to a different kind of community. Instead of presuming an idea of home or homeland, they explored latent spaces, present but not necessarily of identifiable functions. These were emptied-out spaces where the usual operation of power had receded along with its visual operatives; then they were filled with people and events that were not always nameable or representable. This is an unavowable community that celebrated the disembodied body, the corporeality under erasure, in the media space created by the painted board of commercial signage, the shellacked surface of gramophone records, and the print pages of leisure magazines. The coming together of individuals in the media space was carried out only by imagining through texts and their circulation. In an unavowable community, permeability between exterior and interior spaces replaced the intimacy usually attributed to person-to-person interaction in communities, and secretive language substituted for the communicability of language. As a community based on participation, self-creation, and self-generation, participants were defiant in willful disobedience and production of things irregular, erratic, disorderly, and unpredictable.

The privileged mode of subjectivity in this community was speaking, not seeing, because the subject was immersed in the immediate environment without the privilege of a distanced perspective. The cacophony of Seoul was therefore a corporeal performance of the body that desisted a move from sound to speech to allow space for the residual practices of the everyday. It stubbornly returned to haunt the senses and reverberated in chatter, gossip, and laughter. The colonial subject was, therefore, located between speech and speaking, constantly challenging sound and its audibility, and certainly the colonial regime of visuality. This was the terror of speech, "war and madness," according to Blanchot, that crept up in the places left by colonial authority.[8] This metaphor of war, albeit described as a force of disorder, captures how speech can transgress and disorient what orders our senses. In other words, the disorientation of the senses, discussed earlier in terms of misrecognition and blindness's challenge to the completeness of the panorama/narrative, became a task of speech, which took its force of disturbance toward transcendence. That is, in defiance of language's visual ordering of the world, speech was no longer simply speech; it was a transcendence of sight.

Sedimentary History and the Time of Rehearsal

All these discussions about surface matters and speech matters point to a larger question about how colonial power was articulated and contested in Seoul—through temporality. It became apparent that the fiction created by architectural practice was a narrative motored by teleology that is history. Against such history writing in and through Seoul, the book suggested various practices that turned the unprivileged position of colonial subject who is "lagging" into a tactic of desisting the forward trajectory of time via different modes of duration, delay, waiting, and simultaneity. This is what Peter Osborne called a *politics of time*, which "takes the temporal structures of social practices as the specific objects of its transformative (or preservative) intent."[9] Politics of time, in this regard, is a transformative history, and that transformative history does not have to rely on the subject to be the alterity to the universal or try to replace difference with sameness. Rather, it undercuts the distinction between sameness and difference by disturbing the very temporal anchor that secures it. Moreover, politics of time critiques the totality of history precisely from the standpoint of incompleteness because "it is as such—an always incomplete *de*historicization—that the everyday derives its potential as a site for the *re*historicization of experience."[10]

The sedimentary history of Seoul is one such rehistoricization, done through all the multiple temporalities of incompleteness, randomness, and indeterminacy that make up its layers. Copresent and overlayed atop each other, the temporality of sedimentary history is one of "an interlocking of presents, pasts, and futures that retain their depths of other presents, pasts, and futures, each age bearing, altering, and maintaining the previous ones."[11] Such a view of coeval experience between the multiple strata might contradict the common usage of the term *sediment*, accumulated materials over time, which I initially set aside as uncharacteristic of my model. But at this point, it is important to develop this idea further: in the sedimentary history of Seoul, accumulation occurs but not quite in the way that natural sediment works. With natural sediment, the deeper down you go, the farther back in historical time. In place of a spatialized time schema, the accumulated time of sedimentary history indicates the copresence of multiple times—namely, the temporality of experience accumulated through repetition. "Experiences can only be accumulated because they are—as experiences—repeatable,"

writes Koselleck, whereas "history is only able to recognize what continually changes, and what is new, if it has access to the conventions
within which lasting structures are concealed."[12] The sedimented model
of Seoul is, therefore, an accumulation of time not over time. Copious-
ness and redundancy are the markers of experience, so each layer of
sedimentary history is a product of accumulated experience, and the
accumulation of each layer as sedimentary history is meant to mirror
another, never clearly delineated but "irreducible to one another and ab-
solutely not superimposable on one another."[13]

   The book has presented multiperspectival views of Seoul—from
above and below, flowing and fixed, open and concealed, and some in-
between—to uncover a polychronic time in which many things happen
at once, time neither organized by chronometric principles nor accumulated toward an end goal. What is important is that the slices of life that
the book gathered are not a sampling of a moment in the accumulation
of time. Rather, they are the very motor behind enlivening the process of
accumulation to be contingent and irregular. That is, it is the repetition
of experience that enables the accumulation of time, and that accumulation of time enables a history writing whose commitment is politics of
time. To demonstrate the energy of repetition that puts each layer of the
sedimentary history in motion, I turn to the notion of rehearsal, as brilliantly demonstrated by Francis Alÿs; and to better visualize this idea, I
would like to indulge in discussing two of Alÿs's works.

   The idea of rehearsal was first introduced in a work called *Sign-
Painter's Project* (*Rotulistas*).[14] In this, Alÿs collaborated with sign paint-
ers from his neighborhood in Mexico City who produced enlarged copies
of his smaller original paintings. Once they completed their own versions, he produced another model, based on each sign painter's interpretation, and this second "original" was again used for new copies. As the
process was repeated, the hierarchy between origin and copy became
more indistinct. The repeated tasks of painting can be thought of as endless rehearsal.[15] It is an interval space filled with acts of unclosing, never
sequential but constantly repeated and recalibrated toward a new direction so that the conclusion is infinitely delayed. In each delay, unlike
the deferral of the future in teleological time, the moment of pausing,
going back in time, and proceeding again is pregnant with increased creative potential that can reconfigure and change through more iterations.
Ferguson argued that "for Alÿs, that flickering, the movement back and

forth and around an idea, is as productive as a determined path toward a fixed and identifiable goal."[16] For this reason, he described the politics of rehearsal as "a sort of discursive argument . . . staging the experience of time."[17]

The place for Alÿs is Latin America, and the experience of modernity there revolves around a distinctive time structure, as illustrated in *Rehearsal I*.[18] In this work, a video depicts a Volkswagen Beetle tirelessly trying and always failing to climb up a dusty, unpaved hill. A soundtrack plays in the background, a brass band rehearsal session playing on a tape. The car goes uphill while the music is playing, but when the musicians pause, the car stops; then as the musicians are chatting and tuning up their instruments, the car rolls back downhill: and the up-and-down motion of the car repeats. Located in the outskirts of Tijuana, this work gestures at an effort to reach the United States–Mexico border, a task "of working toward an always-deferred result."[19] The voice-over commentary by Cuauhtémoc Medina criticizes Harry Truman's labeling of the United States as "developed" and Latin America as "undeveloped": "Modernity could never be achieved, modernization never accomplished, and Latin America would always be seen to lag behind the north." Yet, showing the loop of the car going up and down like a pendulum movement, it also hints at the latent energy behind that movement, slowing to a halt but speeding once again: "Like a pendulum swaying at the end of its swing, then returning to the center, regaining speed along the way, the stuttering melody governs the period of the car, including its driver into a quasi state of suspension, hypnotized in the repeated act, conveying a state of resilience, of patient, or frustrated absorption."[20]

The belatedness of the colonized is the ultimate lesson of modernity, common across the globe, and Japanese colonialism's fully operating within the logic of modernity also exhibited fantastical expressions of modernity through thingness on the surface, only to then say, "Not yet"—a discourse that "provokes an experience of history as a Sisyphean punishment."[21] However, the task of repetition, as Alÿs showed, is that of resilience. Through endless and unavailing labor, the colonial subject can seize the moment of delay to comment on the deferral of modernity from the colonized and can refuse closure—repetitive, nonconsecutive, fragmentary, inefficient, and suspended. None of these amounts to a unique historical moment or authentic event, and the infinitely repeated present is no longer a transitory point in time connecting past to

future. In the time of rehearsal, one "can go back and forth in time, starting and stopping and beginning again," and in that process, the past is
also "perpetually rewritten—names and events appear, disappear, reap-
pear and disappear again."[22]

The time of rehearsal is also a time of colonial subjects in Seoul,
always incomplete and infinite. This is also a transcendental time, re-
configuring the temporal coordinate that grounds history writing. The
time of rehearsal, in other words, is a politics of time, which can bolster
a historical practice against the usual mode of history writing. The sedimentary history of Seoul is, therefore, a method for colonial subjectivity
that never assumed a privileged position in the production of knowledge.
In the image of the infinite produced by the politics of rehearsal, the
sedimentary history of Seoul aspired to unleash the creative and critical energy of rehearsal, because the unclosing is the very force behind
destabilizing the foreclosing structures of modernity and history. So
in recognizing the limitations of the inquiry into a city besieged by the
foreclosing logic of modernity, the sedimentary history of Seoul recuses
itself from any pretense of offering comprehensive coverage of Seoul
under Japanese colonial rule and remains content in a critique from its
own position of incompleteness.

NOTES

Introduction

1. See "Kyŏngsŏngbu hwijang toan ipsangja simsa palp'yo," *Maeil sinbo*, September 26, 1926.

2. The font style of the character, expressed in bold, simple lines, was done in the "Gothic" style with thick but simple lines for legibility. See "Kyŏngsŏngbu ŭi hwijang," *Maeil sinbo*, June 18, 1918.

3. See "Kyŏngsŏngbu hwijang," *Tonga ilbo*, September 26, 1926.

4. This book follows the categories of signs in the theory of semiotics developed by Charles Sanders Peirce and defines an icon as a sign that has a physical resemblance to the signified; a symbol as a sign relying on connections and consensus produced by culture rather than the resemblance between the signifier and the signified; and an index as a sign that references or points to something else. See Charles S. Peirce, *The Philosophical Writings of Peirce*, ed. Justus Buchler (New York: Dover, 1995).

5. Sŏngjŏsimni refers to an area within ten *ri* from the walls. Here, one *ri* is a unit of measure corresponding to 360 footsteps, approximately 0.4 km. When the city boundary came to be limited within the city walls, Sŏngjŏsimni was transferred to Kyŏnggi Province. Pointing to the exclusion of Sŏngjŏsimni, Baek Yung Kim (Kim Paeg-yŏng) discussed the two-stage transformation of the royal capital of Hansŏng to the colonial city of Kyŏngsŏng in terms of "urban shrinkage strategy" and "urban expansion strategy." The later expansion, mainly in the 1930s, took place only after the initial shrinkage of the city limit with the annexation.

See Baek Yung Kim, "Ruptures and Conflicts in the Colonial Power Bloc: The Great Keijō Plan of the 1920s," *Korea Journal* 48, no. 3 (Autumn 2008): 13.

6. Kim Che-jŏng, "Kŭndae Kyŏngsŏng ŭi yongnye wa kŭ ŭimi ŭi pyŏnhwa," in *1930–40-yŏndae Kyŏngsŏng ŭi tosi ch'ehŏm kwa tosi munje*, ed. Sŏul sirip taehak-kyo tosi munhak yŏn'guso (Seoul: Laum, 2014).

7. "Kyŏngsŏng inya <Keijō> inya," *Tonga ilbo*, January 3, 1927.

8. Jini Kim Watson, *New Asian City: Three-Dimensional Fictions of Space and Urban Form* (Minneapolis: University of Minnesota Press, 2011), 40.

9. "Kukche tosi rossŏ pukkŭrŏul kŏsi ŏpta," *Taehan maeil sinbo*, January 4, 1934.

10. Nōse Iwakichi, "Keijō inshōki," *Chōsen kōron* 14, no. 11 (November 1926): 68–72.

11. The term was coined to be used as an analytic category in reaction to the modernization theory and to propose that modernity and colonialism were simultaneous within the context of capitalist industrial expansion. See Tani Barlow, ed., *Formations of Colonial Modernity in East Asia* (Durham, NC: Duke University Press, 1997). For a review of the debates on colonial modernity since then, see Tani Barlow, "Debates over Colonial Modernity in East Asia and Another Alternative," *Cultural Studies* 26, no. 5 (2012), 617–44.

12. Barlow, "Debates over Colonial Modernity," 624.

13. Naoki Sakai critically spoke of the arbitrary distinction between the West and non-West by showing how it only reinforces the "positive" existence of the West: "Basically, it is just like the name 'Japan,' which reputedly designates a geographic area, a tradition, a national identity, a culture, an ethnos, a market, and so on, yet unlike all the other names associated with geographic particularities, it also implies the refusal of its self-delimitation; it claims that it is capable of sustaining, if not actually transcending, an impulse to transcend all the particularizations." Naoki Sakai, *Translation and Subjectivity: On "Japan" and Cultural Nationalism* (Minneapolis: University of Minnesota Press, 1997), 154.

14. "Africa, because it was and remains that fissure between what the West is, what it thinks it represents, and what it thinks it signifies, is not simply *part of* its imaginary significations, it is *one of* those imaginary significations." Achille Mbembe, *On the Postcolony* (Durham, NC: Duke University Press, 2001), 1–2.

15. See Sarah Nuttall and Achille Mbembe, eds., *Johannesburg: The Elusive Metropolis* (Durham, NC: Duke University Press, 2008), 1.

16. Peter Osborne, *The Politics of Time: Modernity and Avant-Garde* (London: Verso, 1995), ix.

17. Reinhart Koselleck, *Futures Past: On the Semantics of Historical Time* (New York: Columbia University Press, 2004).

18. Ibid., 246.

19. Dipesh Chakrabarty, *Provincializing Europe: Postcolonial Thought and Historical Difference* (Princeton, NJ: Princeton University Press, 2007), 7. Also see Osborne, *The Politics of Time*, 246.

20. Mitchell therefore saw staging as a process through which a series of simulations produce an unmediated and self-sufficient reality, which is particularly

vulnerable to disruption and displacement. See Timothy Mitchell, *Questions of Modernity* (Minneapolis: University of Minnesota Press, 2000). 23. Also see, for more discussion of the concept "world-as-picture," Timothy Mitchell, *Colonising Egypt* (Berkeley: University of California Press, 1991).

21. See Henrik Reeh, *Ornaments of Metropolis: Siegfried Kracauer and Modern Urban Culture* (Cambridge, MA: MIT Press, 2006).

22. In this context, speaking of Korea and other Japanese colonies involves a layered process of temporalizing and othering, as seen in Stephen Tanaka's discussion of Oriental history (*tōyōshi*), which represented China and Korea as Japan's Orient. See Stephen Tanaka, *Japan's Orient: Rendering Pasts into History* (Berkeley: University of California Press, 1993). For Korean nationalism, the shared language of modernity and universal history between colonizer and colonized resulted in a categorical overlap between Korea's own aspiration toward modernity and Japan's exclusive claim. See Andre Schmid, *Korea between Empires, 1895–1919* (New York: Columbia University Press, 2002).

23. Mbembe and Nuttall described the spectacular vision of Johannesburg's modernity in terms of *superfluity*, which refers not to the excess of objects but to how they "hypnotize, overexcite, or paralyze the senses." Seen in the "impressions" of metropolitan modernity are a society's fantasies, they argued, in which the phenomenality of things lies in their ability to substitute, "where the superfluity of objects is converted into a value in and of itself." See Nuttall and Mbembe, *Johannesburg*, 37–67.

24. Nuttall and Mbembe called Johannesburg a metropolis in every sense of the word, but an "elusive metropolis" full of multiplicity that cannot situate it as an African, European, or American city. They employed the term *Afropolitanism* to describe Johannesburg as a city always on the run because cities "always outpace the capacity of the analysts to name them." See Nuttall and Mbembe, *Johannesburg*, 25.

25. My use of the term *urban poetics* is inspired by Pierre Mayol's preface to Michel de Certeau's *The Practice of Everyday Life*, Vol. 2, in which he describes the city as "poeticized" by the subject who has "prefabricated it for his or her own use by undoing the constraints for the urban apparatus and, as a consumer of space, imposes his or her own law on the external order of the city." See Michel de Certeau, Luce Giard, and Pierre Mayol, *The Practice of Everyday Life* (Minneapolis: University of Minnesota Press, 1998), 2:13.

26. During the construction in 2008 of the Kwanghwamun Plaza, an excavation at eight meters deep behind the statue of Yi Sun-sin revealed eleven layers of sand and granite as well as foundations of urbanization from the early to late Chosŏn dynasty underneath the new pavement installed in 1926 during the colonial period. In another area nearby, remnants of iron rails for streetcars that were in use as recently as 1968 were uncovered just one meter under the surface, indicating the long-held practice of simply covering over existing grounds to prepare for new construction. See Sŏul yŏksa pangmulgwan, *Kwanghwamun yŏn'ga sigye rŭl tollida* (Seoul: Sŏul yŏksa pangmulgwan, 2009). See also, for an exhi-

bition about the excavation of the Ch'ŏngjin district, *Asŭp'alt'ŭ arae Unjongga—Ch'ŏngjin palgul ŭi ahop susukkekki* (Seoul: Sŏul yŏksa pangmulgwan, 2020).

27. Reinhart Koselleck employed the concept of "sediments of time," which is a metaphor that was first used in historicizing natural history of the eighteenth century, to human history to "analytically separate different temporal levels upon which people move and events unfold, and thus ask about the longer-term preconditions for such events." He used this theoretical approach to mainly to comment on two prevailing temporalities of history, "the linear-cyclical dichotomy." See Reinhart Koselleck, *Sediments of Time: On Possible Histories*, ed. Sean Franzel and Stefan-Ludwig Hoffmann, Cultural Memory in the Present (Stanford, CA: Stanford University Press, 2018), 3–4.

28. Paul Virilio, *A Landscape of Events* (Cambridge, MA: MIT Press, 2000), x.

29. Walter Benjamin, Howard Eiland, and Michael W. Jennings, eds., *Selected Writings, Vol. 4, 1938–1940* (Cambridge, MA: Harvard University Press, 2003), 392.

30. Giuliana Bruno, *Surface: Matters of Aesthetics, Materiality, and Media* (Chicago: University of Chicago Press, 2014), 3.

31. W.J.T. Mitchell, "Showing Seeing: A Critique of Visual Culture," *Journal of Visual Culture* 1, no. 2 (2012): 165–81. This list is from the section "Eight Counter-Theses on Visual Culture," 170.

32. Walter Benjamin described the objective of this as "to assemble large-scale constructions out of the smallest and most precisely cut components" and "to discover in the analysis of the small individual moment the crystal of the total event." See Benjamin, *The Arcades Project* (Cambridge, MA: Harvard University Press, 2002), 461.

33. Andreas Huyssen, *Miniature Metropolis: Literature in an Age of Photography and Film* (Cambridge, MA: Harvard University, 2015), 3.

34. Other names were: "little pieces" (Kafka) and "aphorisms, witticisms, dreams, thought images" (Benjamin). Ibid., 11.

35. "The new form emerged as anti-form, resistant to the laws of genre as much as to systemic philosophy or urban sociology, crossing the boundaries between poetry, fiction, and philosophy, between commentary and interpretation, and centrally, between the verbal and the visual." Ibid.

36. A good example of the blurred boundary between the verbal and visual is seen in episodic writings called "sketches" (*sŭk'ech'i*). A piece in the magazine *Yŏsŏng*, entitled "A Picture (*manhwa*) without Pictures (*kŭrim*): Nightly Story of Chongno," illustrates how the visual was fused with the verbal even when no visual element accompanied the text; the visual was already an integral part of the verbal. The writer of this piece also drew a contrast from literature, noting that whereas the novel is centered on characters and events that progress and culminate in a climax, iyagi is short, fragmented, and episodic: "Suppose this: when we are so accustomed to the water from the bucket, it is hard to tell its taste. But if we eat ice cream and then drink the water, then we can tell that the water from the bucket is bland. This can be a story (*iyagi*) as well." Cho Punghaeng, "Kŭrim ŏmnŭn manhwa: Chongno yahwa," *Yŏsŏng*, September 1938.

Chapter 1

1. "Tokcha wa kija ŭi tonggi: Pogo sip'ŭn sajin," *Tonga ilbo,* October 9, 1925.

2. Pak Sŏng-jin and U Tong-sŏn, "Ilche kangjŏmgi Kyŏngbokkung chŏn'gak ŭi hoech'ŏl kwa igŏn," *Taehan kŏnch'uk hakhoe nonmunjip* 23, no. 5 (May 2007): 134.

3. One estimate is that 41,800 of the palace's 72,800 p'yŏng was destroyed. One p'yŏng equals 3.3 square meters. See Sŏnu Il and Sŏ Pyŏng-hyŏp, *Chosŏn ch'ongdokpu sich'ŏng onyŏn kinyŏm kongjinhoe sillok* (Kyŏngsŏng: Chōsen Hakubunsha, 1916), 9. Pak Sŏng-jin and U Tong-sŏn noted that many buildings of Kyŏngbok Palace demolished during this exhibition were sold and moved to the South Village or to Japan. See Park and U, "Ilche kangjŏmgi Kyŏngbokkung," 133-40.

4. See Michael Kim, "Collective Memory and Commemorative Space: Reflections on Korean Modernity and Kyongbok Palace Reconstruction 1865-2010," *International Area Review* 13, no. 4 (2010): 75-95.

5. "Kwanghwamun, kŏnch'unmun puktchok ŭro omgigo wŏldae ch'ŏlgŏ," *Tonga ilbo,* July 2, 1926.

6. Cited in Kim, "Collective Memory," 85 (translation by Michael Kim).

7. Ibid. Despite being the main palace in the early years of the dynasty, Kyŏngbok Palace remained largely abandoned after its destruction in 1592 during the Hideyoshi Invasion. Only during the reign of Taewŏn'gun did the reconstruction of the palace begin to bolster the monarchy's power against impinging Western imperialism. Even after its completion in 1867, the palace was again partially destroyed by fire in 1873 and 1876. Although Kojong occupied the palace briefly after its renovation, he retreated to the Russian legation after the assassination of Queen Myŏngsŏng in 1896. When Kojong emerged from the legation in 1897 to proclaim the founding of the Taehan Empire, he chose Tŏksu Palace as the main residence and imperial palace. This means that the choice of the exhibition's site can be explained only as a calculated move on the part of the Government-General to negate the symbolic power of the Chosŏn dynasty while avoiding direct confrontation with the monarchy.

8. In this book, I count the basement as one level, so all the numbers of floors include the basement level unless noted otherwise.

9. "Chosŏn chŏngch'i ŭi kwagŏ wa hyŏnjae" *Kaebyŏk,* March 1925.

10. Kim, "Collective Memory," 88.

11. Jong-Heon Jin, "Demolishing Colony: The Demolition of the Old Government-General Building of Chosŏn," in *Sitings: Critical Approaches to Korean Geography,* ed. Timothy R. Tangherlini and Sallie Yea, (Honolulu: University of Hawai'i Press, 2008), 41.

12. Ibid.

13. For a more detailed history of Tŏksu Palace, see An Ch'ang-mo, *Tŏksugung: Sidae ŭi unmyŏng ŭl an'go cheguk ŭi chungsim e sŏda* (Seoul: Tongnyŏk ch'ulp'ansa, 2009).

14. This road was proposed in 1919 but realized only in 1927, after the death of Sunjong. Kim Paeg-yŏng argued that the monarchy's persistent power made it

difficult to amend the residential palaces of Kojong and Sunjong. See Kim Paeg-yŏng, *Chibae wa konggan* (Seoul: Munhakkwa chisŏngsa, 2009), 366–74.

15. Ibid., 256. For a study of Japanese colonial cities, see Hashiya Hiroshi, *Teikoku nihon to shokuminchi toshi* (Tokyo: Yoshikawa Kōbunkan, 2004).

16. Ibid., 255.

17. For Kim Paeg-yŏng, violent assimilation was a product of the failure of the moderate policy of the protectorate government (1905–1910) and the subsequent establishment of military rule with annexation. Ibid., 322.

18. Chŏn U-yong, "Chongno wa Ponjŏng: Singmin toshi Kyŏngsŏng ŭi tu ŏlgul," *Yŏksa wa hyŏnsil* 40 (June 2001): 163–93.

19. Todd Henry argued that this was a rather contentious process between the colonial government and the settler community, which resulted in uneven development of North Village and South Village with an assimilatory impetus. See Todd A. Henry, *Assimilating Seoul: Japanese Rule and the Politics of Public Space in Colonial Korea, 1910–1945* (Berkeley: University of California Press, 2014).

20. Inha Jung also discussed how the 1912 reform was revised five times before 1928 to include forty-four road reconstruction projects, of which twenty-five were completed during the colonial period. See Inha Jung, *Architecture and Urbanism in Modern Korea* (University of Hawai'i Press, 2013), 11.

21. See Yŏm Pok-kyu, *Sŏul ŭi kiwŏn Kyŏngsŏng ŭi t'ansaeng: 1910–1945: Tosi kyehoek ŭro pon Kyŏngsŏng ŭi yŏksa* (Seoul: Idea, 2016), 34.

22. Gotō Yasushi, "Keijō no gairo kensetsu ni kansuru rekishiteki kenkyū," *Dobokushi kenkyū*, 13 (June 1993): 93–104.

23. Kim Ki-ho, "Namch'on: ilche kangjŏmgi tosi kyehoek kwa tosi kujo ŭi pyŏnhwa," in *Sŏul namch'on: sigan, changso, saram*, eds. Kim Ki-ho, Yang Sŭng-u, Kim Han-bae, Yun In-sŏk, Chŏn U-yong, Mok Su-hyŏn, and Ŭn Ki-su (Seoul: Sŏul sirip taehakkyo sŏurhak yŏn'guso, 2003), 3–18.

24. Chŏn U-yong, "Ilche ha Sŏul namch'on sangga ŭi hyŏngsŏng kwa pyŏnch'ŏn: Ponjŏng ŭl chungsim ŭro," in *Sŏul namch'on: sigan, changso, saram*, 206.

25. Henry, *Assimilating Seoul*.

26. Kim Paeg-yŏng, *Chibae wa konggan*, 376.

27. Gayatri Spivak explains, via Heidegger: "Since the word is inaccurate, it is crossed out. Since it is necessary, it remains legible." See Jacques Derrida, *Of Grammatology*, trans. Gayatari Chakravorty Spivak (Baltimore: Johns Hopkins University Press, 1997), xiv.

28. For Sophie Thomas, ruins "require a simultaneous or double vision whereby the building is perceived both in its ruinous state and in its formerly whole one." See Thomas, *Romanticism and Visuality: Fragments, History, Spectacle* (New York: Routledge, 2007), 51.

29. Translation by Erin Brightwell.

30. The juxtaposition of nature and ruins of stone walls and steps is reminiscent of how Georg Simmel described the ruin aesthetic as always about accommodation between nature and culture and the force of nature that results in the artificial eroding into an organic condition over time. See Georg Simmel,

"The Ruin" (1911), in *Essays on Sociology, Philosophy and Aesthetics*, ed. Kurt H. Wolff (New York: Harper & Row, 1965), 259; cited in Brian Dillon, "Introduction: A Short History of Decay," in *Ruins: Documents of Contemporary Art*, ed. Brian Dillon (Cambridge, MA: MIT Press, 2011), 13.

31. Dillon, "Introduction," 13.

32. Taylor Atkins, *Primitive Selves: Koreana in the Japanese Colonial Gaze, 1910–1945* (Berkeley: University of California Press, 2010), 14.

33. Susan Stewart, *On Longing: Narratives of the Miniature, the Gigantic, the Souvenir, the Collection* (Durham, NC: Duke University Press, 1993), 148.

34. Janet Poole, *When the Future Disappears: The Modernist Imagination in Late Colonial Korea* (New York: Columbia University Press, 2014), 53.

35. Svetlana Boym, *The Future of Nostalgia* (New York: Basic Books, 2001), 41.

36. Ibid.

37. Ibid., 10.

38. Jung, *Architecture and Urbanism*, 36.

39. *Chōsen to kenchiku* (October 1926).

40. Jung, *Architecture and Urbanism*, 38.

41. *Chōsen to kenchiku* (May 1926).

42. Jung, *Architecture and Urbanism*, 46.

43. Han'guk kŏnch'uk yŏksa hakhoe, *Han'guk kŏnch'uksa yŏn'gu 1: punya wa sidae* (Seoul: Parŏn, 2003), 420.

44. Kim Sŏng-man, "Ku-chosŏn ch'ongdokpu ch'ŏngsa ŭi konggan kwa hyŏngt'ae punsŏk e kwanhan yŏn'gu," *Taehan kŏnch'uk hakhoe nonmunjip* 13, no. 4 (1997): 53–63.

45. Sŏul yŏksa p'yŏnch'anwŏn, *Kyŏngsŏngbu kŏnch'uk tomyŏn charyojip* (Seoul: Sŏul ch'aekpang, 2018), 134.

46. *Chōsen to kenchiku* 5 (November 1926), 56; cited in Kim, "Collective Memory," 83.

47. Nishizawa Yasuhiko, "Kŏnch'uksa esŏ ch'ongdokpu: ch'ongsa ŭi wisang," *Sŏulhak yŏn'gu* 73 (November 2018), 156.

48. Pak Kil-yong, "Tae-gyŏngsŏng ŭi kŭndae kŏnch'ungmul chŏnmang," *Samch'ŏlli*, September 1935.

49. Ibid.

50. Pak's criticism extended to most other major colonial buildings. Only two buildings stood out to him: the YMCA building and the Chosŏn Hotel. Pak praised the YMCA building as having the highest aesthetic achievement and style, and the Chosŏn Hotel as a perfect, faultless building that easily adapted Renaissance style to the Asian context. See Pak Kil-yong, "Tae-gyŏngsŏng ppilding kŏnch'uk p'yŏng," *Samch'ŏlli*, October 1935.

51. Ibid.

52. Kim Paeg-yŏng, *Chibae wa konggan*, 178.

53. Kim Chin-song, *Sŏul e ttansŭhol ŭl hŏhara* (Seoul: Hyŏnsil munhwa yŏn'gu, 1999), 169.

54. Adolf Behne was one of the most prominent critics of the elaborate sur-

face of Weimar architecture, who proclaimed in 1925, "No more façade," with the goal of "architectural cleansing" and "purification of the surface." See Janet Ward, *Weimar Surfaces: Urban Visual Culture in 1920s Germany* (Berkeley: University of California Press, 2001), 47.

55. Lewis Mumford, *Sticks and Stones: A Study of American Architecture and Civilization* (New York: Boni & Liveright, 1924), 150; cited in Ward, *Weimar Surfaces*, 22.

56. Travel guides about colonial Korea, developed to aid settlers and later leisure travelers, came to share a standardized narrative by the 1920s, which exoticized Korea as old relics in contrast to the colonial monumental architecture that showed the development of Seoul under Japanese rule. See Hyung-il Pai, "Navigating Modern Keijō—The Typology of Reference Guides and City Landmarks," *Journal of Seoul Studies* 44 (August 2011): 1–39.

57. Cho Chŏng-min, "Singminji sigi sajin yŏpsŏ <Kyŏngsŏng paekkyŏng> ŭi konggan kwa sŏsa chŏllyak," *Ilbon munhwa yŏn'gu* 63 (2017): 11. For discussion of other postcard collections see Kim Sŏn-jŏng, "Kwan'gwang annaedo ro pon kŭndae tosi Kyŏngsŏng: 1920–30 nyŏndae tohae imiji rŭl chungsim ŭro," *Han'guk munhwa yŏn'gu* 33 (2017): 33–62; and Kim Sŏn-hŭi, "Sajin kŭrim yŏpsŏ rŭl t'onghae pon kŭndae Sŏul ŭi kwan'gwang imiji wa p'yosang," *Taehan chiri hakhoeji* 53, no. 4 (August 2018): 569–83.

58. Cho Chŏng-min argued that it played the role of supplementing the usual tourist experience focusing on key landmarks and that these were prefabricated images of Seoul that created the effect of proxy-experience and a sense of reality through the repetition of images; Cho, "Singminji sigi sajin yŏpsŏ," 14.

59. Ch'oe Hyŏn-sik also described it as an aesthetic and psychological system of signs and argued that it aimed to reveal Japanese superiority and Korean inferiority, which I take issue with and explore another discursive potential in architecture. See Ch'oe, "Imiji wa sigak ŭi munhwa chŏngch'ihak (I): Ilche sidae sajin yŏpsŏ ŭi yŏn'gu," *Tongbang hakchi* 175 (2016): 225–65.

60. Translation by Erin Brightwell.

61. It is believed that the song was translated into Japanese by Kim So-un. According to Ch'oe Hyŏn-sik, such textual intervention was a method through which the Japanese subject assumed and mimicked the Korean voice either by "wearing the mask of the Korean self" or by achieving solidarity with the Korean subject through the aestheticization of image and words—both of which are markers of colonial violence. See Ch'oe Hyŏn-sik, "Singmin tosi, chŏnt'ong kwa kŭndae ŭi ijung nasŏn: sajin yŏpsŏ <Kyŏngsŏng paekkyŏng> ŭl chungsim ŭro," *Hyŏndae munhak ŭi yŏn'gu* 67 (2019): 225.

62. Translation by Erin Brightwell.

63. Siegfried Kracauer, *The Mass Ornament: Weimar Essays* (Cambridge, MA: Harvard University Press, 1995), 75.

64. Kim Sŏn-jŏng, "Kwan'gwang annaedo ro," 42–43.

65. Theodore Hughes, *Literature and Film in Cold War South Korea: Freedom's Frontier* (New York: Columbia University Press, 2012), 45.

66. Kim Sŏn-jŏng, "Kwan'gwang annaedo ro."

67. Ibid.

68. Ibid., 46.

69. Drawn by Yoshida Hatsusaburō, who specialized in bird's-eye-view paintings, *Map of the Chōsen Exhibition* is one of twenty-nine maps Yoshida produced about Korea. Yoshida, the painter of this map, favored the "deformer" technique, through which a specific site is emphasized or changed, such as by using an elongated axis, to include sites that you cannot see in real life. See Kim, "Kwan'gwang annaedo ro," 54–55.

70. Kim Kye-wŏn, "P'anorama wa cheguk: kŭndae ilbon ŭi kukka p'yosang kwa p'anorama ŭi sigaksŏng," *Han'guk kŭnhyŏndae misulsahak* 19 (2008): 30–31.

71. Ibid.

72. Angela L. Miller, "The Panorama, the Cinema, and the Emergence of the Spectacular," *Wide Angle* 18, no. 2 (April 1996): 49.

73. Ibid., 46.

74. Ibid., 36.

75. Ibid., 47 and 41.

76. Ibid., 50–55.

77. Crary also noted that the limitless view was essentially a product of "the limitations of subjective vision, or the inadequacy of a human observer," which perpetuated "a pervasive fiction of adequacy." Jonathan Crary, "Géricault, the Panorama, and Sites of Reality in the Early Nineteenth Century," *Grey Room* 9 (Autumn 2002): 21.

78. Hughes, *Literature and Film*, 45.

79. Giuliana Bruno, *Atlas of Emotions: Journeys in Art, Architecture, and Film* (London: Verso, 2018), 180.

80. Ibid., 172. For Bruno, cinema emerged from "transit architecture," which also include railway, arcades, department stores, exhibition pavilions, glass houses, and winter gardens. See ibid., 16–17.

81. David Campany, ed., *The Cinematic: Documents of Contemporary Art* (Cambridge, MA: MIT Press, 2007), 13. Angela Miller, who also described the panorama as "antecedents of the cinema," found the basic characteristics of the cinema in the collapse of the temporal and the spatial—the verbal and the visual. See Miller, "The Panorama," 40–42.

82. Translation by Erin Brightwell.

83. Bruno, *Atlas of Emotions*, 196.

84. Ibid., 202.

85. Ibid., 181.

86. Bruno argued that the desire to capture a site in a panorama, which she called "site-seeing," was about changing the positioning of desire: "It effectively 'located' desire in space and articulated it as a spatial practice." Ibid., 172.

87. Ch'oe Yŏl, *Han'guk kŭndae misul ŭi yŏksa: Han'guk misulsa sajŏn 1800–1945* (P'aju: Yŏrhwadang, 2015).

Chapter 2

1. Mary Linley Taylor, *Chain of Amber* (Lewes: Book Guild, 1991), 159–62.

2. Ibid., 159.

3. Ibid., 162.

4. Ibid., 153.

5. Most missionary accounts of the March First Movement exposed the brutality of the Japanese police toward the Korean people. See, for example, *The Korean Independence Movement: Actual Photographs Showing Peaceful Demonstrations of the Koreans for Independence and Brutal Treatment Accorded Them by Japanese Soldiery* (N.p: n.p., 1919). The British missionary William Heslop, of the Oriental Missionary Society, provided a rare missionary's account of Kojong's funeral. See William Heslop, "Royal Funeral," trans. Han Sŏn-hyŏn, in *Hyŏndae kidokkyo yŏksa yŏn'guso charyo ch'ongsŏ* 5 (Seoul: Hyŏndae kidokkyo yŏksa yŏn'guso, 2003), 197–99.

6. While the few existing studies on the funeral tend to focus on the specialized topics of rites rather than assess the event in the larger historical context, there have been several exhibitions about the funeral: a pop-up photographic exhibition, *Kojong Hwangje ŭi majimak kil chŏnsi*, at Seoul Museum of History (March 3–April 9, 2017), and an exhibition to celebrate its centennial, *100 nyŏn chŏn Kojong Hwangje ŭi kukchang*, at National Palace Museum of Korea (March 1–March 31, 2019). The photo albums of Kojong's and Sunjong's funerals also have been reprinted. See Ch'oe Sun-gwŏn, ed., *Kojong kwa Sunjong ŭi kukchang sajinch'ŏp* (Seoul: Minsogwŏn, 2008).

7. Taylor's comments indicate that even long after his abdication, Kojong still yielded symbolic power for Koreans. This is also noted from the standpoint of urban planning, how only after the passing of the monarch did the physical symbol of his power become subject to erasure. After the funeral, the Tŏksu Palace was emptied out when Kojong's ritual shrine was moved to Ch'angdŏk Palace, as well as his daughters and concubines, and ownership of the palace grounds was divided. Ch'angdŏk Palace met the same fate after Sunjong's death in 1926. See Chang P'il-gu and Chŏn Pong-hŭi, "Kojong changnye kigan Sinsŏnwŏnjŏn ŭi chosŏng kwa Tŏksugung Ch'angdŏkkung kungyŏk ŭi pyŏnhwa," *Taehan kŏnch'uk hakhoe nonmunjip* 29, no. 12 (2013): 197–208.

8. Takashi Fujitani, *Splendid Monarchy: Power and Pageantry in Modern Japan* (Berkeley: University of California Press, 2006).

9. Christine Kim, "Politics and Pageantry in Protectorate Korea (1905–10): The Imperial Progresses of Sunjong," *Journal of Asian Studies* 68, no. 3 (August 2009): 835–59.

10. The funeral for Sunjong, Kojong's heir, also has photographic records such as *Junshō kokusō kinen shashinchō* (Keijō: Keijō shashin tsūshinsha, 1926) and *Gosōgi shashinchō* (Keijō: Chōsen sōtokufu, 1926). Many changes to the record keeping of Kojong's funeral were repeated for Sunjong; so this chapter focuses on the first instance when photography was introduced.

11. See, for an example of colonial Korea, Gyewon Kim, "Unpacking the Ar-

chive: Ichthyology, Photography, and the Archival Record in Japan and Korea,"
Positions 8, no. 9 (2010): 51–88.

12. *Ŭigwe* is variously translated, but I follow the translation, *Royal Protocol of the Chosŏn Dynasty,* used for the UNESCO Memory of the Word Register recommendation in 2007, which explained ŭigwe as "a unique form of documentary heritage, the 'Uigwe' is a collection of Royal Protocols of the over 500 year-long Joseon Dynasty (1392–1910), that both records and prescribes through prose and illustration the major ceremonies and rites of the royal family." The prescriptive aspect is the reason why I use this translation rather than "documents" or "records." See UNESCO, "Uigwe: The Royal Protocol of the Joseon Dynasty," Memory of the World, http://www.unesco.org/new/en/communication-and-information/memory-of-the-world/register/full-list-of-registered-heritage/registered-heritage-page-9/uigwe-the-royal-protocols-of-the-joseon-dynasty/.

13. JaHyun Kim Haboush, "Constructing the Center: The Ritual Controversy and the Search for a New Identity in Seventeenth-Century Korea," in *Culture and the State in Late Chosŏn Korea,* eds. JaHyun Kim Haboush and Martina Deuchler (Cambridge, MA: Harvard University Asia Center, 1999), 49.

14. There is a discrepancy between *sillok* and his funerary ŭigwe in dating Kojong's death. *Kojong T'aehwangje Sillok* (vol. 1, p. 4, register a) says Kojong died on January 21 in Hamnyŏngjŏn in Tŏksu Palace. I follow the date in *Kojong T'aehwangje Sillok,* which is conventionally accepted as the date of his death.

15. The changes in the name from *togam* to *chugam* reflects the status change of the king, because Kojong became emperor of Korea during the Taehan Empire (1897–1910).

16. Kim Yi-sun, *Taehan cheguk hwangje rŭng* (Seoul: Sowadang, 2010), 63–64.

17. See Yi Chi-su and Yi Kyŏng-mi, "Maeil sinbo rŭl t'onghae pon ilche kangjŏmgi sangbok ŭi kŭndaehwa yŏn'gu—1910 nyŏndae kukka changnyesik ŭl chungsim ŭro," *Han'guk poksik hakhoe* 70, no. 3 (June 2020): 148–66. Pak Kye-ri also noted that Kojong's funerary procession featured black mourning garments instead of the traditional pre–Taehan Empire red garments. See Pak Kye-ri, "Ihwa yŏja taehakkyo pangmulgwan sojang <Myŏngsŏng Hwanghu parin panch'ado> yŏn'gu," *Misulsa nondan,* no. 35 (December 2012): 91–115.

18. Changes to royal rites were not new in 1919, and Japan had already attempted to reduce the king's symbolic power by regulating state rites since the Kabo reform of 1894. See Yi Uk, "Kŭndae kukka ŭi mosaek kwa kukka ŭirye ŭi pyŏnhwa: 1894–1908 nyŏn kukka chesa ŭi pyŏnhwa rŭl chungsim ŭro," *Chŏngsin munhwa yŏn'gu* 27, no. 2 (2004): 59–94.

19. The art historian Pak Kye-ri has noted how the route change transformed the concept of death and the fundamentals of Chosŏn funerary rites by symbolically separating the body from its spirit. See Pak Kye-ri, "'Myŏngsŏng Hwanghu parin panch'ado wa parin haengnyŏng," *Misulsa hakbo* (2016): 20.

20. The origin of the word *ŭigwe* combines the roots *ŭi* 儀 (ritual) and *kwe* 軌 (standard; examples of ways of doing things). The word *ŭigwe* was used to refer to the rules for monks in Buddhist rituals, but the founders of the Chosŏn dy-

nasty used the term to write rules and protocols for Neo-Confucian rituals for the new dynasty. See Sin Myŏng-ho, "Chosŏn ch'ogi ŭigwe p'yŏnch'an ŭi paegyŏng kwa ŭiŭi," *Chosŏn sidaesa hakpo* 59 (December 2011): 5–53.

21. Yi Sŏng-mi, *Wangsil karye togam ŭigwe wa misulsa* (Sowadang, 2008), 218.

22. For one, many panch'ado participants were wearing modernized attire and carrying swords. Other examples showed the adoption of customs from the Chinese imperial court and items that had not been used in previous weddings. This was the first ŭigwe where the palanquin (*yŏn*) was replaced with a phoenix palanquin (*ponggyo*), with the golden phoenix on the top and bird ornaments at the four corners. This ŭigwe also included the surname of the mother of the bride for the first time, following Chinese imperial custom, as a way to claim Korea's status as an empire equal to China by appropriating customs once exclusively reserved for the imperial family in China. Ibid., 236–37.

23. Ibid., 347–38.

24. See Pak Chŏng-hye, "Changsŏgak sojang ilche kangjŏmgi ŭigwe ŭi misulsa chŏk yŏn'gu," *Misulsa yŏn'gu* 259 (2008): 117–50.

25. Another *ŭigwe, Kojong T'aehwangje Myŏngsŏng T'aehwanghu pumyo chugam ŭigwe* (Ritual Manual for the Ancestral Tablet for Emperor Kojong and Empress Myŏngsŏng) was published in 1921.

26. See Che Song-hŭi, "19-segi chŏnban ŭigwe panch'ado ŭi sin kyŏnghyang," *Misul sahak yŏn'gu* 288 (2015): 89–120.

27. *Maeil sinbo*, January 24 and 26, 1919.

28. *Maeil sinbo*, February 3, 1919.

29. Yi Ji-su and Yi Kyŏng-mi, "Maeil sinbo," 159.

30. *Maeil sinbo*, March 2, 1919.

31. One exception is a famous photograph of Cho Tong-yun following Ito Hirokuni in Japanese attire for the *hōkokusai* ritual on February 10.

32. *Maeil sinbo*, January 21, 1920.

33. *Maeil sinbo*, March 4, 1919.

34. Ibid.

35. The films are: *Kojong insan silgyŏng* and *Kyŏngsŏng kyooe chŏn'gyŏng*, both of which were produced by Tansŏngsa in 1919. Although neither film survives, there exists a twelve-minute-long film about Sunjong's funeral, *Junshō kōtai insan shūyi* (1926, 35mm), which was remastered in 1958.

36. Jean Baudrillard, *Simulacra and Simulation* (Ann Arbor: University of Michigan Press, 2004), 48.

37. Roland Barthes, *Camera Lucida: Reflections on Photography* (New York: Hill and Wang, 1980), 4.

38. This commemorative album was possibly published following the footsteps of the photo album of the funeral of the Meiji Emperor. See Ogawa Kazumasa, *Meiji tennō gotaisō shashinchō* (Tokyo: n.p, 1912). Unlike the *Tŏksu Album*, the photo album of the Meiji Emperor tends to focus exclusively on the funeral itself. There are also other photo albums for Kojong's funeral, but they were not collectibles available for sale and thus lack the kind of editorial intervention

seen in the *Tŏksu Album*. For instance, *Ri taiō denka sōgi shashinchō*, in care of the Seoul National University Museum, shows multiple photographs of the same scene with no effort to edit them. The Keijō Newspaper Company also published for Sunjong's funeral, *Sunjong kukchang nok* (Keijō: Chōsen Hakubunsha, 1926), which is not a photo album but a record that included over 75 pages of photographs along with over 220 pages of text; the choice of language also differed in this one, using the Korean mixed script. For more on this, see Yun Chong-sŏn, "<Sunjong kukchangnok> yŏn'gu," *Journal of Korean Culture* 51 (2020): 221–54.

39. See, for example, the advertisement in *Maeil sinbo* on March 10, 1919. The intended readers were not Japanese only. The *kanbun* text in the introduction was also accessible to Korean literati, and Japanese-language photo captions included Korean translations of prepositions and conjugated verbs written in *hiragana*, as well as some detailed translations of phrases in Korean-mixed script, obviously intended for Korean readers.

40. Yi Hyŏn-jong, *Taehan cheguk Kojong Hwangje kukchang hwach'ŏp* (Seoul: Chimun'gak, 1975).

41. In her study of the Meiji emperor's imperial progress from 1872 to 1886, Gyewon Kim argued that the photographs replicated the imperial gaze in appearing to be taken from the perspective of the emperor himself. This gaze, I argue though, could not have been replicated for the dead king; any power he had was ceded to the camera-eye of the invisible photographer. See Gyewon Kim, "Tracing the Emperor: Photography, Famous Places, and the Imperial Progresses in Prewar Japan," *Representations* 120, no. 1 (Fall 2012): 115–50.

42. Although Barthes spoke of newspaper photographs in general as unary for transforming reality without the power to disturb or wound, I find that punctum in Taylor's photographs despite his profession as journalist. Barthes, *Camera Lucida*, 47.

43. Siegfried Kracauer described this as "partly patterned, partly amorphous—a consequence, in both cases, of the half-cooked state of our everyday world." "A genuine photograph," then, "precludes the notion of completeness" and "points beyond that frame, referring to a multitude of real-life phenomena which cannot possibly be encompassed in their entirety." Kracauer, *History: The Last Things before the Last* (Princeton, NJ: Markus Wiener Publishers, 1995), 58–9.

44. A different example of how readers' engagement worked is seen in another piece of memorabilia, *The Grand Ritual of the Great King Yi's State Funeral* (Ri taiō denka kokusō seigi), which shows a collage view of fourteen photographs. In this, any narrative born of the collector's engagement with the photos would have been composed by nonlinear association and connections to the photographs. Another postcard collection, *Ko Ri taiō tenka go sōgi kōkei e hagaki* similarly allowed subjective narrative formation, although this collection only includes images of the funeral procession. In other cases, a single image had to create meaning and narrative on its own. For example, the cover of the Italian newspaper *La Domenica del Corriere* published an image on June 1, 1919, of

horse figurines used in the funerary procession, for which the caption described the king, his reign, and his funeral in detail.

45. Siegfried Kracauer, "Photography," in *The Mass Ornament: Weimar Essays*, ed. Thomas Y. Levin (Cambridge, MA: Harvard University Press, 1995), 49.

46. Susan Sontag, *On Photography* (London: Penguin Books, 1979), 23.

Chapter 3

1. "Sangt'ujaengi kanp'an," *Tonga ilbo*, March 28, 1929.

2. Although this study focuses on signage as signposts added to architecture, there was specific architecture built for the purpose of advertisement during this time called "billboard architecture." For more information, see Kim Pyŏng-ju and Sŏk Kang-hŭi, "Ilche kangjŏmgi kanp'an kŏnch'uk e kwanhan yŏn'gu," *Han'guk munhwa konggan kŏnch'uk hakhoe nonmunjip* 66 (May 2019): 189–99.

3. Chōsen Shōtokufu, *Chōsenjin no shōgyō* (1929), cited in Kwak Myŏng-hŭi, "Ilche kangjŏmgi kanp'an munhwa ŭi t'ŭkching e kwanhan yŏn'gu," in *Ogwoe k'wanggohak yŏn'gu* 1, no. 1 (February 2004): 10.

4. Ibid., 17.

5. O Chu-ŭn, "Ilche kangjŏmgi kanp'an tijain ŭi sigaksŏng," *Archives of Design Research* 30, no. 2 (May 2017): 192.

6. Ibid., 186–91.

7. Henrik Reeh, *Ornaments of the Metropolis: Siegfried Kracauer and Modern Urban Culture* (Cambridge, MA: MIT Press, 2006), 5. Jacques Derrida also spoke of ornament in terms of a supplemental structure that is not exclusively tied to architecture, and he included anything added to a structure, such as title, preface, metaphor, and signature. However, that ornament is supplementary does not make it secondary. Mark Wigley, *The Architecture of Deconstruction: Derrida's Haunt* (Cambridge, MA: MIT Press, 1995), 84.

8. Roland Barthes, *Travels in China* (Cambridge, MA: Polity, 2013).

9. Derrida, *Of Grammatology*, 90.

10. Michel Foucault, *Order of Things: An Archaeology of the Human Science* (New York: Vintage, 1994), xv.

11. Ibid., xvi.

12. Ibid., xix.

13. Longxi Zhang, "The Myth of the Other: China in the Eyes of the West," *Critical Inquiry* 15, no. 1 (Autumn 1988): 111.

14. See Elizabeth Kaske, *The Politics of Language in Chinese Education: 1895–1919* (Boston: Brill, 2008).

15. Lu, *Silent China: Selected Writings of Lu Xun*, ed. Gladys Yang (London: Oxford University Press, 1973), 163–64.

16. Ibid., 167.

17. Nobukuni Koyasu, "Kŭndae ilbon ŭi hanja wa chagugŏ insik," in *Hŭndŭllinŭn ŏnŏdŭl: ŏnŏ ŭi kŭndae wa kungmin kukka*, ed. Im Hyŏng-t'aek, Han Ki-hyŏng, Ryu Chun-p'il, and Yi Hye-ryŏng. (Seoul: Sŏnggyun'gwan taehakkyo taedong munhwa yŏn'guwŏn, 2008), 43–58.

18. "Kungmullon," *Tongnip sinmun*, April 22, 1877. See also Ko Yŏng-jin, Kim Pyŏng-mun, Cho T'ae-rin, Kim Ha-su, and Im Kyŏng-hwa, eds., *Singminji sigi chŏnhu ŭi ŏnŏ munje* (Seoul: Somyŏng ch'ulp'an, 2012).

19. "Hanja ŭm ssŭnŭn pŏp ŭi illyŏl," *Tonggwang*, January 1927.

20. Pak Chin-su, "Hanja munhwa wa kŭndae tong-asia ŭi ŏnŏ: ŏnŏ minjok-chuŭi rŭl nŏmŏsŏ," *Asia munhwa yŏn'gu* 11 (December 2006): 36.

21. Yŏ Hŭi-jŏng, "Ilche kangjŏmgi chŏnt'ong chisigin ŭi ijung ŏnŏ kŭlssŭgi: kukhakcha Chŏng In-bo ŭi han'gŭl kŭlssŭgi wa hanmun kŭlssŭgi ŭi kwan'gye rŭl chungsim ŭro," *Chŏngsin munhwa yŏn'gu* 38 no. 3 (September 2015): 180, 185. Hwang Ho-dŏk's study presented an in-depth look at the discourses on national language in modern Korea, particularly interesting in regard to treaties and travelogues. See Hwang Ho-dŏk, *Kŭndae neisyŏn kwa kŭ p'yosang dŭl* (Seoul: Somyŏng ch'ulp'an, 2005). For more studies about language and literature, see Kwŏn Bodŭrae, "1910 nyŏndae ŭi ijungŏ sanghwang kwa munhak ŏnŏ," *Han'gugŏ munhak yŏn'gu*, 54 (2010): 5–43. For a study about the use of *hanmun* and mixed script in newspapers, see Ch'oe Yŏng-ch'ŏl and Hŏ Chae-yŏng, "Kaehang ihu hakche toip ijŏn kkaji ŭi han'guk kŭndae hangmullon kwa ŏmun munje: <Hansŏng sunbo> wa <Hansŏng jubo> rŭl chungsim ŭro," *Inmun kwahak yŏn'gu* 40 (March 2014): 181–207.

22. Yŏ Hŭi-jŏng, "Ilche kangjŏmgi chŏnt'ong," 185.

23. Ha Yŏng-sam, *Hanja wa ek'ŭrit'wirŭ* (Seoul: Ak'anet, 2001), 19.

24. Ibid.

25. Bergson called this "the survival of the past," where accumulating memory is preserved. This notion of memory should be differentiated from the kind of reflective and recollective memory discussed in part 1 of this book. Bergson argued: "Memory . . . is not a faculty of putting away recollections in a drawer or of inscribing them in a register. There is no register, no drawer; there is not even, properly speaking, a faculty, for a faculty works intermittently, when it will or when it can, whilst the piling up of the past upon the past goes on without relaxation." Henri Bergson, *Creative Evolution* (Mineola, NY: Dover Publications, 1998), 4–5.

26. Homi Bhabha, "Dissemination," in *Nation and Narration* (London; New York: Routledge, 1990), 297.

27. See for example, Chŏn U-yong, "Chongno wa Ponjŏng," 163–193. Through a close reading of Ch'ae Man-sik's *"Chongno ŭi chumin,"* Hwang Ho-dŏk also argued for the colonizing process through the linguistic policy that forcibly assimilated Koreans through the national language (*kuk'ŏ*)—Japanese. In this bilingual space that privileged Japanese over Korean, Honmachi is considered a space of travel and Chongno a space of residence. See Hwang Ho-dŏk, "Kyŏngsŏng chiriji, ijung ŏnŏ ŭi changsoron—Ch'ae Man-sik ŭi 'Chongno ŭi chumin' kwa singmin tosi ŭi (ŏnŏ) kamgak," *Taedong munhwa yŏn'gu* 51 (2005): 107–41. Yi Hwa-jin also discussed bilingual (*ijung ŏnŏ*) spaces in Seoul along ethnic lines (*tongjogŏ konggan*) and argued that bilingual performance gradually gave way to the rigid boundary between Korean and Japanese in theaters. See Yi Hwa-

jin, *Sori ŭi chŏngch'i: Singminji Chosŏn ŭi kŭkchang kwa cheguk ŭi kwan'gaek* (Seoul: Hyŏnsil munhwa, 2016).

28. Neon signs in Seoul became immensely popular in the 1930s. See Kang Chun-man, "Han'guk kanp'an munhwa ŭi yŏksa: wae Han'gugin ŭn kanp'an e moksum ŭl kŏnŭn'ga?" *Inmul kwa sasang* 117 (January 2008): 154–204. See also the three installments of articles called "Syowindo yong kwanggo kigu" in *Tonga ilbo* about how to DIY manufacture mechanical signage, including a neon sign, on May 20, 25, and 29, 1938.

29. The difference between writing and lettering may not be all that distinguishable for most observers, because many letterforms and typefaces incorporated and imitated handwriting styles. Even though typography was mechanized and some typefaces used simpler, geometric shapes, hand-drawn letterform and calligraphy continued to be popular, as many typefaces simulated and stylized the rhythm and motion of brushstrokes. Gennifer Weisenfeld has noted, for instance, how early typefaces in Japan were based on hand-drawn lettering and purposefully emulated calligraphic forms of the past for aesthetic reasons. See Gennifer Weisenfeld, "Japanese Typographic Design and the Art of Letterforms," in *Bridges to Heaven: Essays on East Asian Art in Honor of Professor Wen C. Fong*, eds. Jerome Silbergeld, Dora C. Y. Ching, Judith G. Smith, and Alfreda Murck (Princeton: P. Y. and Kinmay W. Tang Center for East Asian Art, Department of Art and Archaeology, Princeton University, in association with Princeton University Press, 2011), 836–37.

30. Gerrit Noordzij, *The Stroke: Theory of Writing* (London: Hyphen Press, 2009), 39.

31. Ibid., 9.

32. Henri Michaux, *Ideograms in China*, trans. Gustaf Sobin (Cambridge: New Directions, 2002).

33. Weisenfeld, "Japanese Typographic Design," 840.

34. "Kyŏngsŏng kak sangjŏm kanp'an p'ump'yŏnghoe," *Pyŏlgŏn'gon*, January 1927.

35. An Sŏk-chu was the real name of An Sŏk-yŏng, a famed cartoonist of the time.

36. "Kyŏngsŏng kak sangjŏm." Kwangmudae was a theater established in 1912 by Pak Sŭng-p'il and other Korean entrepreneurs that by the 1920s specialized in traditional theater.

37. Although Stewart's topic is a craft-form miniature that provokes nostalgia, the metonymic impulse that refers to the context outside of the text and refuses the production of subjectivity through narrativity is also important in understanding the signage in Seoul. Susan Stewart, *On Longing: Narratives of the Miniature, the Gigantic, the Souvenir, the Collection* (Durham, NC: Duke University Press, 1993), 45.

38. Charles Sanders Peirce, *Collected Paper of Charles Sanders Peirce*, ed. Charles Hartshorne and Paul Weiss, (Cambridge, MA: Harvard University Press, 1932), 3:361.

39. Ibid.

40. *Pyŏlgŏn'gon*, January 1927.

41. Miyako Inoue, "Things That Speak: Peirce, Benjamin, and the Kinesthetics of Commodity Advertisement in Japanese Women's Magazines, 1900 to the 1930s," *Positions* 15, no. 3 (Winter 2007): 512.

42. Ibid., 544.

43. Ibid.

44. Ibid.

45. Although Inoue is referring to the naturalization of an unequal relationship for women's speech in Japan by the memory of a politically and culturally constructed past, I use the notion of time lag in the vernacular space of signage differently. See Miyako Inoue, "What Does Language Remember? Indexical Inversion and the Naturalized History of Japanese Women," *Journal of Linguistic Anthropology* 14, no. 1 (2004): 39.

Chapter 4

1. *Maeil sinbo*, January 3, 1935.

2. A Korean ironing stone was a fulling block on which a garment was placed and beaten by two wooden sticks to dewrinkle it.

3. The sales number is an estimate from an advertisement of this album in *Chosŏn ilbo* on February 21, 1933. This number has been re-estimated as a total sales number of Okeh records by some scholars. See, for instance, Yi Sŭng-hŭi, "Paeu Sin Pul-ch'ul, usŭm ŭi chŏngch'i," *Han'guk kŭgyesul yŏn'gu* 33 (2011): 29–30. Its popularity led it to be released by another label, Chieron, in 1933, and it became the biggest seller among Chieron records, selling over 10,000. (Sin Pul-ch'ul and Kim Yŏn-sil, *Iksal majŭn taemŏri* [*kongsan myŏngwŏl*] Chieron 79-A). This led to the rerelease of the Okeh recording with Yun Paek-nam in 1936 under a different title, Sin Pul-ch'ul and Kim Yŏn-sil, *Taemŏri* (*Kongsan myŏngwŏl*) (Korai, 1051 A/B). See U Su-jin, "Chaedam kwa mandam, 'Pi-ŭimi' wa 'Chinsil' ŭi hyŏngsik: Pak Ch'un-jae wa Sin Pul-ch'ul ŭl chungsim ŭro," *Han'guk yŏn'gŭkhak* 1, no. 64 (2017): 29.

4. Pae Yŏn-hyŏng. *Han'guk yusŏnggi ŭmban munhwasa* (Seoul: Chisŏngsa, 2019), 337.

5. This number is an estimate by Pae, ibid., 571. Of over two hundred stores countrywide, fifty-one were located in Seoul. For a full list of gramophone record stores in Korea, see ibid., 558–62.

6. Ibid., 569.

7. Up until this point, censorship mainly applied to the print media and film. This is relatively late given the popularity of gramophone recordings since the late 1920s, creating a vacuum from state control and interference during the period of the initial expansion. Unlike the censorship of print media, which had to get the approval of the censorship bureau before publication, censorship of recording mainly targeted consumption and distribution after the release. See Yi Chun-hŭi, "Ilche sidae ŭmban kŏmyŏl," in *Singminji kŏmyŏl: chedo, t'eksŭt'ŭ, silch'ŏn*, ed. *Kŏmyŏl yŏn'guhoe* (Seoul: Somyŏng ch'ulp'an, 2011), 450–51.

8. An article in *Samch'ŏlli* in 1936 provided a list of all the records that were censored between 1933 and 1936. According to it, forty-five recordings were censored for the offense against public decency and forty-four recordings for the interference with public order. See "Ŏttŏhan rek'odŭ ka kŏmyŏl ŭl tanghana," *Samch'ŏlli*, April, 1936.

9. Pan Chae-sik, ed., *Mandam paengnyŏnsa* (Seoul: Paekchungdang, 2000), 205.

10. Ibid., 67.

11. Sin became a central member of the Alliance of Literature and Art in North Korea in 1957 and founded a research institute of mandam named after himself in 1961. Ŏm Hyŏn-sŏp, "Sin Pul-ch'ul taejung munyeron yŏn'gu," *Comparative Korean Studies* 17, no. 3 (2009): 315–48.

12. A reporter for *Samch'ŏlli* explained in the following way: "My first impression about Sin Pul-ch'ul's mandam is that it is something that can only be expressed by speaking, not by writing. If we try to express mandam in the format of manmun, it is not only impossible, but it will also seem like it merely imitated one aspect of it. Mandam is a separate entity with its own unique beauty." "Sin Pul-ch'ul ssi mandam pangch'ŏnggi: Kwandaehan namp'yŏn," *Samch'ŏlli*, August 1935.

13. "Ungbyŏn kwa mandam," *Samch'ŏlli*, June 1935.

14. Ibid.

15. Ibid.

16. Ibid.

17. "Mandam ŏnŏ anin ŏnŏ," *Samch'ŏlli*, November 1935.

18. *Chung'ang*, February 1934 cited in Pan, *Mandam paengnyŏnsa*, 115.

19. "Pom kwa rek'odŭ" in *Pyolgŏn'gon*, April 1934; *Tonggwang*, October 1932, cited in Pan, *Mandam paengnyŏnsa*, 114.

20. *Chosŏn chungang ilbo*, May 11, 1934 cited in Pan, *Mandam paengnyŏnsa*, 187.

21. Ibid.

22. Ibid.

23. "Ungbyŏn kwa mandam"

24. Rudolf Mrázek, *Engineers of Happy Land: Technology and Nationalism in a Colony* (Princeton, NJ: Princeton University Press, 2002), xviii.

25. "Ungbyŏn kwa mandam."

26. "Mandam ŏnŏ anin ŏnŏ."

27. Sin Pul-ch'ul (performer), "Ŏngt'ŏri yŏnsŏl," recorded on May 5,1937, Victor KJ1107A, shellac record, 1937.

28. Kang Nae-hŭi, "Mimicry and Difference: A Spectralogy for the Neo-Colonial Intellectual," *Traces* 1 (2000): 151. Sin's mandam, "Laugh and Let Blessing Come" (Somun manbongnae) for instance, deployed this idea of coming belatedly to mock the one who proceeded one by featuring a father-in-law and a son-in-law who repeated what the father-in-law said verbatim, which in the end caused confusion in the identities of the two. See Sin Pul-ch'ul (performer),

"Somun manbongnae," with Na P'um-sim, Sin Il-sŏn, and Sŏng Kwang-hyŏn, Okeh 1611 A/B, shellac record, 1933.

29. Sin Pul-ch'ul (performer), "Yojŏl Simch'ŏngjŏn," with Sŏng Kwang-hyŏn, Okeh 1634-AB, shellac record, 1934. Another mandam, "The Dog-Shit Grandmother," in which the grandmother is searching for a son-in-law who excels in language play, presented many examples of homonyms written in different hanja, such as *pangmun* (a visit; a door), *chido* (to teach; a map), *chŏldo* (to rob; a broken knife), *tangsŏn* (to be elected; a Tang-style fan), *susang* (suspicious; water merchant), and *yanghae* (to be forgiving; a western sea). Sin Pul-ch'ul (performer), "Kaettong halmŏni," with Kim Chin-mun, Okeh 1701 AB, Shellac record, 1934.

30. Sin Pul-ch'ul (performer), "Kyŏnmal yŏlssoet'ong," with Sin Ŭn-bong, Chieron 83-B, shellac record, 1933.

31. In the very beginning of the recording, the modern boy described his financial condition as *puch'ae puch'ae*. *Puch'ae* is a hanja word meaning "bankruptcy" but also has a homonym that means "fan" in Korean. By repeating the word, he invoked a gesture of waving a fan and commented on his financial trouble through a doubling remark on the weather. Other examples of metaphorization through visualization followed this remark: an unchanging situation is described as *pulbyŏn saek* (unchanging color) and *sup'yŏngsŏn* (the horizon).

32. "Kŭl ŏpnŭn Chongno manhwa," *Yŏsŏng* (September 1938).

33. Arthur Rimbaud, "Delirium II: Alchemy of the Word," in *A Season in Hell and Illuminations*, trans. Bertrand Mathieu (Rochester: BOA Editions, 1991), 33–35.

34. Inez Hedges, "Surrealist Metaphor: Frame Theory and Componential Analysis," *Poetics Today* 4, no. 2 (1983): 275.

35. For Anna Balakian, "Metaphor and Metamorphosis in Andre Breton's Poetics," *French Studies* 19, no. 1 (1965): 36.

36. "Kaettong halmŏni," Okeh 1701 AB.

37. Sin Pul-ch'ul (performer), "Chŏnjang ŭi paekhaphwa," with Sin Ŭn-bong, Chieron 83-A, shellac record, 1933. This recording became subject to censorship for taking the Sino-Japanese War as its subject. See Yi Chun-hŭi, "Ilche sidae ŭmban kŏmyŏl," 478.

38. Sin Pul-ch'ul, "Kŏjŭnmal," *Samch'ŏlli*, June, 1936.

39. G.W. F.Hegel, *Phenomenology of Spirit*, trans. A. V. Miller (Oxford: Oxford University Press, 1977).

40. Sin Pul-ch'ul (performer), "Iksalmajŭn taemŏri," with Yun Paek-dam, Okeh 1518-A, shellac record, 1933.

41. This visual language play is also seen in the sequel to this piece, "Pockmark-Face Melody," which similarly makes fun of an old man at the shop for his face's resemblance to a checkerboard, brick wall, bullet hole, and so forth. See Sin Pul-ch'ul (performer), "Kombo t'aryŏng," with Sin Ŭn-bong, Okeh 1585A, shellac record, 1933. Ch'ŏn Chŏng-hwan explained how "The Funny Bald Man" was a self-satire, which in turn made him the fiercest defender of his body from attack.

See Ch'ŏn Chŏng-hwan, "Singminji Chosŏnin ŭi usŭm: <Samch'ŏlli> sojae sohwa wa Sin Pul-ch'ul mandam ŭi yŏngu," Yŏksa wa munhwa 18 (September 2009): 7–38.

42. José Gil, Metamorphosis of the Body (Minneapolis: University of Minnesota Press, 1998), 144.

43. Ibid.

44. Yi Sŭng-hŭi explained the success of "The Funny Bald Man" in terms of its economized narrative structure and utilization of sound making it effective for the medium of gramophone. Yi Sŭng-hŭi, "Paeu Sin Pul-ch'ul."

45. Hwang Chae-gyŏng (performer), "Yŏldugaji usŭm," Columbia 40699-A, shellac record, 1936. René Descartes also explained laughter as a physiological phenomenon that involves a complicated process of the interruption of breath that creates an explosion of sound. See René Descartes, The Passions of the Soul, trans. Stephen Voss (Indianapolis: Hackett, 1989) cited in Simon Critchley, On Humor (London: Routledge, 2002), 8.

46. Sin Pul-ch'ul (performer), "Irŏk'e usŏra," with Kim Chin-mun, Okeh 1691 A, shellac record.

47. Mikhail Bakhtin, Rabelais and His World, trans. Helene Iswolsky (Indianapolis: Indiana University Press, 1984), 26.

48. Ibid., 8 and 10.

49. R. Murray Schafer, The Soundscape: Our Sonic Environment and the Tuning of the World (Rochester, NY: Destiny Books, 1993), 90–91.

50. Walter Ong, Orality and Literacy: The Technologizing of the Word, ed. Terence Hawkes. New Accent (New York: Methuen, 1988).

51. "Paekhwajŏm pom p'unggyŏng sagyŏng," Chogwang, April 1938.

52. Deception was how the seductive power of commodity operated, evident in another story of the same trope of the old man touring the department store that fittingly added the word for "lies" as an adjective to the department store, as "the fake (kŏjinmal) department store." See "Kŏjŭnmal ŭi tep'at'ŭment'ŭ," Chogwang, October, 1936.

53. Critchley, On Humor, 17.

54. According to Walter Ong, the sense of hearing is privileged over seeing because of its evanescence: "Sound is more real or existential than other sense objects, despite the fact that it is also more evanescent. Sound itself is related to present actuality rather than to past or future; sounds exist only as they go out of existence." Walter Ong, Presence of the Word: Some Prolegomena for Cultural and Religious History, 2nd ed. (Binghamton, NY: Global Publications, Binghamton University, 2000), 111.

55. Walter Benjamin, "Theses on the Philosophy of History," in Illuminations, ed. Hannah Arendt, 253–64 (New York: Schocken Books, 1969).

56. The censored album is Sŏul kugyŏng (Okeh 1519A). It reappeared in Okeh 1527 A, and later a sequel to this was released in Sinjak Sŏul kugyŏng by Sin Pul-ch'ul and Kim Hyo-san (Okeh 1773 A/B). For more information about Sin's trouble with censorship, see Im T'ae-hun, "Unnŭn mandam rek'odŭ wa haep'ŭning

ŭi midiŏ: Sin Pulch'ul ŭi <Iksalmajin taemŏri> (1933) e kwanhayŏ," *Inmunhak yŏn'gu* 59 (2020): 427–58.

57. Some examples about the old man from the countryside found in magazines are "Sŏul kugyŏng on noin," *Tonggwang*, January 1932, and "Sigol ajŏssi ŭi Sŏul kugyŏng," *Pyŏlgŏn'gon*, July 1932.

58. Kim Sŏng-un (performer), "Mŏngt'ŏngguri Sŏul yŏhaeng," with Sim Yŏng, Kim Sŏn-ch'o, and Kim Sŏn-yŏng, Columbia 40458 AB, shellac record, 1933. Other recordings about touring Seoul include "Sŭigolttŭgi utchimaso" (Regal C195) and "Sikchauhwa" (Regal C 195 B).

59. Kim Sŏng-un (performer), "Mŏngt'ŏngguri tongmurwŏn kugyŏng," with Sŏk Kŭm-sŏng, Regal C330, shellac record, 1936.

Chapter 5

1. "Kija ch'ong ch'uldong Kyŏngsŏng paekchu amhaenggi cheirhoe <ilssigan sahoe t'ambang>," *Pyŏlgŏn'gon*, December 1926.

2. Ibid.

3. Ibid.

4. I translate *ch'wimi chapchi* as "leisure magazines." *Ch'wimi* usually means hobby, taste, or interest. According to Ch'ŏn Chŏng-hwan and Yi Yong-nam, *ch'wimi* was a neologism that was likely introduced by Japan, and the usage usually indicated whether or not one had *ch'wimi* rather than what one's particular *ch'wimi* was. The term has a close relationship with how modern life was divided into labor and leisure, so I translate it to underscore the cultivated aspect of life that stands apart from labor and to distinguish it from reading matters for mere entertainment. See Ch'ŏn Chŏng-hwan and Yi Yong-nam, "Kŭndae chŏk taejung munhwa ŭi paljŏn kwa ch'wimi," *Minjon munhaksa yŏn'gu*, 30 (2006): 227–65.

5. "Kaebyŏksa yaksa," *Pyŏlgŏn'gon*, July 1930.

6. Although *Pyŏlgŏn'gon* attempted to acclimatize to the changing landscape of publishing in the 1930s and to compete with full-fledged popular magazines like *Hyesŏng* (It rebranded itself as a "5-chŏn magazine" in 1931, then closed in 1934), it was still best known as the leisure magazine that marked the beginning of a shift toward the masses.

7. For this reason, Kim Ye-rim argued that *Pyŏlgŏn'gon*, as in the reading culture of the mid- to late 1920s, was primarily created for consumer-readers. Kim Ye-rim, *1930 nyŏndae huban kŭndae insik ŭi t'ŭl kwa miŭisik* (Seoul: Somyŏng ch'ulp'an, 2004), 265–66. For studies that explored the reading culture of this time through the lens of childhood and gender, see Dafna Zur, *Figuring Korean Futures: Children's Literature in Modern Korea* (Stanford, CA: Stanford University Press, 2017) and Ji-Eun Lee, *Women: Pre-scripted: Forging Modern Roles through Korean Print* (Honolulu: University of Hawai'i Press, 2015).

8. The overall number of publication increased from 522 in 1919 to 1,272 in 1925, but the majority of publications during this time consisted of old tales (*ku sosŏl*) and family registers (*chokpo*). See Chŏng Kŭn-sik and Ch'oe Kyŏng-hŭi, "Tosŏgwa ŭi sŏlch'i wa ilche singminji ch'ulp'an kyŏngch'al ŭi ch'egyehwa,

1926–1929," in *Singminji kŏmyŏl: chedo, t'eksŭt'ŭ, silch'ŏn*, ed. *Kŏmyŏl yŏn'guhoe* (Seoul: Somyŏng ch'ulp'an, 2012), 64–136.

9. After the closure of *Kaebyŏk*, much of the socialism-related topics were published by *Chosŏn chi kwang*. For further information about this magazine and the effect of censorship, see Han Ki-hyŏng, "Singminji kŏmyŏl chŏngch'aek kwa sahoejuŭi kwallyŏn chapchi ŭi chŏngch'i yŏkhal," *Singminji kŏmyŏl: chedo, t'eksŭt'ŭ, silch'ŏn*, ed. *Kŏmyŏl yŏn'guhoe* (Seoul: Somyŏng ch'ulp'an, 2012), 168–99.

10. When newspapers and general magazines had to follow censorship regulations for newspapers, other magazines could be regulated by general publication laws; *Pyŏlgŏn'gon* was published under the general publication law for its content focusing on lifestyle and leisure, absent of social or political commentary. Kim Chillyang, "Kŭndae chapchi <Pyŏlgŏn'gon> ŭi 'ch'wimi tamnon' kwa kŭlssŭgi ŭi t'ŭksŏng," *Ŏmunhak* (June 2005), 339. For a discussion of censorship of *Pyŏlgŏn'gon*, see Kim To-gyŏng, "Singminji kŏmyŏl kwa taejung chapchi *Pyŏlgŏn'gon* ŭi puronsŏng," *Ŏmunhak* 130 (December 2005): 111–32.

11. Ch'ŏn and Yi, "Kŭndae chŏk taejung," 251.

12. Yi Kyŏng-don, "*Pyŏlgŏn'gon* kwa kŭndae ch'wimi tongmul," *Taedong munhwa yŏn'gu* 46, (2004): 258.

13. "Pin ch'wimi jŭng mansŏng ŭi Chosŏnin" *Pyŏlgŏn'gon*, November 1926.

14. Ibid.

15. Ibid.

16. Roughly translated as "fairy land," it is synonymous with *pyŏlch'ŏnji* or *pyŏlsegye*.

17. Yi, "*Pyŏlgŏn'gon* kwa kŭndae," 259.

18. Ibid., 260–61.

19. Chŏn Ŭn-gyŏng, "'Ssŭinŭn t'eksŭt'ŭ rosŏ ŭi *Pyŏlgŏn'gon* kwa taejung munhak tokcha ŭi hyŏngsŏng," *Hakhoe ŏmunhak* 125 (September 2014): 389–435. For more on the reportage genre in general, see Sunyoung Park, "A Forgotten Aesthetic: Reportage in Colonial Korea 1920s-1930s," *Comparative Korean Studies* 19, no. 2 (2011): 35–69.

20. Yi Kyŏng-don, "*Pyŏlgŏn'gon* kwa kŭndae," 269.

21. An example of other types of stories about the city is seen in the series "Viva Kyŏngsŏng (Kyŏngsŏng paeksŭng)" that ran for fifty days beginning on June 25, 1924 in *Tonga ilbo*. The series was crowdsourced, which received more than 1,200 entries, and introduced about one hundred districts in Seoul. Published stories were selected for their most unique representation of the place. Although the *Pyŏlgŏn'gon* reportage and the *Tonga ilbo* series shared some similarities—both represented Seoul in multiple views through collective participation—they were different in that the *Tonga ilbo* series defined the neighborhood by administrative districts and told stories about places, legends, and history by tracing the neighborhood's origin. See Kim Hae-yŏng and Yu Chu-ŭn, "'Nae tongni myŏngmul ŭl t'onghae pon ilche kangjŏmgi Kyŏngsŏng simin ŭi kyŏnggwan insik," *Hyangt'o Sŏul*, no. 87 (2014): 218–21.

22. "Kija ch'ong ch'uldong Kyŏngsŏng paekchu ŭamhaenggi cheihoe <ilssigan

sahoe t'ambang>," *Pyŏlgŏn'gon*, February 1927; "Kija tae ch'uldong 1sigan t'ambang tae Kyŏngsŏng paekchu amhaenggi, 3-wŏl 29-il ohu 2-si 30-pun but'ŏ 3-si 30-pun kkaji," *Pyŏlgŏn'gon*, April 1929.

23. See Adrian Rifkin, *Street Noises: Parisian Pleasure, 1900–40* (Manchester: Manchester University Press, 1995). Miriam Silverberg argued that the "principle of montage" was "central to popular consciousness" in capturing the sense of fragmentation and dynamism of Japanese mass culture. See Miriam Silverberg, *Erotic Grotesque Nonsense: The Mass Culture of Japanese Modern Times* (Berkeley: University of California Press, 2009).

24. André Breton, "Manifesto of Surrealism (1924)," in *Manifestoes of Surrealism*, trans. Richard Seaver and Helen R. Lane (Ann Arbor: University of Michigan Press, 1972), 26.

25. Guy Debord, "Theory of the Dérive," in *The Situationists and the City*, ed. Tom McDonough (London: Verso, 2009), 78, originally published in *Les Lèvres Nues*, no. 9 (November 1956) and reprinted in *Internationale Situationniste*, no. 2 (December 1958).

26. Simon Sadler, *The Situationist City* (Cambridge, MA: MIT Press, 1998), 94.

27. Michel de Certeau, *The Practice of Everyday Life* (Berkeley: University of California Press, 1984), 97–99.

28. Vincent Kaufmann, *Guy Debord: Revolution in the Service of Poetry* (Minneapolis: University of Minnesota Press, 2006), 111. See also McKenzie Wark, *The Beach beneath the Street: The Everyday Life and Glorious Times of the Situationist International* (London: Verso, 2011), 57–58.

29. Although surrealism was mainly an artistic practice that sought to liberate the consciousness trapped in a work of art, Walter Benjamin understood it to be liberating historical energy that was trapped in commodity form and translated the psychic form of surrealism into the social form. This is also what allowed the refiguring of experience into a new form of historical life, according to Osborne. See Osborne, *Politics of Time*, 183.

30. Tom McDonough, *Guy Debord and the Situationist International: Texts and Documents* (Cambridge, MA: MIT Press, 2002), 259.

31. De Certeau, *The Practice of Everyday Life*, 37.

32. Ibid.

33. Griselda Pollock, *Visions and Difference* (London: Routledge, 1988), 67, cited in Tom McDonough, *Guy Debord*, 257.

34. Debord, "Theory of the Dérive," 78

35. Margaret Iversen, *Chance: Documents of Contemporary Art* (Cambridge, MA: MIT Press, 2010), 23.

36. Rebecca Solnit, *Wanderlust: A History of Walking* (New York: Penguin Books, 2000), 72.

37. *Pyŏlgŏn'gon*, December 1926.

38. Claire Doherty, ed., *Situation: Documents of Contemporary Art* (Cambridge, MA: MIT Press, 2009), 13.

39. *Pyŏlgŏn'gon*, February 1, 1927.

40. Lewis Mumford, *Technics and Civilization* (Chicago: University of Chicago Press, 2010), 13–15.

41. Karl Marx, *The Poverty of Philosophy*, in Karl Marx and Frederick Engels, *Collected Works*, vol. 6, *1845–1848* (London: Lawrence & Wishart, 1976), 127.

42. *Pyŏlgŏn'gon*, March 1929.

43. Punctuation in the translation is mine for the sake of clarification. *Pyŏlgŏn'gon*, February 1927.

44. E. H. Gombrich, "Standards of Truth: The Arrested Image and the Moving Eye," in *The Language of Images*, ed. W.J.T. Mitchell (Chicago: University of Chicago Press, 1981), 181.

45. Ibid.

46. Ibid., 195.

47. Ibid., 197.

48. Christopher Isherwood, in his 1939 *Goodbye to Berlin*, described the passivity of the camera-eye in a similar way: "I am a camera. I am a camera with its shutter open, quite passive, recording, not thinking." Although Isherwood expressed a wish to put the disparate images he captured into an ordered system—developed, printed, and fixed—the passivity in the camera-eye is what allowed the insignificant details of reality to appear unfiltered. See Christopher Isherwood, *Goodbye to Berlin* (New York: New Directions, 2012), 3.

49. McDonough, *Guy Debord*, 259.

50. Ibid.

51. *Pyŏlgŏn'gon*, December 1926.

52. Ibid.

53. Maurice Blanchot, "Everyday Speech," trans. Susan Hanson, *Yale French Studies* 73 (1987): 15.

54. Ibid.

55. Ibid.

56. Although this kind of "oblivion-enhancing" waiting is contrasted with "active urban waiting" characteristic of urban intellectuals, Kracauer saw the potential of openness in both. Ibid., 132.

57. Ibid., 16.

58. Reeh, *Ornaments of Metropolis*, 130–31.

59. Ibid., 134.

60. As Ian James noted, "community is recast not as the intimate sharing of an essence or identity but rather as the opening of an absence of identity in the spacing of a shared finitude." Ian James, "Naming the Nothing: Nancy and Blanchot on Community," *Culture, Theory, & Critique* 51, no. 2 (2010): 173.

61. *Pyŏlgŏn'gon*, April 1929.

62. George Perec, *An Attempt at Exhausting a Place in Paris* (Cambridge, MA: Wakefield Press, 2002), 3.

63. Ibid.

64. George Perec, "Approach to What?" in *The Everyday Life Reader*, ed. Ben Highmore (London: Routledge, 2002), 177.

65. Highmore, ed., *The Everyday Life Reader* (London: Routledge, 2002), 176.

66. Ibid.

67. Wark explained this through the etymology of the word *dérive*, whose Latin root *derivare*, makes aquatic reference; with this, he characterizes drifting as a time of liquid movement. Wark, *Beach beneath the Street*, 22.

Chapter 6

1. "Tae Kyŏngsŏng sambugok," *Pyŏlgŏn'gon*, September 1929.

2. Translation by Erin Brightwell. Keijō Denki Kabushiki Kaisha, *Nobiyuku Keijō Denki* (Keijō-fu: Keijō Denki Kabushiki Kaisha, 1935), 59.

3. A similar presentation is seen in a previous publication by the same company. See Keijō Denki Kabushiki Kaisha, *Keijō Denki Kabushiki Kaisha nijūnen enkakushi* (Tōkyō-shi: Keijō Denki Kabushiki Kaisha, 1929).

4. "Pullyang namnyŏ ilmang t'ajin: pyŏnjang kija yagan t'ambanggi," *Pyŏlgŏn'gon*, February 1928.

5. "Sŭwit'ŭ hom Yi Kwang-su ssi kajŏng pangmun'gi," *Pyŏlgŏn'gon*, November 1930.

6. "Ŭihak paksa Yi Kap-se ŭi chut'aek,"*Chogwang*, September 1937.

7. "Sŭwit'ŭ hom ch'ang ŭl nŏmŏ ponda," *Yŏsŏng*, September 1936.

8. Lefebvre claimed the existence of "a global structure" or "totality" made up by the dialectical system of leisure, work, and private life: even time and space away from work were organized and integrated into the modern capitalist structure of production and consumption. See Henry Lefebvre, *Critique of Everyday Life*, vol. 1, *Introduction* (London: Verso, 1991), 30.

9. Alain Corbin, *Time, Desire, and Horror: Toward a History of the Senses*, ed. Jean Birrell (Cambridge, UK: Polity Press, 1995), 8.

10. Ibid., 7.

11. Herbert Marcuse, *Eros and Civilization* (London: Routledge, 1998), 195. Georges Bataille also declared: "Transgression is a game. In the world of play, philosophy disintegrates." Georges Bataille, *Erotism: Death and Sensibility* (New York: City Lights Publishers, 1986), 275.

12. In the aftermath of the March First Movement, the Japanese police system was radically restructured, the military police abolished, and the general police system installed in its place. With this change, however, the police force and police duties expanded gradually, as police came to assume administrative duties and to educate Koreans, and had the power to prosecute, sequester, and use weapons. This change to a general police force took place on August 20, 1919, which placed most police personnel, including military police, in the position of *sunsa*. See Cho Sŏng-t'aek, "Ilche kangjŏmgi kyŏngch'al ŭi yŏkhal e kwanhan yŏn'gu," *Han'guk haengjŏng sahakchi* 37 (2015): 79–102.

13. "Odae kija ch'uldong (siil 10 wŏl 25 il), chajŏng hu ŭi tae Kyŏngsŏng t'ambang," *Pyŏlgŏn'gon*, November 1932.

14. Tom Gunning, "Tracing the Individual Body: Photography, Detectives,

and Early Cinema," in *Cinema and the Invention of Modern Life*, ed. Leo Charney and Vanessa Schwartz (University of California Press, 1995), 20.

15. Ibid.

16. *Pyŏlgŏn'gon*, November 1932.

17. Gunning likened the criminal to a forged banknote: "In new systems of mobility and circulation, the criminal who could hide beneath an assumed identity functioned like a forged banknote, exploiting the rapid exchange of modern currency while undermining the confidence on which it depended." See Gunning, "Tracing the Individual Body," 20.

18. Georg Simmel, "The Metropolis and Mental Life," in *The Blackwell City Reader*, ed. Gary Bridge and Sophie Watson (Oxford: Wiley-Blackwell, 2002), 15.

19. Ibid., 12.

20. "Pu'in kija ŭmhaeng'gi: yŏja kohaksaeng ŭro pyŏnjang hago haksaeng hasukch'on simbang'gi: sihŏm ttae ŭi haksaeng saenghwal," *Pyŏlgŏn'gon*, January 1929.

21. Ibid.

22. Michel de Certeau, Luce Giard, and Pierre Mayol, *The Practice of Everyday Life*. Vol. 2: *Living and Cooking*, trans. Timothy J. Tomasik (Minneapolis: University of Minnesota Press, 1998), 2:9–10.

23. Ibid., 9.

24. De Certeau discussed that the neighborhood was initially located in between the public and private but underwent a gradual privatizing process. Ibid.

25. See Michael Warner, *Public and Counterpublic* (London: Zone Books, 2002).

26. Michael Warner, "Public and Counterpublic," *Public Culture* 14, no. 1 (2002): 49.

27. Ibid.

28. Warner, *Public and Counterpublic*, 75.

29. Ibid., 11.

30. "Pimil myŏngnyŏng wanyŏng," *Pyŏlgŏn'gon*, December 1928.

31. Other examples include a series called "Local Colors" (*chibangsaek*) which exclusively published stories about different localities submitted by readers beginning in December 1926. In July 1927 a subsequent series, "Postcard Communication" (*yŏpsŏ t'ongsin*), featured shorter stories of light gossip and miscellaneous, non-serious topics.

32. Chŏn Ŭn-gyŏng, "Ssŭinŭn t'eksŭt'ŭ rosŏ ŭi *Pyŏlgŏn'gon*": 428.

33. Kim Chil-lyang, "Kŭndae chapchi <Pyŏlgŏn'gon>": 344.

34. *Pyŏlgŏn'gon*, January 1929.

35. Warner, "Public and Counterpublic," 77.

36. Michael Bakhtin, *The Dialogic Imagination: Four Essays*, trans. Caryl Emerson and Michael Holoquist (Austin: University of Texas Press, 1981), 289, cited in Warner, "Public and Counterpublic," 78.

37. Warner, *Public and Counterpublic*, 78.

38. Max Gluckman spoke about membership in gossip reinforced through

shared secrecy, claiming that gossip is a "hallmark of membership." Max Gluck-man, "Paper in Honor of Melville J. Herskovits: Gossip and Scandal," *Current Anthropology* 4, no. 3 (1963): 313.

39. Maurice Blanchot, *The Infinite Conversation* (Minneapolis: University of Minnesota Press, 1993), 31.

40. Ibid.

41. Ibid., 28.

42. Ibid., 28–29.

43. Virgil, *Aeneid* IV.173–90, cited in Francesco Careri, "The Storyteller," in *Francis Alÿs, A Story of Deception*, ed. Mark Godfrey, Klaus Biesenbach, and Kerryn Greenberg (London: Tate Publishing, 2010), 183–86.

44. Russell Ferguson and Francis Alÿs, *Francis Alÿs: Politics of Rehearsal* (Los Angeles: Hammer Museum, 2007), 29.

45. See a conversation between Francis Alÿs and James Lingwood in "Making Seven Walks: Rumours," *Artangel*, https://www.artangel.org.uk/seven-walks/rumours/#part-3.

46. Careri, "The Storyteller."

Epilogue

1. The mid- to late 1920s can be seen as a vacuum from the perspective of urban planning. Keijō City Planning Research Association published two pro-posals in 1926 and 1928, each of which incorporated scientifically oriented thinking geared toward efficient management of the city, unlike earlier piece-meal reform projects. However, they were never implemented because of budget-ary reasons and existed only on paper until 1934, when a more comprehensive urban plan redrew the city boundary. For a more details, see Todd Henry, *Assimilating Seoul*, 42–61.

2. Derrida explains how deconstruction does not supervene "afterwards, from outside, one fine day." Nor is it located in the center, but rather in an "eccen-tric center, in a corner whose eccentricity assures the solid concentration of the system, participating in the construction of what it, at the same time, threatens to deconstruct." See Jacques Derrida, *Mémoires: For Paul de Man* (New York: Co-lumbia University Press, 1986), 73.

3. Keith Mitnick, *Artificial Light: A Narrative Inquiry into the Nature of Ab-straction, Immediacy, and Other Architectural Fictions* (New York: Princeton Ar-chitectural Press, 2008), 42.

4. Ibid., 34. Emphasis in original.

5. Jonathan Crary, "Géricault, the Panorama, and Sites of Reality in the Early Nineteenth Century," *Grey Room* 9 (Autumn, 2002): 18–19.

6. Marilyn Ivy, *Discourse of the Vanishing: Modernity, Phantasm, Japan* (Chicago: University of Chicago Press, 1995), 16–17. The question of language is poignant because of the "crisis of representation," as Christopher Hanscom discussed, which was situated in the "juncture between language and knowing, the (in)ability to say what one meant," in the context of a universal mode of enun-

ciation that "occluded the voice and situation of the colonized in any attempt at enunciation as a condition of its universality." This was compounded by the "conundrum of language" that Aimee Kwon discussed in terms of how the colonial subject was "burdened by the coercive lure of the normative universality of the imperial language." Even though the latter case was more acutely felt during wartime, ample evidence points to efforts to privilege Japanese as the correct reading of the shared script of hanja/kanji during this time. See Christopher Hanscom, *The Real Modern: Literary Modernism and the Crisis of Representation in Colonial Korea* (Cambridge, MA: Harvard University Asia Center, 2013), 174; Nayoung Aimee Kwon, *Intimate Empire Collaboration and Colonial Modernity in Korea and Japan* (Durham, NC: Duke University Press, 2015), 12.

7. According to Bliss Cua Lim: "To maintain that the future holds the same thing for everyone, that the future is already known (the achievement of progress, secular disenchantment, and rationality), and hence to anticipate that the primitive will one day be like the modern observer ('their' future can be extrapolated from 'our' past), would in Bergosonian terms, amount to a fundamentally timeless view of time." See Lim, *Translating Time: Cinema, the Fantastic, and Temporal Critique* (Durham, NC: Duke University Press, 2009), 14.

8. Maurice Blanchot, *The Infinite Conversation* (Minneapolis: University of Minnesota Press, 1993), 28.

9. Peter Osborne, *The Politics of Time: Modernity and Avant-Garde* (London & New York: Verso, 1995), xii.

10. Ibid., 196.

11. Mbembe discussed this as "living in the concrete world." See Achille Mbembe, *On the Postcolony* (Durham, NC: Duke University Press, 2001), 16–17.

12. Reinhart Koselleck, *Futures Past: On the Semantics of Historical Time* (New York: Columbia University Press, 2004), 288.

13. Michel Foucault, "Of Other Spaces: Utopias and Heterotopias," trans. Jay Miskowiec, *Architecture/Mouvement/Continuité* (October 1984): 3.

14. Francis Alÿs, *Sign-Painter's Project (Rotulistas)*, Mexico City, 1993–97. See Francis Alÿs, Juan García, Enrique Huerta, and Emilio Rivera, *Francis Alÿs: Sign Painting Project* (Göttingen, Sweden: Steidl; Basel, Switzerland: Schaulager, 2011).

15. The critic Russell Ferguson discussed rehearsal as a creative period imbued with critical possibilities—"the specifically artistic moment" for the actor to conceive, efface, repeat, and ruminate. Russel Ferguson, *Francis Alÿs: Politics of Rehearsal* (Los Angeles: Hammer Museum, 2007), 12.

16. Ibid.

17. Ibid., 11.

18. Francis Alÿs, *Rehearsal I (El Ensayo)*, 1999-2001, in collaboration with Rafael Ortega, four video (color and black-and-white, sound, 29:34 min), one painting, forty-four drawings, fifteen photographs, three prints.

19. Alÿs, Francis, Mark Godfrey, Klaus Biesenbach, and Kerryn Greenberg, *Francis Alÿs: A Story of Deception* (London: Tate Publishing, 2010), 18–19.

20. Francis Alÿs, "Politics of Rehearsal," in *blueOrange 2004* (Köln: Walther König, 2004), 10, as cited in Ferguson, *Francis Alÿs*, 88.

21. Alÿs et al., *Francis Alÿs*, 19.

22. Ferguson, *Francis Alÿs*, 106; Boris Groy, "How to Do Time with Art," in *Francis Alÿs: A Story of Deception*, 151.

BIBLIOGRAPHY

PRIMARY SOURCES
Periodicals
Chogwang
Chōsen to kenchiku
Chōsen kōron
Chosŏn chi kwang
La Domenica del Corriere
Hyesŏng
Kaebyŏk
Maeil sinbo
Pyŏlgŏn'gon
Samch'ŏlli
Taehan maeil sinbo
Tonga ilbo
Tonggwang
Tongnip sinmun
Yŏsŏng

Books and Other Publications
Chōsen Hakubunsha. *Sunjong kukchangnok*. Seoul: Chōsen Hakubunsha, 1926.
Chōsen Shōtokufu. *Chōsenjin no shōgyō*. Seoul: n.p., 1929.
Heslop, William. "Royal Funeral." Translated by Han Sŏn-hyŏn. *Hyŏndae kidok-kyo yŏksa yŏn'guso charyo ch'ongsŏ* 5, 197–199. Seoul: Hyŏndae kidokkyo yŏksa yŏn'guso, 2003.

Keijō Denki Kabushiki Kaisha. *Keijō Denki Kabushiki Kaisha nijūnen enkakushi.* Tokyo: Keijō Denki Kabushiki Kaisha, 1929. Reprint. Tokyo: Yumani Shobō, 2003.

——. *Nobiyuku Keijō Denki.* Keijō-fu: Keijō Denki Kabushiki Kaisha, 1935. Reprint. Tokyo: Yumani Shobō, 2003.

Kojong T'aehwangje Myŏngsŏng T'aehwanghu pumyo chugam ŭigwe.

Kojong T'aehwangje ŏjang chugam ŭigwe.

Kojong T'aehwangje pinjŏn honjŏn chugam ŭigwe.

Kojong T'aehwangje sallŭng chugam ŭigwe.

Kojong T'aehwangje sillok.

Lu Xun. *Silent China: Selected Writings of Lu Xun.* Edited and translated by Gladys Yang. London: Oxford University Press, 1973.

Myŏngsŏng Hwanghu kukchang togam ŭigwe.

Sŏnu Il, and Sŏ Pyŏng-hyŏp, eds. *Chosŏn ch'ongdokpu sich'ŏng onyŏn kinyŏm kongjinhoe sillok.* Keijō: Chōsen Hakubunsha, 1916.

Taylor, Mary Linley. *Chain of Amber.* Lewes: The Book Guild, 1991.

Illustrative Materials

Alÿs, Francis. *Rehearsal I (El Ensayo).* 1999–2001. In collaboration with Rafael Ortega. Four videos (color and black-and-white, sound, 29:34 min.), 1 painting, 44 drawings, 15 photographs, and 3 prints.

Ch'oe Sun-gwŏn, ed. *Kojong kwa Sunjong ŭi kukchang sajinch'ŏp.* Seoul: Minsogwŏn, 2008.

Chūō jōhō senman shisha, ed. *Dai-keijō shashinchō.* Keijō: Chūō jōhō senman shisha, 1937.

Gosōgi shashinchō. Keijō: Chōsen sōtokufu, 1926.

Junshō kokusō kinen shashinchō. Keijō: Keijō shashin tsūshinsha, 1926.

Keijō hyakkei. Taishō Hatō. ca. 1930s. Postcards. 14.2 x 9 cm. Busan Museum, Pusan.

The Korean Independence Movement: Actual Photographs Showing Peaceful Demonstrations of the Koreans for Independence and Brutal Treatment Accorded Them by Japanese Soldiery. N.p: n.p., 1919.

Ko Ri taiō tenka go sōgi kōkei e hagaki. 1919. Postcards. 9.7 x 15.3 cm. Seoul History Museum, Seoul.

Ogawa Kazumasa. *Meiji tennō gotaisō shashinchō.* Tokyo: n.p., 1912.

Ri taiō denka kokusō seigi. 1919. Print on paper. 54 x 39 cm. The Independence Hall, Ch'ŏnan-si.

Ri taiō denka sōgi shashinchō. Print on paper. 28 x 37 cm. Seoul National University Museum, Seoul.

Taehan cheguk Kojong Hwangje kukchang hwach'ŏp. Seoul: Chimun'gak. 1975.

Tokujukyū kokusō gachō. 1919. 49 pages. 28.8 x 21.6 cm. Keijō: Keijō Nippō. Seoul History Museum, Seoul.

Visual Recordings

Junshō kōtai insan shūi. 1926. 12 min. 35 mm.

Sound Recordings

Hwang Chae-gyŏng (performer). "Yŏldugaji usŭm." Columbia 40699-A. Shellac record. 1936.

Kim Sŏng-un (performer). "Mŏngt'ŏngguri Sŏul yŏhaeng." With Sim Yŏng, Kim Sŏn-ch'o, and Kim Sŏn-yŏng. Columbia 40458 AB. Shellac record. 1933.

Kim Sŏng-un (performer). "Mŏngt'ŏngguri tongmurwŏn kugyŏng." With Sŏk Kŭm-sŏng. Regal C330. Shellac record. 1936.

Sin Pul-ch'ul (performer). "Chŏnjang ŭi paekhaphwa." With Sin Ŭn-bong. Chieron 83-A. Shellac Record. 1933.

Sin Pul-ch'ul (performer). "Iksalmajŭn taemŏri." With Yun Paek-dam. Okeh 1518-A. Shellac record. 1933.

Sin Pul-ch'ul (performer). "Iksalmajŭn taemŏri [kongsanmyŏngwŏl]". With Kim Yŏn-sil. Chieron 79-A. 1933.

Sin Pul-ch'ul (performer). "Kaettong halmŏni." With Kim Chin-mun. Okeh 1701 AB. Shellac record. 1934.

Sin Pul-ch'ul (performer). "Kombo t'aryŏng." With and Sin Ŭn-bong. Okeh 1585A. Shellac record. 1933.

Sin Pul-ch'ul (performer). "Kyŏnmal yŏlssoet'ong." With Sin Ŭn-bong. Chieron 83-B, Shellac record. 1933.

Sin Pul-ch'ul (performer). "Ŏngt'ŏri yŏnsŏl." Recorded on May 5, 1937. Victor KJ1107A. Shellac record, 1937.

Sin Pul-ch'ul (performer). "Somun manbongnae." With Na P'um-sim, Sin Il-sŏn, and Sŏng Kwang-hyŏn. Okeh 1611 A/B. Shellac record. 1933.

Sin Pul-ch'ul. "Taemŏri (Kongsanmyŏngwŏl)." With Kim Yŏn-sil. Korai, 1051 A/B. 1936.

Sin Pul-ch'ul (performer). "Yojŏl Simch'ŏngjŏn." With Sŏng Kwang-hyŏn. Okeh 1634-AB. Shellac record. 1934.

SECONDARY SOURCES
Korean

An Ch'ang-mo. *Tŏksugung: Sidae ŭi unmyŏng ŭl an'go cheguk ŭi chungsim e sŏda.* Seoul: Tongnyŏk ch'ulp'ansa, 2009.

Chang P'il-gu and Chŏn Pong-hŭi. "Kojong changnye kigan Sinsŏnwŏnjŏn ŭi chosŏng kwa Tŏksugung Ch'angdŏkkung kungyŏk ŭi pyŏnhwa." *Taehan kŏnch'uk hakhoe nonmunjip* 29, no. 12 (2013): 197–208.

Che Song-hŭi. "19-segi chŏnban ŭigwe panch'ado ŭi sin kyŏnghyang." *Misulsahak yŏn'gu* 288 (2015): 89–120.

Cho Chŏng-min. "Singminji sigi sajin yŏpsŏ <Kyŏngsŏng paekkyŏng> ŭi konggan kwa sŏsa chŏllyak," *Ilbon munhwa yŏn'gu,*" 63 (2017): 5–26.

Cho Sŏng-t'aek. "Ilche kangjŏmgi kyŏngch'al ŭi yŏkhal e kwanhan yŏn'gu." *Han'guk haengjŏng sahakchi* 37 (2015): 79–102.

Ch'oe Hyŏn-sik. "Imiji wa sigak ŭi munhwa chŏngch'ihak (I): Ilche sidae sajin yŏpsŏ ŭi yŏngu." *Tongbang hakchi* 175 (2016): 225–65.

——. "Singmin tosi, chŏnt'ong kwa kŭndae ŭi ijung nasŏn: sajin yŏpsŏ <Kyŏngsŏng paekkyŏng> ŭl chungsim ŭro." *Hyŏndae munhak ŭi yŏn'gu* 67 (2019): 193–268.

Ch'oe Sun-gwŏn, ed. *Kojong kwa Sunjong ŭi kukchang sajinch'ŏp.* Seoul: Minsogwŏn, 2008.

Ch'oe Yŏl. *Han'guk kŭndae misul ŭi yŏksa: Han'guk misulsa sajŏn* 1800–1945. P'aju: Yŏrhwadang, 2015

Ch'oe Yŏng-ch'ŏl and Hŏ Chae-yŏng. "Kaehang ihu hakche toip ijŏn kkaji ŭi han'guk kŭndae hangmullon kwa ŏmun munje: <Hansŏng sunbo> wa <Hansŏng jubo> rŭl chungsim ŭro." *Inmun kwahak yŏn'gu* 40 (March 2014): 181–207.

Ch'ŏn Chŏng-hwan. "Singminji Chosŏnin ŭi usŭm: <Samch'ŏlli> sojae sohwa wa Sin Pul-ch'ul mandam ŭi yŏngu." *Yŏksa wa munhwa* 18 (September 2009): 7–38.

Ch'ŏn Chŏng-hwan and Yi Yong-nam. "Kŭndae chŏk taejung munhwa ŭi paljŏn kwa ch'wimi." *Minjon munhaksa yŏn'gu,* 30 (2006): 227–65.

Chŏn U-yong. "Chongno wa Ponjŏng: singmin toshi Kyŏngsŏng ŭi tu ŏlgul." *Yŏksa wa hyŏnsil* 40 (June 2001): 163–93.

——. "Ilche ha Sŏul namch'on sangga ŭi hyŏngsŏng kwa pyŏnch'ŏn: Ponjŏng ŭl chungsim ŭro." In *Sŏul namch'on: sigan, changso, saram,* edited by Kim Ki-o, Yang Sŭng-u, Kim Han-bae, Yun In-sŏk, Chŏn U-yong, Mok Su-hyŏn, and Ŭn Ki-su, 173–235. Seoul: Sŏul sirip taehaekkyo pusŏl sŏurhak yŏn'guso, 2003.

Chŏn Ŭn-gyŏng. "'Ssŭinŭn t'eksŭt'ŭ rosŏ ŭi *Pyŏlgŏn'gon* kwa taejung munhak tokcha ŭi hyŏngsŏng." *Hakhoe ŏmunhak* 125 (September 2014): 389–435.

Chŏng Kŭn-sik and Ch'oe Kyŏng-hŭi. "Tosŏgwa ŭi sŏlch'i wa ilche singminji ch'ulp'an kyŏngch'al ŭi ch'egyehwa, 1926–1929." In *Singminji kŏmyŏl: chedo, t'eksŭt'ŭ, silch'ŏn,* edited by Kŏmyŏl yŏn'guhoe, 64–136. Seoul: Somyŏng ch'ulp'an, 2012.

Ha Yŏng-sam. *Hanja wa ek'ŭrit'wirŭ.* Seoul: Ak'anet, 2001.

Han Ki-hyŏng. "Singminji kŏmyŏl chŏngch'aek kwa sahoejuŭi kwallyŏn chapchi ŭi chŏngch'i yŏkhal." *Singminji kŏmyŏl: chedo, t'eksŭt'ŭ, silch'ŏn,* edited by Kŏmyŏl yŏn'guhoe, 168–99. Seoul: Somyŏng ch'ulp'an, 2012.

Han'guk kŏnch'uk yŏksa hakhoe. *Han'guk kŏnch'uksa yŏn'gu 1: punya wa sidae.* Seoul: Parŏn, 2003.

Hwang Ho-dŏk. *Kŭndae neisyŏn kwa kŭ p'yosang tŭl.* Seoul: Somyŏng ch'ulp'an, 2005.

——. "Kyŏngsŏng chiriji, ijung ŏnŏ ŭi changsoron—Ch'ae Man-sik ŭi 'Chongno ŭi chumin' kwa singmin tosi ŭi (ŏnŏ) kamgak." *Taedong munhwa yŏn'gu* 51 (2005): 107–41.

Im T'ae-hun. "Unnŭn mandam rek'odŭ wa haep'ŭning ŭi midiŏ: Sin Pulch'ul ŭi <Iksalmajin taemŏri>(1933) e kwanhayŏ." *Inmunhak yŏn'gu* 59 (2020): 427–58.

Kang Chun-man. "Han'guk kanp'an munhwa ŭi yŏksa: wae Han'gugin ŭn kanp'an e moksum ŭl kŏnŭn'ga?" *Inmul kwa sasang* 117 (January 2008): 154–204.

Kim Che-jŏng. "Kŭndae Kyŏngsŏng ŭi yongnye wa kŭ ŭimi ŭi pyŏnhwa." In *1930–40-yŏndae Kyŏngsŏng ŭi tosi ch'ehŏm kwa tosi munje*, ed. Sŏul sirip tae-hakkyo tosi munhag yŏn'guso. Seoul: Laum, 2014.

Kim Chil-lyang. "Kŭndae chapchi <Pyŏlgŏn'gon> ŭi 'ch'wimi tamnon' kwa kŭlssŭgi ŭi t'ŭksŏng." *Ŏmunhak* (June 2005): 331–52.

Kim Chin-song. *Sŏul e ttansŭhol ŭl hŏhara*. Seoul: Hyŏnsil munhwa yŏn'gu, 1999.

Kim Hae-yŏng and Yu Chu-ŭn. "'Nae dongni myŏngmul ŭl t'onghae pon ilche kangjŏmgi Kyŏngsŏng simin ŭi kyŏnggwan insik." *Hyangt'o Sŏul*, no. 87 (2014): 218–21.

Kim Ki-ho. "Namch'on: ilche kangjŏmgi tosi kyehoek kwa tosi kujo ŭi pyŏnhwa." In *Sŏul namch'on: sigan, changso, saram*, edited by Kim Ki-o, Yang Sŭng-u, Kim Han-bae, Yun In-sŏk, Chŏn U-yong, Mok Su-hyŏn, and Ŭn Ki-su, 1–35. Seoul: Sŏul sirip taehaekkyo pusŏl sŏurhak yŏn'guso, 2003.

Kim Kye-wŏn. "P'anorama wa cheguk: kŭndae ilbon ŭi kukka p'yosang kwa p'anorama ŭi sigaksŏng." *Han'guk kŭnhyŏndae misulsahak* 19 (2008): 29–49.

Kim Paeg-yŏng. *Chibae wa konggan*. Seoul: Munhak kwa chisŏngsa, 2009.

Kim Pyŏng-ju and Sŏk Kang-hŭi. "Ilche kangjŏmgi kanp'an kŏnch'uk e kwan-han yŏn'gu." *Han'guk munhwa konggan kŏnch'ukhakhoe nonmunjip* 66 (May 2019): 189–99.

Kim Sŏng-man. "Ku-chosŏn ch'ongdokpu ch'ŏngsa ŭi konggan kwa hyŏngt'ae punsŏk e kwanhan yŏn'gu." *Taehan kŏnch'uk hakhoe nonmunjip* 13, no. 4 (1997): 53–63.

Kim Sŏn-hŭi. "Sajin kŭrim yŏpsŏ rŭl t'onghae pon kŭndae Sŏul ŭi kwan'gwang imiji wa p'yosang." *Taehan chiri hakhoeji* 53, no. 4 (August 2018): 569–83.

Kim Sŏn-jŏng. "Kwan'gwang annaedo ro pon kŭndae tosi Kyŏngsŏng: 1920–30 nyŏndae tohae imiji rŭl chungsim ŭro." *Han'guk munhwa yŏn'gu* 33 (2017): 33–62.

Kim Sŭng and Yang Mi-suk, eds. *Sinp'yŏn pusan taegwan*. Seoul: Sŏnin mun-hwasa, 2010.

Kim To-gyŏng. "Singminji kŏmyŏl kwa taejung chapchi Pyŏlgŏn'gon ŭi puronsŏng." *Ŏmunhak* 130 (December 2005): 111–32.

Kim Ye-rim. *1930 nyŏndae huban kŭndae insik ŭi t'ŭl kwa miŭisik*. Seoul: Somyŏng ch'ulp'an, 2004.

Kim Yi-sun. *Taehan cheguk hwangje rŭng*. Seoul: Sowadang, 2010.

Ko Yŏng-jin, Kim Pyŏng-mun, Cho T'ae-rin, Kim Ha-su, and Im Kyŏng-hwa, eds. *Singminji sigi chŏnhu ŭi ŏnŏ munje*. Seoul: Somyŏng ch'ulp'an, 2012.

Kwak Myŏng-hŭi. "Ilche kangjŏmgi kanp'an munhwa ŭi t'ŭkching e kwanhan yŏn'gu." *Ogwoe k'wanggohak yŏn'gu* 1, no. 1 (February 2004): 7–21.

Kwŏn Bodŭrae. "1910 nyŏndae ŭi ijungŏ sanghwang kwa munhak ŏnŏ." *Han'gugŏ munhak yŏn'gu* 54 (2010): 5–43.

Nishizawa Yasuhiko. "Kŏnch'uksa esŏ ch'ongdokpu: ch'ongsa ŭi wisang." *Sŏul-hak yŏn'gu* 73 (November 2018), 155–57.

Nobukuni Koyasu. "Kŭndae ilbon ŭi hanja wa chagugŏ insik." In *Hŭndŭllinŭn ŏnŏdŭl: ŏnŏ ŭi kŭndae wa kungmin kukka*, edited by Im Hyŏng-t'aek, Han Ki-hyŏng, Ryu Chun-p'il, and Yi Hye-ryŏng, 43–58. Seoul: Sŏnggyun'gwan taehakkyo taedong munhwa yŏn'guwŏn, 2008.

O Chu-ŭn. "Ilche kangjŏmgi kanp'an tijain ŭi sigaksŏng." *Archives of Design Research* 30, no. 2 (May 2017): 183–95.

Ŏm Hyŏn-sŏp. "Sin Pul-ch'ul taejung munyeron yŏn'gu." *Comparative Korean Studies* 17, no. 3 (2009): 315–48.

Pae Yŏn-hyŏng. *Han'guk yusŏnggi ŭmban munhwasa*. Seoul: Chisŏngsa, 2019.

Pak Chin-su. "Hanja munhwa wa kŭndae tong-asia ŭi ŏnŏ: ŏnŏ minjokchuŭi rŭl nŏmŏsŏ." *Asia munhwa yŏn'gu* 11 (December 2006): 31–46.

Pak Chŏng-hye. "Changsŏgak sojang ilche kangjŏmgi ŭigwe ŭi misulsa chŏk yŏn'gu." *Misulsa yŏn'gu* 259 (2008): 117–50.

Pak Kye-ri. "Ihwa yŏja taehakkyo pangmulgwan sojang <Myŏngsŏng Hwanghu parin panch'ado> yŏn'gu." *Misulsa nondan*, no. 35 (December 2012): 91–115.

——. "'Myŏngsŏng Hwanghu parin panch'ado wa parin haengnyŏng." *Misulsa hakbo* (2016): 7–26.

Pak Sŏng-jin and U Tong-sŏn. "Ilche kangjŏmgi Kyŏngbokkung chŏn'gag ŭi hwech'ŏl kwa igŏn." *Taehan kŏnch'uk hakhoe nonmunjip* 23, no. 5 (May 2007): 133–40.

Pan Chae-sik, ed. *Mandam paengnyŏnsa*. Seoul: Paekchungdang, 2000.

Sin Myŏng-ho. "Chosŏn ch'ogi ŭigwe p'yŏnch'an ŭi paegyŏng kwa ŭiŭi." *Chosŏnsidaesa hakpo* 59 (December 2011): 5–53.

Sŏul yŏksa pangmulgwan. *Asŭp'alt'ŭ arae Unjongga—Ch'ŏngjin palgul ŭi ahop susukkekki*. Seoul: Sŏul yŏksa pangmulgwan, 2020.

——. *Kwanghwamun yŏn'ga sigye rŭl tollida*. Seoul: Sŏul yŏksa pangmulgwan, 2009.

Sŏul yŏksa p'yŏnch'anwŏn. *Kyŏngsŏngbu kŏnch'uk tomyŏn charyojip*. Seoul: Sŏul ch'aekpang, 2018.

U Su-jin. "Chaedam kwa mandam, 'Pi-ŭimi' wa 'Chinsil' ŭi hyŏngsik: Pak Ch'unjae wa Sin Pulch'ul ŭl chungsim ŭro." *Han'guk yŏn'gŭkhak* 1, no. 64 (2017): 5–40.

Yi Chi-su and Yi Kyŏng-mi. "Maeil sinbo rŭl t'onghae pon ilche kangjŏmgi sangbok ŭi kŭndaehwa yŏn'gu—1910 nyŏndae kukka changnyesik ŭl chungsim ŭro." *Han'guk poksik hakhoe* 70, no. 3 (June 2020): 148–66.

Yi Chun-hŭi. "Ilche sidae ŭmban kŏmyŏl." In *Singminji kŏmyŏl: chedo, t'eksŭt'ŭ, silch'ŏn*, edited by Kŏmyŏl yŏn'guhoe. Seoul: Somyŏng ch'ulp'an, 2011.

Yi Hwa-jin. *Sori ŭi chŏngch'i: Singminji Chosŏn ŭi kŭkchang kwa cheguk ŭi kwan'gaek*. Seoul: Hyŏnsil munhwa, 2016.

Yi Hyŏn-jong. *Taehan cheguk Kojong Hwangje kukchang hwach'ŏp*. Seoul: Chimun'gak, 1975.

Yi Kyŏng-don. "*Pyŏlgŏn'gon* kwa kŭndae ch'wimi tongmul." *Taedong munhwa yŏn'gu* 46, (2004): 249–87.

Yi Sŏng-mi. *Wangsil karye togam ŭigwe wa misulsa*. Seoul: Sowadang, 2008.

Yi Sŭng-hŭi. "Paeu Sin Pul-ch'ul, usŭm ŭi chŏngch'i." *Han'guk kŭgyesul yŏn'gu* 33 (2011): 13–49.

Yi Uk. "Kŭndae kukka ŭi mosaek kwa kukka ŭirye ŭi pyŏnhwa: 1894–1908 nyŏn kukka chesa ŭi pyŏnhwa rŭl chungsim ŭro." *Chŏngsin munhwa yŏn'gu* 27, no. 2 (2004): 59–94.

Yŏ Hŭi-jŏng. "Ilche kangjŏmgi chŏnt'ong chisigin ŭi ijung ŏnŏ kŭlssŭgi: kukhakcha Chŏng In-bo ŭi han'gŭl kŭlssŭgi wa hanmun kŭlssŭgi ŭi kwan'gye rŭl chungsim ŭro." *Chŏngsin munhwa yŏn'gu* 38, no. 3 (September 2015): 179–208.

Yŏm Pok-kyu. *Sŏul ŭi kiwŏn Kyŏngsŏng ŭi t'ansaeng—1910–1945: Tosi kyehoek ŭro pon Kyŏngsŏng ŭi yŏksa.* Seoul: Idea, 2016.

Yun Chong-sŏn. "<Sunjong kukchangnok> yŏn'gu." *Journal of Korean Culture* 51 (2020): 221–54.

Japanese

Gotō Yasushi. "Keijō no gairo kensetsu ni kansuru rekishiteki kenkyū." *Dobokushi kenkyū* 13 (1993): 93–104.

Hashiya Hiroshi. *Teikoku nihon to shokuminchi toshi.* Tokyo: Yoshikawa Kōbunkan, 2004.

English

Alÿs, Francis. *blueOrange 2004.* Köln: Walther König, 2004.

Alÿs, Francis, Juan García, Enrique Huerta, and Emilio Rivera. *Francis Alÿs: Sign Painting Project.* Göttingen: Steidl; Basel: Schaulager, 2011.

Alÿs, Francis, Mark Godfrey, Klaus Biesenbach, and Kerryn Greenberg. *Francis Alÿs: A Story of Deception.* London: Tate Publishing, 2010.

Atkins, Taylor. *Primitive Selves: Koreana in the Japanese Colonial Gaze, 1910–1945.* Berkeley: University of California Press, 2010.

Bakhtin, Mikhail. *The Dialogic Imagination: Four Essays.* Translated by Caryl Emerson and Michael Holoquist. Austin: University of Texas Press, 1981.

——. *Rabelais and His World.* Translated by Helene Iswolsky. Indianapolis: Indiana University Press, 1984.

Balakian, Anna. "Metaphor and Metamorphosis in Andre Breton's Poetics." *French Studies* 19, no. 1 (1965): 34–41.

Barlow, Tani, ed. "Debates over Colonial Modernity in East Asia and Another Alternative." *Cultural Studies* 26, no. 5 (2012): 617–44.

——. *Formations of Colonial Modernity in East Asia.* Durham, NC: Duke University Press, 1997.

Barthes, Roland. *Camera Lucida: Reflections on Photography.* New York: Hill and Wang, 1980.

——. *Travels in China.* Cambridge, MA: Polity, 2013.

Bataille, Georges. *Erotism: Death and Sensibility.* New York: City Lights Publishers, 1986.

Baudrillard, Jean. *Simulacra and Simulation.* Ann Arbor: University of Michigan Press, 2004.

Bhabha, Homi. *Nation and Narration.* London; New York: Routledge, 1990.

Benjamin, Walter. *The Arcades Project.* Translated by Howard Eiland and Kevin McLaughlin. Cambridge, MA: Harvard University Press, 2002.

——. "Theses on the Philosophy of History." In *Illuminations,* edited by Hannah Arendt, 253–64. New York: Schocken Books, 1969.

Benjamin, Walter, Howard Eiland, and Michael W. Jennings eds. *Selected Writings, Vol. 4, 1938–1940.* Cambridge, MA: Harvard University Press, 2003.

Bergson, Henri. *Creative Evolution.* Mineola, NY: Dover Publications, 1998.

Blanchot, Maurice. "Everyday Speech." Translated by Susan Hanson,. *Yale French Studies* 73 (1987): 12–20.

——. *The Infinite Conversation.* Minneapolis: University of Minnesota Press, 1993.

Boym, Svetlana. *The Future of Nostalgia.* New York: Basic Books, 2001.

Breton, André. "Manifesto of Surrealism (1924)." In *Manifestoes of Surrealism,* translated by Richard Seaver and Helen R. Lane, 3–41. Ann Arbor: University of Michigan Press, 1972.

Bruno, Giuliana. *Atlas of Emotions: Journeys in Art, Architecture, and Film.* London: Verso, 2018.

——. *Surface: Matters of Aesthetics, Materiality, and Media.* Chicago: University of Chicago Press, 2014.

Campany, David, ed. *The Cinematic: Documents of Contemporary Art.* Cambridge, MA: MIT Press, 2007.

Careri, Francesco. "The Storyteller." In *Francis Alÿs, A Story of Deception,* edited by Mark Godfrey, Klaus Biesenbach, and Kerryn Greenberg, 183–86. London: Tate Publishing, 2010.

Chakrabarty, Dipesh. *Provincializing Europe: Postcolonial Thought and Historical Difference.* Princeton, NJ: Princeton University Press, 2007.

Corbin, Alain. *Time, Desire, and Horror: Toward a History of the Senses.* Edited by Jean Birrell. Cambridge: Polity Press, 1995.

Crary, Jonathan. "Géricault, the Panorama, and Sites of Reality in the Early Nineteenth Century." *Grey Room* 9 (Autumn, 2002): 5–25.

Critchley, Simon. *On Humor.* London: Routledge. 2002.

Debord, Guy. "Theory of the Dérive." In *The Situationists and the City: A Reader,* edited by Tom McDonough, 77–85. London: Verso, 2009. Originally published in *Les Lèvres Nues,* no. 9 (November 1956) and reprinted in *Internationale Situationniste,* no. 2 (December 1958).

De Certeau, Michel. *The Practice of Everyday Life.* Berkeley: University of California Press, 1984.

De Certeau, Michel, Luce Giard, and Pierre Mayol. *The Practice of Everyday Life. Vol. 2: Living and Cooking.* Translated by Timothy J. Tomasik. Minneapolis: University of Minnesota Press, 1998.

Derrida, Jacques. *Of Grammatology.* Translated by Gayatari Chakravorty Spivak. Baltimore: Johns Hopkins University Press, 1997.

Derrida, Jacques, and Paul De Man. *Mémoires: For Paul de Man.* New York: Columbia University Press, 1986.

Descartes, René. *The Passions of the Soul.* Translated by Stephen Voss. Indianapolis: Hackett Publishing, 1989.

Dillon, Brian. "Introduction: A Short History of Decay." In *Ruins: Documents of Contemporary Art,* edited by Brian Dillon, 10–19. Cambridge, MA: MIT Press, 2011.

Doherty, Claire, ed. *Situation: Documents of Contemporary Art.* Cambridge, MA: MIT Press, 2009.

Ferguson, Russell, and Francis Alÿs. *Francis Alÿs: The Politics of Rehearsal.* Göttingen: Steidl, 2007.

Foucault, Michel. "Of Other Spaces: Utopias and Heterotopias." *Diacritics* 16, no. 1 (1986): 22–27; "Des Espace Autres," *Architecture /Mouvement/ Continuité* 5 (October 1984): 46–49. Translated by Jay Miskowiec. http://web.mit.edu/allanmc/www/foucault1.pdf.

———. *Order of Things: An Archaeology of the Human Science.* New York: Vintage, 1994.

Fujitani, Takashi. *Splendid Monarchy: Power and Pageantry in Modern Japan.* Berkeley: University of California Press, 2006.

Gil, José. *Metamorphosis of the Body.* Minneapolis: University of Minnesota Press, 1998.

Gluckman, Max. "Paper in Honor of Melville J. Herskovits: Gossip and Scandal." *Current Anthropology* 4, no. 3 (1963): 307–16.

Gombrich, E. H. "Standards of Truth: The Arrested Image and the Moving Eye." In *The Language of Images,* edited by W.J.T. Mitchell, 181–217. Chicago: University of Chicago Press, 1981.

Gunning, Tom. "Tracing the Individual Body: Photography, Detectives, and Early Cinema." In *Cinema and the Invention of Modern Life,* edited by Leo Charney and Vanessa Schwartz, 15–45. Berkeley: University of California Press, 1995.

Haboush, JaHyun Kim. "Constructing the Center: The Ritual Controversy and the Search for a New Identity in Seventeenth-Century Korea." In *Culture and the State in Late Chosŏn Korea,* edited by JaHyun Kim Haboush and Martina Deuchler, 46–91. Cambridge, MA: Harvard University Asia Center, 1999.

Hanscom, Christopher P. *The Real Modern: Literary Modernism and the Crisis of Representation in Colonial Korea.* Harvard East Asian Monographs 357. Cambridge, MA: Harvard University Asia Center, 2013.

Hedges, Inez. "Surrealist Metaphor: Frame Theory and Componential Analysis." *Poetics Today* 4, no. 2 (1983): 275–95.

Hegel, G.W.F. *Phenomenology of Spirit.* Translated by A. V. Miller. Oxford: Oxford University Press, 1977.

Henry, Todd A. *Assimilating Seoul: Japanese Rule and the Politics of Public Space in Colonial Korea, 1910–1945.* Berkeley: University of California Press, 2014.

Highmore, Ben, ed. *The Everyday Life Reader.* London: Routledge, 2002.

Hughes, Theodore. *Literature and Film in Cold War South Korea: Freedom's Frontier.* New York: Columbia University Press, 2012.

Huyssen, Andreas. *Miniature Metropolis: Literature in an Age of Photography and Film.* Cambridge, MA: Harvard University Press, 2015.

Inoue, Miyako. "Things That Speak: Peirce, Benjamin, and the Kinesthetics of Commodity Advertisement in Japanese Women's Magazines, 1900 to the 1930s." *Positions* 15, no. 3 (Winter 2007): 511–52.

———. "What Does Language Remember? Indexical Inversion and the Naturalized History of Japanese Women." *Journal of Linguistic Anthropology* 14, no. 1 (2004): 39–56.

Isherwood, Christopher. *Goodbye to Berlin*. New York: New Directions, 2012.

Iversen, Margaret. *Chance: Documents of Contemporary Art*. Cambridge, MA: MIT Press, 2010.

Ivy, Marilyn. *Discourses of the Vanishing Modernity, Phantasm, Japan*. Chicago: University of Chicago Press, 1995.

James, Ian. "Naming the Nothing: Nancy and Blanchot on Community." *Culture, Theory, & Critique* 51, no. 2 (2010): 171–87.

Jin, Jong-Heon. "Demolishing Colony: The Demolition of the Old Government-General Building of Chosŏn." In *Sitings: Critical Approaches to Korean Geography*, edited by Timothy R. Tangherlini and Sallie Yea, 39–58. Honolulu: University of Hawai'i Press, 2008.

Jung, Inha. *Architecture and Urbanism in Modern Korea*. Honolulu: University of Hawai'i Press, 2013.

Kang Nae-hŭi. "Mimicry and Difference: A Spectralogy for the Neo-Colonial Intellectual." *Traces* 1 (2000): 123--58.

Kaske, Elizabeth. *The Politics of Language in Chinese Education: 1895–1919*. Boston: Brill, 2008.

Kaufmann, Vincent. *Guy Debord: Revolution in the Service of Poetry*. Minneapolis: University of Minnesota Press, 2006.

Kim, Baek Yung. "Ruptures and Conflicts in the Colonial Power Bloc: The Great Keijō Plan of the 1920s." *Korea Journal* 48, no. 3 (Autumn 2008): 10–40.

Kim, Christine. "Politics and Pageantry in Protectorate Korea (1905–10): The Imperial Progresses of Sunjong." *Journal of Asian Studies* 68, no. 3 (August 2009): 835–59.

Kim, Gyewon. "Unpacking the Archive: Ichthyology, Photography, and the Archival Record in Japan and Korea." *Positions* 8, no. 9 (2010): 51–88.

———. "Tracing the Emperor: Photography, Famous Places, and the Imperial Progresses in Prewar Japan." *Representations* 120, no. 1 (Fall 2012): 115–50.

Kim, Michael. "Collective Memory and Commemorative Space: Reflections on Korean Modernity and Kyongbok Palace Reconstruction 1865–2010." *International Area Review* 13, no. 4 (2010): 75–95.

Koselleck, Reinhart. *Futures Past: On the Semantics of Historical Time*. New York: Columbia University Press, 2004.

———. *Sediments of Time: On Possible Histories*. Edited by Sean Franzel and Stefan-Ludwig Hoffmann. Cultural Memory in the Present. Stanford, CA: Stanford University Press, 2018.

Kracauer, Siegfried. *History: The Last Things before the Last*. Princeton, NJ: Markus Wiener Publishers, 1995.

——. *The Mass Ornament: Weimar Essays*. Edited and translated by Thomas Y. Levin. Cambridge, MA: Harvard University Press, 1995.

——. "Photography." In *The Mass Ornament: Weimar Essays*. Edited and translated by Thomas Y. Levin, 47–63. Cambridge, MA: Harvard University Press, 1995.

Kwon, Nayoung Aimee. *Intimate Empire: Collaboration and Colonial Modernity in Korea and Japan*. Durham, NC: Duke University Press, 2015.

Lee, Ji-Eun. *Women: Pre-scripted: Forging Modern Roles through Korean Print*. Honolulu: University of Hawai'i Press, 2015.

Lefebvre, Henry. *Critique of Everyday Life, Vol. 1: Introduction*. London: Verso, 1991.

Lim, Bliss Cua. *Translating Time : Cinema, the Fantastic, and Temporal Critique*. Durham, NC: Duke University Press, 2009.

Marcuse, Herbert. *Eros and Civilization*. London: Routledge, 1998.

Marx, Karl, and Frederick Engels. *Collected Works, Volume 6, 1845–1848*. London: Lawrence & Wishart, 1976.

Mbembe, Achille. *On the Postcolony*. Durham, NC: Duke University Press, 2001.

McDonough, Tom, ed. *Guy Debord and the Situationist International: Texts and Documents*. Cambridge, MA: MIT Press, 2002.

——. *The Situationists and the City*. London: Verso, 2009.

Michaux, Henri. *Ideograms in China*. Translated by Gustaf Sobin. Cambridge: New Directions, 2002.

Miller, Angela L. "The Panorama, the Cinema, and the Emergence of the Spectacular." *Wide Angle* 18, no. 2 (April 1996): 34–69.

Mitchell, Timothy. *Colonising Egypt*. Berkeley: University of California Press, 1991.

——. *Questions of Modernity*. Minneapolis: University of Minnesota Press, 2000.

Mitchell, W.J.T. "Showing Seeing: A Critique of Visual Culture." *Journal of Visual Culture* 1, no. 2 (2012): 165–81.

Mitnick, Keith. *Artificial Light: A Narrative Inquiry into the Nature of Abstraction, Immediacy, and Other Architectural Fictions*. New York: Princeton Architectural Press, 2008.

Mrázek, Rudolf. *Engineers of Happy Land: Technology and Nationalism in a Colony*. Princeton, NJ: Princeton University Press, 2002.

Mumford, Lewis. *Sticks and Stones: A Study of American Architecture and Civilization*. New York: Boni & Liveright, 1924.

——. *Technics and Civilization*. Chicago: University of Chicago Press, 2010.

Noordzij, Gerrit. *The Stroke: Theory of Writing*. London: Hyphen Press, 2009.

Nuttall, Sarah, and Achille Mbembe, eds. *Johannesburg: The Elusive Metropolis*. Durham, NC: Duke University Press, 2008.

Ong, Walter. *Orality and Literacy: The Technologizing of the Word*. Edited by Terence Hawkes. New Accent. New York: Methuen, 1988.

——. *Presence of the Word: Some Prolegomena for Cultural and Religious History*, 2nd ed. Binghamton, NY: Global Publications, Binghamton University, 2000.

Osborne, Peter. *The Politics of Time: Modernity and Avant-Garde.* London & New York: Verso, 1995.

Pai, Hyung-il. "Navigating Modern Keijō—The Typology of Reference Guides and City Landmarks." *Journal of Seoul Studies* 44 (August 2011): 1–39.

Park, Sunyoung. "A Forgotten Aesthetic: Reportage in Colonial Korea 1920s–1930s." *Comparative Korean Studies* 19, no. 2 (2011): 35–69.

Peirce, Charles Sanders. *Collected Paper of Charles Sanders Peirce.* Edited by Charles Hartshorne and Paul Weiss. Vol. 3. Cambridge, MA: Harvard University Press, 1932.

——. *The Philosophical Writings of Peirce.* Edited by Justus Buchler. New York: Dover, 1995.

Perec, George. "Approach to What?" In *The Everyday Life Reader*, edited by Ben Highmore, 176–78. London: Routledge, 2002.

——. *An Attempt at Exhausting a Place in Paris.* Cambridge, MA: Wakefield Press, 2002.

Pollock, Griselda. *Visions and Difference.* London: Routledge, 1988.

Poole, Janet. *When the Future Disappears: The Modernist Imagination in Late Colonial Korea.* New York: Columbia University Press, 2014.

Reeh, Henrik. *Ornaments of the Metropolis: Siegfried Kracauer and Modern Urban Culture.* Cambridge, MA: MIT Press, 2006.

Rifkin, Adrian. *Street Noises: Parisian Pleasure, 1900–40.* Manchester: Manchester University Press, 1995.

Rimbaud, Arthur. "Delirium II: Alchemy of the Word." In *A Season in Hell and Illuminations*, translated by Bertrand Mathieu, 33–35. Rochester, NY: BOA Editions, 1991.

Sadler, Simon. *The Situationist City.* Cambridge, MA: MIT Press, 1998.

Sakai, Naoki. *Translation and Subjectivity: On "Japan" and Cultural Nationalism.* Minneapolis: University of Minnesota Press, 1997.

Schafer, R. Murray. *The Soundscape: Our Sonic Environment and the Tuning of the World.* Rochester, NY: Destiny Books, 1993.

Schmid, Andre. *Korea between Empires, 1895–1919.* New York: Columbia University Press, 2002.

Silverberg, Miriam. *Erotic Grotesque Nonsense: The Mass Culture of Japanese Modern Times.* Berkeley: University of California Press, 2009.

Simmel, Georg. "The Metropolis and Mental Life." In *The Blackwell City Reader*, edited by Gary Bridge and Sophie Watson, 103–10. Oxford: Wiley-Blackwell, 2002.

——. "The Ruin" (1911). In *Essays on Sociology, Philosophy and Aesthetics*, edited by Kurt H. Wolff, 259–66. New York: Harper & Row, 1965.

Solnit, Rebecca. *Wanderlust: A History of Walking.* New York: Penguin Books, 2000.

Sontag, Susan. *On Photography.* London: Penguin Books, 1979.

Stewart, Susan. *On Longing: Narratives of the Miniature, the Gigantic, the Souvenir, the Collection.* Durham, NC: Duke University Press, 1993.

Tanaka, Stephen. *Japan's Orient: Rendering Pasts into History*. Berkeley: University of California Press, 1993.

Taylor, Mary Linley. *Chain of Amber*. Lewes: Book Guild, 1991.

Thomas, Sophie. *Romanticism and Visuality: Fragments, History, Spectacle*. New York: Routledge, 2007.

Virilio, Paul. *A Landscape of Events*. Boston: MIT Press, 2000.

Ward, Janet. *Weimar Surfaces: Urban Visual Culture in 1920s Germany*. Berkeley: University of California Press, 2001.

Wark, McKenzie. *The Beach beneath the Street: The Everyday Life and Glorious Times of the Situationist International*. London: Verso, 2011.

Warner, Michael. *Public and Counterpublic*. London: Zone Books, 2002.

———. "Public and Counterpublic," *Public Culture* 14, no. 1 (2002): 49–90.

Watson, Jini Kim. *New Asian City: Three-Dimensional Fictions of Space and Urban Form*. Minneapolis: University of Minnesota Press, 2011.

Weisenfeld, Gennifer. "Japanese Typographic Design and the Art of Letterforms." In *Bridges to Heaven: Essays on East Asian Art in Honor of Professor Wen C. Fong*, edited by Jerome Silbergeld, Dora C. Y. Ching, Judith G. Smith, and Alfreda Murck, 827–48. Princeton, NJ: P. Y. and Kinmay W. Tang Center for East Asian Art, Department of Art and Archaeology, Princeton University, in association with Princeton University Press, 2011.

Wigley, Mark. *The Architecture of Deconstruction: Derrida's Haunt*. Cambridge, MA: MIT Press, 1995.

Zhang, Longxi. "The Myth of the Other: China in the Eyes of the West." *Critical Inquiry* 15, no. 1 (Autumn 1988): 108–31.

Zur, Dafna. *Figuring Korean Futures: Children's Literature in Modern Korea*. Stanford, CA: Stanford University Press, 2017.

Websites

"Making Seven Walks: Rumours." *Artangel: Extrodinary Art, Unexpected Places*. https://www.artangel.org.uk/seven-walks/rumours/#part-3.

"Uigwe: The Royal Protocol of the Joseon Dynasty." Memory of the World. UNESCO. http://www.unesco.org/new/en/communication-and-information/memory-of-the-world/register/full-list-of-registered-heritage/registered-heritage-page-9/uigwe-the-royal-protocols-of-the-joseon-dynasty/.

INDEX

Acousmatic sound, 139
Advertising: for Lion toothpaste, 113 (fig.); orality, 112; reading, 120; scripts, 111–12, 118; for Taeryuk Rubber Company, 118–20, 119 (fig.); for *Tŏksu State Funeral Photo Album*, 77–78; word-images, 118–20. *See also* Signage
Africa: Johannesburg, 205nn23–24; Western views of, 12, 204n14
Alÿs, Francis, 189–90; *Rehearsal I*, 201; *Sign-Painter's Project (Rotulistas)*, 200–201
An Sŏk-chu, 114–18, 218n35
An Mountain, panoramic photographs taken from, 48
Anonymity, in urban space, 179, 181
Architecture: cinema and, 53–55; deceptions, 193–94; under Japanese rule, 30–31, 32–37, 193–94; modern materials and construction, 37–38, 40; ornamentation, 37, 38, 40–42, 46, 47, 95, 216n7; relationship to

surroundings, 29–30; ruins, 14, 34, 35–36, 57–58, 208n30; as text, 13; urban space and, 29–30; Weimar, 41–42, 209–10n54; Western styles, 13, 37, 38, 40–42, 193, 209n50. *See also* Government-General Building; Monumental architecture
Atkins, Taylor, 36

Bakhtin, Mikhail, 139
Bank of Chosŏn, 37; square in front of, 32, 53, 55–57, 56 (fig.)
Barthes, Roland, 85, 97–98, 215n42
Bataille, Georges, 227n11
Baudrillard, Jean, 77
Behne, Adolf, 209–10n54
Benjamin, Walter, 17–18, 121, 179, 206n32, 225n29
Bergson, Henri, 100–101, 217n25
Bhabha, Homi, 101
Blanchot, Maurice, 161–62, 188–89, 198
Bloch, Ernst, 19–20

The authorized representative in the EU for product safety and compliance is:
Mare Nostrum Group
B.V Doelen 72
4831 GR Breda
The Netherlands

www.ingramcontent.com/pod-product-compliance
Lightning Source LLC
Chambersburg PA
CBHW020844270326
41928CB00006B/536

9781503635524